THE SUNDAY TIMES
HISTORY OF
THE
World
CUP

Brian Glanville

written with the
co-operation of FIFA with
a foreword by its president
SIR STANLEY ROUS

Times Newspapers Limited

First published in Great Britain in 1973 by Times Newspapers
Limited, Printing House Square, London EC4P 4DE

© Brian Glanville 1973

ISBN 0 7230 0103 0

Designed by Ivan and Robin Dodd

Printed in Great Britain by
Hazell Watson and Viney Ltd, Aylesbury, Buckinghamshire

Acknowledgements
The author and publishers are particularly grateful to the staff of
FIFA for all their help; they would also like to thank Penelope
Brown, who did the picture research, and Colin Kyte for
compiling the index. They are glad to acknowledge the following
owners and copyright holders of illustrations reproduced in the
book:
ANP-Foto, Amsterdam (pp. 166, 168, 169, 173, 206/7, 209); the
Associated Press Ltd (pp. 54, 58, 59, 60, 61, 62, 64, 65, 71, 72, 75,
85, 93, 94, 99, 100, 103, 111, 113, 123, 125, 130, 132, 134, 157);
the Brazilian Embassy's Photographic Archive (p. 56); Editora
Abril, São Paulo (pp. 38, 40, 42, 43, 63, 67, 135, 160, 166, 193);
Keystone Press Agency Ltd (pp. 7, 10, 14, 16, 18/19, 19, 28, 29,
30, 31, 32, 34/35, 44, 46, 47, 48, 80, 84, 86, 109, 110, 112, 117, 118,
119, 120, 121, 124, 126, 141, 145, 146, 151, 153, 155, 156, 159,
172/173, 175, 178, 181, 183, 185, 192, 195, 198, 201, 208, 220, 222,
223, 231, 232, 233, 235); Novosti Press Agency (pp. 131, 151);
Paris Match (p. 184); Press Association Ltd (pp. 188, 203, 209);
Presse Sports, Paris (pp. 8, 114, 115, 128, 134, 137, 245); Paul
Popper Ltd (p. 205); Sportinformation, Zurich (pp. 20, 25, 35, 38,
74/75, 76, 81, 82, 84, 86, 89, 91, 94, 100, 101, 102, 107, 117, 136,
191, 224); Sven Simon, Munich (pp. 103, 204, 205, 208, 226);
Syndication International Ltd (cover colour illustrations; pp. 175,
177, 182, 187, 189, 190, 194, 196, 197, 198, 199, 200, 201, 202, 207,
212/213, 217, 218, 219, 225, 236, 237, 240, 243, 248, 251);
Ullstein Bilderdienst (pp. 6/7); United Press International (UK)
Ltd (pp. 15, 69, 136, 140/141, 146, 150, 154, 156, 160, 163, 164,
166, 213, 229, 231, 235, 236, 238, 244, 247, 248, 249, 250).

In a few instances it has proved impossible to trace the source of
photographs; it is hoped that anybody inadvertently omitted from
the list will accept this general acknowledgement.

Contents

Foreword

Interest in international football began in 1872, when the first match between any two countries was played. This was Scotland v. England in Glasgow. Fifty-eight years later, in 1930, Uruguay staged the first World Cup tournament in which thirteen countries took part, only three being from Europe, presumably because in those days a two to three week sea voyage was involved.

As a member of the FIFA World Cup Organising Committee since 1950, when the first post-war competition was staged in Brazil, and as President during four tournaments, I feel qualified to write a foreword to this history of the greatest sports event in the world, second only to the Olympic Games. I am pleased to do so because in this ever-changing world of sport the history of international events becomes lost unless it is recorded. Not only the statistics, but the atmosphere in which the games were played; outstanding players, referees, administrators should be remembered. So, too, should the interest which the resident ambassadors and their respective staffs show in their team's participation. On no-match days receptions, invitations to visit other sports clubs and sometimes to private homes are arranged; these breaks from training and the constant togetherness are generally regarded as of great benefit to the team.

In this volume, Brian Glanville has sought to revive the memories of old times and provide interesting information for all those who will want to have details of all previous competitions at the time of the World Cup to be staged in the Federal Republic of Germany in 1974.

In this book the reader will learn of the changes in the competition from those early days to the last and most trouble-free event in Mexico in 1970. He will recall the great players who have taken part, the exciting matches, one of the most skilful being between Brazil and Sweden in Stockholm in 1958 when Pelé, an unknown player, was in devastating form; of the enlarged and splendidly equipped stadia built to house the ever-increasing number of spectators wishing to witness the matches.

From 1974 the World Cup trophy will be named simply 'The FIFA World Cup'. I was asked by Brazil to allow them to present a gold cup to be called the 'Stanley Rous Cup' but although I was grateful for the gesture I asked the Executive Committee to refuse the generous offer because I have always been averse to trophies bearing names of persons. Invariably, a trophy with a name attached is referred to with a shortened title such as 'The World Cup' and that is what the new cup will be styled. That does not mean that Jules Rimet and his fellow pioneers will be forgotten. They would certainly have been surprised at the development of the competition they founded, considering the number of countries involved and the changes in the regulations in the present competition.

It is important that enthusiasts for the game should know and understand how the World Cup is organised in other countries and continents. As President of an international federation I am sure that this history of the World Cup will enlighten the readers about football as it is played in all parts of the world. The information about the world's greatest football tournament as set out in the pages of this book is welcome and I recommend it to be widely read and as a useful addition to the bookshelf and library of all those who are interested in the game of soccer.

Stanley Rous

URUGUAY 1930

Background to 1930

Like so many of the best ideas in football, that of the World Cup was conceived in France. Its true parents were, indeed, two Frenchmen: Jules Rimet, after whom it was eventually named, and Henri Delaunay. Rimet was President of the French Federation, FFF, for thirty years from its beginning in 1919, and President of FIFA, the Fédération Internationale des Football Associations, from 1920 to 1954; an extraordinary record. Delaunay, who had been concerned with running French football from 1908, was officially Secretary from 1919 till his death in 1956, a little before the death of the 83-year-old Rimet.

Jules Rimet, father of the World Cup.

Henri Delaunay, another French World Cup pioneer.

These two men complemented each other: Rimet the persuader, the diplomat, sometimes intransigent, always devoted to the game; Delaunay the worker, visionary and energetic. Sometimes they quarrelled, but they were the pioneers of French football, European football – and the World Cup.

The very first meeting of FIFA took place in Paris in 1904 – without the benefit of British attendance – and decided rather grandly that it alone had the right to organise a world championship. This right was not to be exercised for twenty-six years. In 1920, at FIFA's Antwerp congress, concurrent with the Olympic Games, the idea of a World Cup, previously much debated, was accepted in principle. In 1924, at the Paris Olympics, the FIFA meeting discussed it in more serious detail, while a dazzling and hitherto obscure Uruguayan side walked off with the soccer tournament.

Two years later, at FIFA's congress, Delaunay proclaimed: 'Today international football can no longer be held within the confines of the Olympics; and many countries where professionalism is now recognised and organised cannot any longer be represented there by their best players.'

This had always been true of Britain, which even before the war had been represented by genuine amateurs and which in a couple of years would withdraw from FIFA over the question of broken time payments. Now, it was keeping out such rising countries as Austria and Hungary, while many of those which competed were professionals in all but name. In 1928, in Amsterdam, where Uruguay retained their title against a strong challenge from Argentina, Delaunay's resolution that the World Cup be set on foot at once was adopted. But where should it be played?

There were five aspirants: Italy, Holland, Spain, Sweden and Uruguay. Tiny Uruguay, with its proud footballing tradition – 'Other countries have their history,' their team manager, Viera, would say at the 1966 World Cup, 'Uruguay has its football' – made an offer extraordinary for a country of merely two million people. They would pay all travelling and hotel expenses for the visiting teams, and they would build a new stadium for the tournament. It would be in central Montevideo, and would be called the Centenary Stadium, for Uruguay in 1930 would be celebrating a hundred years of independence. It would be built in only eight months, three of which included the rainy season.

Faced by such transcendent enthusiasm, what could the European countries do but withdraw – altogether? None of the four disappointed hosts made the trip to Uruguay, which in those days took a wearying three weeks.

The contenders

Allotted the World Cup at FIFA's 1929 congress in Barcelona, Uruguay found themselves, two months before it was due to kick off, without a single European entrant. In addition to the four we have mentioned, the Austrians, Hungarians, Germans, Swiss and Czechs said no; the British were out of FIFA. Belgium, Romania and Yugoslavia vacillated, as did France, though after Rimet's appointment to the FIFA presidency, and Uruguay's 1924 appearance in Paris, the moral imperatives were strong.

Embittered, insulted, the Latin American federations threatened to withdraw from FIFA; a threat they would be making many times in the years to come. Belgium and Romania at last adhered – Belgium under the pressure of the veteran FIFA Vice-President, Rodolphe William Seeldrayers, Romania under that of King Carol himself. Though the German-speaking king was

The centenary stadium in Uruguay, unfinished when the World Cup began.

never popular in Romania, he had always had much to do with Romanian sport. One of his first acts, on coming to the throne, was to grant an amnesty to all suspended Romanian footballers. Now he picked the Romanian team himself and brought pressure on the companies which employed them to give them time off for Uruguay. Yugoslavia also agreed to go, so there would be four European entrants; but not even by the greatest feat of imagination could they be ranked among the élite. The bitterness in Montevideo was scarcely assuaged.

In the 1924 Olympics Uruguay had thrashed Yugoslavia 7–0 and France 5–1. In 1928, Belgium had been beaten by Argentina 6–3; and now they were travelling without three of their best players, including Bastin.

Argentina, traditional rivals of Uruguay in the Lipton Cup, would be there, however, and would be doughty rivals. In 1928, it had taken a replay before they succumbed 2–1 in the Olympic Final. They had lost their dazzling left-winger, Raimondo Orsi, to Juventus and the Italian national side, but there was still the muscular, ruthless, attacking centre-half, Luisito Monti, the 'man who strolls', a splendid centre-forward in Ferreira, dangerous wingers in Carlos Peucelle and Mario Evaristo.

The United States would be there too; moreover, they were one of the teams seeded in the four qualifying pools, which had been set up only when it was realised there wouldn't be enough countries to make a knock-out competition possible. At this time there was still professional football of a sort in the States, the rump of the attempt by such as Bethlehem Steel to put the sport on its feet in the 1920s. The American team, managed by Jack Coll of Brooklyn Wanderers, was made up largely of British and Scots pros: Alec Wood, James Gallacher, Andrew Auld, James Brown and Bart McGhee from Scotland, George Moorhouse from England. They were powerfully-built men whom the French players nicknamed 'the shot-putters'.

'They always amused us when we saw them training,' said Maurice Pinel, the talented young French centre-half, 'for they were always clad in tiny shorts which revealed enormous thighs like tree-trunks, and they would go lapping and slogging round and round a track like long-distance runners.'

Brazil were present, but it was not long since the gates had been opened to the black player and the game there was still somewhat in a condition of inspired anarchy. Chile and Mexico, who made up Pool I with Argentina and France; Bolivia, in Pool II with Brazil and Yugoslavia; Peru, in Pool III with Uruguay and Romania; Paraguay, in Pool IV with the USA and Belgium completed the entry of thirteen. The four Pool winners would go into the semi-finals.

Uruguay's World Cup team, 1930
Left to right, back row
Alvaro Gestido, José Nasazzi
Enrique Ballesteros
Ernesto Masqueroni
José Leandro Andrade
Lorenzo Fernandez; front row
Pablo Dorado, Hector Scarone
Hector Castro, Pedro Cea
Santos Iriarte

The Uruguayan team badge.

Uruguay

Uruguay were unquestionably the favourites, though their fine team of the 1924 and 1928 Olympics was fractionally past its peak; in the image of its famous centre-forward, Pedro Petrone. Nevertheless, it had home advantage and its still abundant talent in its favour, and it is arguable that it would have won the tournament whatever European teams had come, even England, Scotland and the formidable Austrian Wunderteam.

Like every other side in the competition, Uruguay played with an attacking centre-half – Lorenzo Fernandez. The wing-halves, playing on the flanks, were the famous José Andrade, a tiny negro with a conjuror's control of the ball, and the strongly-built, good-looking Alvaro Gestido, less given to feats of juggling but a superb passer of the ball. José Nasazzi, captain and right-back, was infinitely reliable, while the slender, red-haired Hector Scarone, physically frail, was yet a terror near goal.

Even in those distant times, training camps and their rigours were no strangers to Uruguay, whose own was set up in an expensive hotel in the middle of Montevideo's Prado park. When Mazzali, their excellent goalkeeper, sneaked in late one night, shoes in hand, and was caught by his manager he was banished, his place going to his reserve, Enrique Ballesteros.

The solidarity and camaraderie between these Uruguayan footballing heroes was extraordinary. As late as 1969 one could meet a group of elderly survivors, Andrade and Mazzali among them, in a Montevideo television studio, called together to celebrate publicly the twenty-fifth anniversary of their victory in Paris, chaffing each other like old soldiers.

The earlier matches

The four European teams, whose boat had picked up the Brazilians en route, were tumultuously welcomed in Montevideo, though none had been seeded head of a group; a distinction reserved for Uruguay, Argentina, Brazil and the USA. The Centenary Stadium was, alas, still unfinished, thanks to heavy rain; early matches had to be played on the grounds of the Penarol and Nacional clubs, Pocito and Central Park. On Sunday afternoon, July 13, France opened the tournament against Mexico with a 4–1 win; although their admirable and unspectacular goalkeeper, Alex Thépot, was kicked on the jaw after ten minutes, giving way to his left-half, Chantrel. (There would be no substitutes for another forty years.) The French team was a good and lively one, with Etienne Mattler, who would play so well for France for so long, at right-back, Pinel as pivot, and a captain, Alex Villaplane, the right-half, who would ultimately be shot by the French Resistance for collaborating with the Nazis.

Two days later, France faced the gifted Argentinians – and

were most unlucky to go down by 1–0. Monti was at his most ferocious, hurting the ankle of Lucien Laurent, France's inside-left, early in the game, and giving Pinel, who largely overplayed him, some kind of a knock every time they met. Monti it was who scored the goal, nine minutes from time. Argentina were given a free kick, twenty yards out. As Monti took it, Pinel stepped to his right, unsighting the excellent Thépot – and the shot flashed into the net.

Three minutes later, with Maschinot, the centre-forward, limping after another tackle by Monti, Marcel Langiller raced the length of the field. It might have been the equaliser, but Almeida Rego, the Brazilian referee, suddenly blew for time. Instant chaos. While Argentina's fans invaded the field of Central Park, the French players assailed the referee, insisting there were six minutes left. Mounted police galloped on to the field, Senhor Rego consulted his watch and his linesmen, and at last, raising his arms, cried to the heavens that he had erred in good faith. Cierro, the Argentinian inside-left, fainted, and the game resumed, and the remaining minutes petered uneventfully away.

Afterwards, Uruguay's watching players declared that France deserved to win, Thépot and Pinel were carried off shoulder high, and the Argentinians complained accordingly to the Organising Committee, threatening to go home; thus sounding what would become another tediously familiar note.

In their next match, against Mexico, deprived of Manuel Ferreira, taking – oh, pioneering days – a university exam, they brought in young Guillermo Stabile, *El Infiltrador*, destined to become the competition's leading scorer and eventually his country's team manager.

This was a match in which the Bolivian referee, Ulysses Saucedo, gave no fewer than five penalties – Monti was not playing! – of which perhaps two were justified.

Stabile, who had scored three goals against Mexico, kept his place for a tempestuous game against Chile, Ferreira coming in as inside-left. Two minutes from half-time Monti, back again, kicked at Torres, Chile's left-half, as he jumped to head the ball. Torres retaliated, and both teams indulged in a protracted brawl, broken up with great difficulty by the police. Not one player was sent off; but alas, this was to be the precursor of so many battles in World Cup matches to come, a warning that whatever else the tournament might inculcate, it would not be friendship between nations.

Argentina, Stabile scoring twice more, won 3–1 and advanced to the semi-finals. A tired France had anti-climactically gone down 1–0 to Chile, managed by the old Hungarian star, George Orth.

Uruguay did not enter the fray till July 18, when the Centenary Stadium was at last ready to receive them. Not unexpectedly, perhaps, the game against Peru was a disappointment. Peru's defence held out well, and where Romania had scored three against them, Uruguay could manage only one; a late one by Castro – a player who had lost the lower part of one arm.

For their next match, against Romania, Uruguay brought in Scarone and their new star, Pelegrin Anselmo, for Castro and Petrone, respectively, winning 4–0 in a canter to qualify.

In Group II, Yugoslavia unexpectedly toppled Brazil 2–1 in their first game. Brazil were individually cleverer, collectively inferior; another theme to be resumed, *grosso modo*, till the 1958 World Cup. Two of the Yugoslav team, Beck and Stefanovic, had just helped Sète win the French Cup. Seculic, who played in France for Montpellier, would later be national team manager, as would Tirnanic, who replaced him on the eve of the 1954 World Cup. Tirnanic and Beck scored in the first half-hour, another goal was disallowed for offside, and Brazil could muster but one reply through their captain, Neto. Each team then beat Bolivia 4–0, and the Yugoslavs went through.

So did the United States, their strong defence and breakaway attacks routing Belgium and Paraguay in turn by 3–0. In the semi-final, alas, the much greater pace and sophistication of the Argentinians simply overwhelmed them and they crashed 6–1; precisely the score by which Uruguay trounced Yugoslavia. The half-time score was only 1–0, a goal credited to Monti, but in the second half the Americans simply fell apart, conceding five more, the last three within nine minutes, two to the swift right-winger, Peucelle. Brown, their own outside-right, got their only goal, but the richest moment of the match had little to do with football.

John Langenus, the celebrated Belgian referee who officiated, whatever the heat, in cap and plus fours, gave a foul against an American. At this the team's medical attendant raced, bellicose, on to the field, to berate Langenus. Having had his say, he flung his box of medicines to the ground, the box burst open, various bottles smashed, including one full of chloroform, and its fumes rose to overpower the American. He was helped from the field.

Eighty thousand spectators watched Uruguay despatch Yugoslavia after sustaining the shock of a fourth-minute goal by Seculic. Cea and Anselmo made it 2–1 by the interval, and Yugoslavia were then refused, on a controversial offside decision, what would have been their equaliser.

So, in the second half, Uruguay scored four. Fernandez caught the Yugoslav defence off guard with a cleverly lobbed free kick which Iriarte converted, then Cea, the inside-left, scored two more, the first after a mistake by Yugoslavia's captain and right-back, Ivkovic. Next day, Argentina joined them in a Final which would be a repetition of the Olympic Final of 1928.

The display poster used for the first World Cup.

John Langenus, the Belgian referee, in his perpetual plus fours, watches Nasazzi, Uruguay's captain, shake hands with Ferreira of Argentina before the Final.

Uruguay's four goals in the World Cup Final against Argentina scored by (top to bottom) Dorado, Cea, Iriarte and Castro.

The Final Uruguay v. Argentina

In Buenos Aires the excitement was phenomenal. Ten packet-boats were chartered to take fans across the River Plate to Montevideo, but they were insufficient; thousands of desperate supporters thronged the centre of Buenos Aires, clamouring for more boats. When they eventually sailed, at ten o'clock on the eve of the Final, a great crowd thronged the quayside to see them off, letting off fireworks and chanting, '*Argentina si, Uruguay no!* Victory or death!' Arriving in Montevideo, the Argentinians were searched for revolvers by customs and police; and searched again at the entrance to the Centenary Stadium. The kick-off was scheduled for two o'clock; the gates were opened at eight in the morning, and by noon the ground was packed. Though it could take 100,000, the attendance was limited to 90,000 – with memories of an inaugural day when the police had been over-

1930 final: Guillermo Stabile, Argentina's centre-forward, equalises at 1–1 against Uruguay.

whelmed by the crowds and the ticket offices, now closed with metal grilles, were assailed.

John Langenus, chosen, as had been expected, to referee the match, demanded that the safety of himself and his linesmen be guaranteed, and only a few hours before kick-off did his fellow referees authorise him to preside. The Argentinian players had been under a police guard day and night, mounted police escorting their coach to and from each training session. Around the stadium, soldiers with fixed bayonets kept the crowds moving; and after all this there was still the question of the match ball.

Each team insisted on a ball of native manufacture; a point which had not been covered in the regulations. It was finally decided that Langenus should toss up on the field. To a fusillade of firecrackers, he did. Argentina won.

Though Uruguay clearly had to be favoured on their own stadium, before their own crowd, the team had not played with the assurance of its predecessors. Moreover, Pelegrin Anselmo was unfit and was replaced at centre-forward by Castro; Petrone's sun had definitely set. Argentina might have missed Orsi, but they had found Stabile, and their forward play had been excellent; full of fast, sweeping, intelligent movements, the traditionally fine ball control allied to subtle positioning. In goal, however, there was a manifest weakness. Angelo Bossio's flashy, unreliable play had led to his being dropped from the semi-final, but his replacement, Juan Botasso, was no great improvement.

The first half was pregnant with surprises. After only twelve minutes, Pablo Dorado, the Uruguayan right-winger, gave his country the lead, but Paucelle, his opposite number, equalised, and ten minutes from half-time John Langenus boldly sanctioned a goal by Stabile which Nasazzi, Uruguay's captain, fiercely insisted was offside. Crowds being unpredictable organisms, there was no attempt to invade the pitch this time, merely a stunned acceptance.

The crowd came to life again ten minutes after the interval, when Pedro Cea capped an insidious dribble with the equalising goal. Uruguay had broken the spell. Ten minutes more and the young Uruguayan outside-left, Santos Iriarte, put them ahead, and finally Castro, Anselmo's understudy, smashed the ball into the roof of the net in the concluding seconds. Uruguay had won an exciting and surprisingly good-tempered game.

Motor horns blared in triumph, ships blew their sirens in the port, flags and banners flew, the next day was proclaimed a national holiday. The golden, 50,000-franc Cup, designed by a French sculptor, Abel Lafleur, was consigned to Nasazzi by Jules Rimet.

In Buenos Aires, the Uruguayan Consulate was stoned by an infuriated mob until the police dispersed it by opening fire. The World Cup was well and truly launched.

Lorenzo Fernandez, Pedro Cea and Hector Scarone celebrate Uruguay's victory in the Final.

Uruguay 1930

Pool I

France 4, Mexico 1 (HT 3/0)
Argentina 1, France 0 (HT 0/0)
Chile 3, Mexico 0 (HT 1/0)
Chile 1, France 0 (HT 0/0)
Argentina 6, Mexico 3 (HT 3/0)
Argentina 3, Chile 1 (HT 2/1)

	P	W	D	L	F	A	Pts
Argentina	3	3	0	0	10	4	6
Chile	3	2	0	1	5	3	4
France	3	1	0	2	4	3	2
Mexico	3	0	0	3	4	13	0

Pool II

Yugoslavia 2, Brazil 1 (HT 2/0)
Yugoslavia 4, Bolivia 0 (HT 0/0)
Brazil 4, Bolivia 0 (HT 1/0)

	P	W	D	L	F	A	Pts
Yugoslavia	2	2	0	0	6	1	4
Brazil	2	1	0	1	5	2	2
Bolivia	2	0	0	2	0	8	0

Pool III

Romania 3, Peru 1 (HT 1/0)
Uruguay 1, Peru 0 (HT 0/0)
Uruguay 4, Romania 0 (HT 4/0)

	P	W	D	L	F	A	Pts
Uruguay	2	2	0	0	5	0	4
Romania	2	1	0	1	3	5	2
Peru	2	0	0	2	1	4	0

Pool IV

United States 3, Belgium 0 (HT 2/0)
United States 3, Paraguay 0 (HT 2/0)
Paraguay 1, Belgium 0 (HT 1/0)

	P	W	D	L	F	A	Pts
United States	2	2	0	0	6	0	4
Paraguay	2	1	0	1	1	3	2
Belgium	2	0	0	2	0	4	0

Semi-finals

Argentina 6
Botasso; Della Torre,
Paternoster; Evaristo, J.,
Monti, Orlandini;
Peucelle, Scopelli, Stabile,
Ferreira (capt.),
Evaristo, M.

United States 1
Douglas; Wood,
Moorhouse; Gallacher,
Tracey, Auld; Brown,
Gonsalvez, Patenaude,
Florie (capt.), McGhee.

SCORERS
Monti, Scopelli, Stabile (2), Peucelle (2), for Argentina
Brown for United States
HT 1/0

Uruguay 6
Ballesteros; Nasazzi
(capt.), Mascheroni;
Andrade, Fernandez,
Gestido; Dorado, Scarone,
Anselmo, Cea, Iriarte.

Yugoslavia 1
Yavocic; Ivkovic (capt.),
Milhailovic; Arsenievic,
Stefanovic, Djokic;
Tirnanic, Marianovic,
Beck, Vujadinovic, Seculic.

SCORERS
Cea (3), Anselmo (2), Iriarte for Uruguay
Seculic for Yugoslavia
HT 3/1

Final

Uruguay 4
Ballesteros; Nasazzi
(capt.), Mascheroni;
Andrade, Fernandez,
Gestido; Dorado, Scarone,
Castro, Cea, Iriarte.

Argentina 2
Botasso; Della Torre,
Paternoster; Evaristo, J.,
Monti, Suarez; Peucelle,
Varallo, Stabile, Ferreira
(capt.), Evaristo, M.

SCORERS
Dorado, Cea, Iriarte, Castro for Uruguay
Peucelle, Stabile for Argentina
HT 1/2

ITALY 1934

Background to Italy

It would be twenty years before the World Cup returned to South America – and to Uruguay. The 1934 tournament was altogether more high-powered and highly competitive, though for the first and only time so far the holders did not defend. Uruguay, still piqued by the defection of the European 'powers' in 1930, plagued, too, by one of those periodic players' strikes which would still torment them over forty years later, stayed at home. Italy organised it, Italy won, prompting the reflection of John Langenus: 'In the majority of countries, the World Championship was called a sporting fiasco, because beside the desire to win all other sporting considerations were non-existent, and because, moreover, a certain spirit brooded over the whole Championship. Italy wanted to win, it was natural, but they allowed it to be seen too clearly.'

The Italian team badge.

Given the Fascist climate of the times, it was perhaps inevitable. The Italian team, the *azzurri* (blues) were 'Mussolini's *azzurri*', the Duce himself would appear, heavy-chinned and smirking under a yachting cap, at Rome's Stadio Torino. Vittorio Pozzo, the Italian *Commissario Tecnico*, a great anglophile but a great authoritarian, unquestionably used the inflated spirit of the times to promote an atmosphere, a discipline, which subsequent Italian managers have envied, and which would never have been possible without it; any more than Pozzo himself, the revered father figure.

He and the equally authoritarian anglophile Hugo Meisl of Austria, were the dominant figures in European football between the wars, sharing the friendship of Herbert Chapman, the remarkable Yorkshireman who built up Arsenal. The 'natural' final would have been between Italy and Meisl's so-called Wunderteam, fractionally past its peak but still a fine side, which

The Stadio Torino in Rome, where the Final took place.

had whacked Italy 4–2 in Turin only months before the World Cup began. They would meet in the semi-final.

This time, it would be a knock-out competition with sixteen teams in the first round; a dispensation which meant that Brazil and Argentina came some eight thousand miles to play just one game. There had been, besides, a qualifying competition, in which, curiously, even the Italians were obliged to take part. They beat Greece in Milan, a match in which Nereo Rocco of Triestina, later the outstanding manager of Milan, played his only (half) game for his country.

The tournament had been assigned to Italy at the Stockholm congress of 1932. It was realised that it could no longer be confined to a single city, nor to a country without huge resources. Uruguay had in fact paid everyone's expenses and still made a comfortable profit in 1930, but the scale was growing. 'The Italian Federation', promised its delegate, *Avvocato* Mauro, 'is capable of sustaining these burdens, and even in the case of an adverse balance wants to hold the entire final stages of the tournament, using as its theatre the numerous and flourishing Italian cities, all provided with magnificent stadiums.' Behind the hard-working Mauro and his pleasant energetic colleague, Engineer Barassi, the Fascist government stood ready to pick up the cheque.

Italy and Pozzo

Pozzo, an immensely shrewd, practical psychologist and a clever tactician, whipped his temperamental players off to Lago Maggiore, then to the Tuscan watering place of Roveta, where they behaved impeccably. The struggle for the Italian Championship between Inter and Juventus had left scars. Pozzo's remedy was skilful: he would set players whom he knew had quarrelled to share the same room. When they complained, he would reply that he knew all about it, 'but we are trying to build a *team*. You must convince yourself that this man is not an enemy but a friend.' Next morning, he poked his teddy bear's head around their doors to ask: 'Well, cannibals, have you eaten each other yet?' Embarrassed grunts. Later, each would take him aside to say, 'He isn't such a bad fellow. The public set me against him.'

Another of Pozzo's stratagems for dealing with a spoiled player – a French writer called him 'the poor captain of a company of millionaires' – was to give a man orders in a training game then, if he argued, to let it go. Later in the game, which he was refereeing, he would approach him again and say, 'You know, you were right just now. I've been thinking about it. You *should* do so-and-so' – so-and-so being what Pozzo himself had wanted. 'King, with a strong hand,' he would say. 'If I let them make mistakes, I lose my authority.' He also believed that 'English

Special souvenir trophies and stamps commemorating the World Cup.

players can be treated collectively, Italian players must always be treated individually. They like to know you are on their side.'

Pozzo, a sturdy, small, athletic man, was a Piedmontese, an *alpino*. Before the Great War he studied in Switzerland, then came to England and liked it so much that he refused his family's calls to come home. When they cut off his allowance he made a living by teaching English all over the Midlands. Meanwhile, he watched and admired the fine Manchester United team on whose tactics he would later model Italy's; at a time when English football had abandoned them. Charlie Roberts, United's famous attacking centre-half, was a particular hero. One day Pozzo shyly waited outside the ground for him after a match, asked if they might speak together, and began a germinal series of conversations. He also became acquainted with the mighty goal-scorer Steve Bloomer.

It was only by a bluff that Pozzo's family got him back, sending him a return ticket to attend a wedding, then refusing to let him leave Turin. He kept the surviving half of that ticket for the rest of his life. In Turin, he helped to found the Torino football club, became Secretary of the Italian Federation, took a team to the Olympic tournament of 1912 in Stockholm at the last moment, and made Hugo Meisl's acquaintance when Austria beat them 5–1. The following year he arranged a return in Turin, to the horror of the Prefect ('Have you ever been in an asylum?'). There was no trouble.

The third back game, entrenched in England for some five years, was still largely unknown in Europe, and of all the entrants only the methodical but somewhat uninspired Germans played it. If Uruguay had refused to come, Argentina, infuriated and made fearful by Italy's poaching of their players, sent a weakened team. Pozzo's justification for picking *oriundi*, foreign players of Italian extraction such as Monti and Orsi, was that 'if they can die for Italy, they can play for Italy', meaning that they were liable for military service. This rationalisation would look a little sick when, on the eve of the Abyssinian war, three *oriundi*, including the World Cup winger, Guaita, having been ordered to report for their Army medical, were caught trying to sneak across the border.

Pozzo would reproach himself for the next four years over the way he made up his team, taking a huge squad into training camp, then gradually and painfully whittling them down. In 1938 he went to the other extreme, firmly choosing his twenty-two and sticking by them, although in the case of Depetrini it meant excluding a player in form.

Needing cover for Monti at centre-half, he decided upon the Roman player, Attilio Ferraris IV, though he knew him to be unfit. He was, however, a combatant of the type Pozzo admired, so he went to the capital to see him and talked to him on the top step of Rome stadium's terraces. 'Do you think I can still do it?' Ferraris asked him.

'Certainly, if you do what I tell you.'

'I'm smoking thirty to forty cigarettes a day.'

'We'll cut them down gradually.'

'Let's try,' said Ferraris.

'Let's try,' responded Pozzo.

In goal, the veteran Giampiero Combi had been replaced by the marvellously acrobatic Carlo Ceresoli of Inter. Then, during a training game at Fiorentina's splendid stadium beneath the trees, hills and villas of Fiesole, while Pozzo leaned against his very goal post, Ceresoli made a daring save; and broke his arm. Combi watched him leave for hospital and said to Pozzo: 'Then it's up to me?'

Umberto Caligaris, the left-back with fifty-nine caps, was very distressed to have lost his place to the younger Allemandi. Viri Rosetta, his partner in so many internationals, was himself to be replaced by Monzeglio, who would in turn be deposed by Alfredo Foni during the 1938 tournament. Caligaris was afraid his record number of caps would be beaten by the dazzling, dark young Meazza of Inter, a player of infinite skills and exceptional finishing power, despite a slight physique – though in fact the record was unbroken till 1971, when it was beaten by another left-back, Giacinto Facchetti.

At Roveta, the only complaint to be heard was about the noise made by the peacocks. 'Why did they ever save two of them for the Ark?' demanded the Bologna centre-forward, Schiavio, who would play with Meazza – really a centre – on his right.

Oddly, the team was jeered by local hooligans when it got to Chiusi on its way to Rome, an insult which very nearly provoked violence. The temperature would change.

Austria and Meisl

Meisl's background was very different from Pozzo's, and to some extent those backgrounds, each with its assumptions and influences, were reflected in the teams. Italy, for all the artistry of brilliant individual players – Meazza, Orsi, Ferrari – was a robust, forcing side. Ever since he had watched Charlie Roberts, Pozzo had wanted a strong centre-half capable of swinging the ball far to the wings, and he eventually found him in . . . Luisito Monti, having meanwhile jettisoned Fulvio Bernardini, the most elegant of all Italian centre-half-backs.

It was no chance, no coincidence, that Monti should abominate the Austrian international centre-forward Mathias Sindelar, the 'man of paper', for each in his own way embodied the philosophy of his own team. Sindelar, tall, blond and ghostly thin, was the quintessence of the Vienna school, evolved and inspired by Meisl, the son of a wealthy Viennese Jewish business-man, and little Jimmy Hogan, his remarkable Lancastrian coach. Sindelar's lovely control, his graceful movements, his evanescent swerve, infuriated and tormented the robust Monti, whom Juventus had brought to Italy fat, ageing and unfit, but who with typical determination had trained himself back into form. 'When I see Sindelar,' he told Pozzo, 'I see red.' Once, in an international match, he hit him.

Hugo Meisl's passion for football was overriding; so much so that his disapproving father 'banished' him to work in Trieste. To no avail. Meisl continued to correspond with a leading Viennese player, Johann Leute, and when he returned to do his military service he was just as conversant as before with all that was going on in Austrian football.

He brought Hogan to Vienna and, after the Englishman's first coaching session had failed, inspired him to become a great coach; the man to whom both the Austrians and the Hungarians would dedicate their later victories. Hogan believed in the Scottish style of scientific, largely short-passing, football. So did Meisl. There was one great crisis, a few years after the Great War, when Austria were thrashed on a snow-covered pitch at Nuremberg by South Germany. All through the fifteen-hour journey home, Meisl and his men discussed the validity, or otherwise, of their delicate style, and decided at last to keep it. The foundations of the Wunderteam had been laid.

In 1932 the team came to Chelsea, and gave a powerful England side a dreadful fright, losing by four goals to three. Sindelar, Smistik, the brilliant captain and attacking centre-half; Zischek, the clever young winger known as 'the Ghost'; Schall, the hard-shooting inside-left (a rarity, this, in the Vienna school); and Seszta, the muscular left-back, were all still present, though Rudi Hiden, the great goalkeeper, had gone.

But 1934 was a bad year for Austrian football. The team was tired and out of form, and Meisl brought it to Italy only out of loyalty to Pozzo. 'We have no chance,' he told his brother Willy, once Austria's goalkeeper but by then a famous journalist who would end his career in London. 'England', he added, 'could not win this Championship. I don't know whether they could reach the semi-final.' Fair enough comment, when England had just lost by 2–1 away to Hungary and Czechoslovakia, strong contenders for the World Cup. Meisl insisted, however, that if he could have just one English player, the Arsenal forward Cliff Bastin, Austria would walk away with the tournament.

The opening games

There was still, curiously, an eliminating match to play before the tournament proper could begin; curiously because it took place in Rome between two countries as distant as Mexico and the United States. The Americans, with only two survivors from their 1930 semi-final team, won, but were thrashed 7–1 in the same Stadio Torino by Italy in the following game. Schiavio scored three, Orsi two, while Donelli, an Italo-American, hammer of the Mexicans, fulfilled his ambition by scoring America's only goal. Thirty-two teams had entered the qualifying tournament; twenty-two from Europe, eight from the Americas, one each from Asia and Africa – none from Britain.

Both South American teams went out at once. In Genoa, Spain, captained by their celebrated goalkeeper Ricardo Zamora, now a veteran, were 3–1 up against Brazil at half-time, a score which did not change. Brazil, without their full-backs, were once again a haphazard agglomeration of shimmering talent, including the little, black, acrobatic centre-forward Leonidas, whose time would come four years later. Silva and de Britto – later the mentor of Pelé – were spectacular inside-forwards, Silva scoring Brazil's goal, but the obviously nervous de Britto missed a penalty after a bad foul by Quincoces, the Spanish back.

Argentina went down 3–2 to Sweden, their team including not a single member of the 1930 side. Indeed, its one representative in the tournament was Monti – playing for Italy. Belis gave Argentina the lead with a powerful twenty-five-yard free kick, but the less individually gifted Swedes prevailed through more solid teamwork and better use of the wings. Galateo, a superb ball player, almost scored for Argentina after beating five men, and did score after a similar run just after half-time, but Argentina still had goalkeeping trouble. Freschi missed Rosen's lob, Sweden were back in the game, and Kroon got the winner ten minutes from time.

The World Cup poster, signed by the winning Italian team.

In Turin, France provided the chief surprise of the round, doing far better than had been expected against the Austrians, and confirming the Cup-fighting abilities they had displayed in Uruguay. They still had Alex Thépot in goal, Mattler at full-back, and Austria, who had most of the luck that was going, won only in extra time with a most dubious goal. Schall scored it, looking blatantly offside – he thought so himself, but the Dutch referee Van Moorsel let it stand. French critics maintained that he had been upset by just hearing the news that Holland had unexpectedly been knocked out by the Swiss. That made it 2–1, France's only goal having been scored by their injured centre-forward, Jean Nicolas. Bican added a third, Verriest replying with a penalty for hands. Austria had, as Meisl anticipated, looked tired and stale.

The Germans, who had prepared thoroughly, whittling down their team from thirty-eight possibles, and were captained by the versatile, blond Franz Szepan ('Saucepan' to English teams) were startled by Belgium in Florence, but recovered strongly. The Belgians had squeezed through ahead of Eire only by ·09 of a goal, had been out of form for some time and had lost their star left-winger, Stanley van den Eynde, who broke a leg in Dublin. Nonetheless, Voorhoof scored twice in the first half to give them a 2–1 lead; then the team blew up. Conen, Germany's centre-forward, completed a hat trick, and his side won 5–2.

In Trieste the fancied Czechs, with another famous veteran, Frantisek Planicka, in goal, were troubled by the Romanians. It was as well, indeed, that Planicka was there, for he made two marvellous saves. Dobai scored for Romania after eleven minutes, but Puc, the thrustful Czech left-winger, and Nejedly, their dangerous, graceful inside-left, replied in the second half. The winner was rather a lucky goal, for Nejedly received the ball after Sobotka won it in a bounce-up.

Hungary were given a surprisingly hard time of it by Egypt in Naples, winning only 4–2; small compensation after their astonishing 3–0 defeat by Egypt in the 1924 Olympic tournament. Skilful and fluent as ever in attack, they did not, however, play their gifted centre-forward, Dr George Sarosi.

Switzerland beat the Dutch 3–2 in Milan; one of their goals, by the bespectacled centre-forward Kielholz, came from a shot which hit a bump in the ground and was crazily diverted.

The second round

The second round included two fascinating pairings: Italy would play Spain in Florence; Austria and Hungary, those old foes, would meet at Bologna.

Throughout the Italian peninsula, in every café and *botti-glieria*, the talk was of Zamora, thirty-three years old now, a rare stumbling block to Italy in the past. How would he play in Florence? At least he had mellowed. Whereas in 1924, on the eve of the Paris Olympics, he had assured a journalist: 'We shall win, of course!', he now told the same questioner: 'I've no idea. Who can tell?'

In the event, he played the game of his life, but was so roughly treated by the Italian forwards that he missed the replay. For a hundred and twenty minutes he defied the strong, ruthless Italian attack, minimally protected by the Swiss Mercet, a craven referee later suspended by his own federation. By half-time, the Italians had forced sixteen corners to the Spaniards' six, but Zamora was 'eating' corners. On the only occasion he was beaten, Quincoces kicked off the line. Not that the Spaniards always played a drawing-room game. Once in the series Quincoces and his fellow full-back tried to sandwich the slender Orsi, but he nipped between them, and they knocked each other flat. '*Ai, mi madre!*' cried the right-back.

Spain took the lead with a goal which might have demoralised a less resilient team than Italy. When Langara, the centre-forward, took a free kick, Regueiro – whose son would play for Mexico in the 1968 Olympics – swung at the ball, miskicked it utterly, and in miskicking beat the wrong-footed Combi.

A minute after the interval, Italy were lucky to equalise when Pizziolo, the right-half, took another free kick. Zamora, obstructed by Schiavio, could only push the ball out, and Ferrari drove it home.

In extra time, Pozzo switched Schiavio and Guaita, as he would in the Final, but now it was unproductive. After the game he called each of his players, one by one, into the salon of the hotel where they were staying on the Lungarno. For the replay the following day he wanted only volunteers, and there were three changes. Pizziolo had broken his leg – another blow Italy had ridden with aplomb – and gave way to Ferraris IV, while de Maria and Borel had their only game of the competition, in attack. Spain by contrast were able to use only four of their previous team. Noguet, a young reserve, stood in for Zamora, and Bosch, the left-winger, was hurt as early as the fourth minute.

Eight minutes later Meazza, always dangerous in the air, rose gracefully to Orsi's corner and headed Italy into the semi-finals. Noguet, knee-padded and courageous, was excellent, but there was no replacing the sheer moral impact Zamora had on both sides. Early in the second half, Monti briefly lost form and Spain seemed to have a chance, but Italy survived and he recovered.

In Bologna, Hugo Meisl picked the busy little inside-forward Horwarth and he, though no Sindelar, gave the team fresh drive in what Meisl described as 'a brawl, not an exhibition of football'. After only seven minutes, Horwarth raced in to convert Zischek's cross, and with Sarosi well under form Hungary found it hard to get back into the game.

Six minutes after half-time, Zischek, in the centre, drove in Bican's pass to make it 2–0, and the match began to get rough. Sarosi reduced the lead from a penalty, things grew rougher still, and Markos, Hungary's right-winger, foolishly got himself sent off just when his team threatened to equalise. As it was, they pressed gamely on till the end, though the most dangerous shot was Sindelar's, gloriously saved by Szabo. Austria, calmer and better together, had deserved their win, and had found new life.

In Milan, heavy rain did not prevent a large crowd, mushroomed with umbrellas and chequered with swastika flags, from attending the Germany–Sweden game. Germany, with one inside-forward lying deep, the other upfield, met in Sweden a team of similar Nordic propensities, solid rather than skilful, and had slightly the better of the first half.

Twelve minutes after the break, Rosen, the Swedish centre-half, found Kroon, his left-winger, unmarked ten yards from goal. Kroon shot wide, and Sweden's chance had gone. Three minutes later, when Rydberg, who had made two fine saves in the first half, could only push a ball out, Hohmann, Germany's insight-right, scored. Another three minutes and he got a far more spectacular goal, beating both Swedish backs and drawing Rydberg out of goal before placing his shot coolly past him.

Sweden soon afterwards lost their left-half, E. Andersson, who was hurt, but they kept on gamely and Dunker scored them a consoling if irrelevant goal.

At Turin, the Czechs won the best match of the round against the combative Swiss. The game swung and swayed, but the Czechs always seemed to have the resources of skill, stamina and confidence to regain the lead, running out winners by 3–2.

The bespectacled Kielholz gave Switzerland, who had many vociferous supporters there, the lead in a breakaway after eighteen minutes. Six minutes later, the clever Czech forwards Svoboda and Sobotka interpassed through the Swiss defence for Svoboda to equalise. After half-time, the Czechs besieged the Swiss goal, and within four minutes Svoboda and Cambal, the attacking centre-half, had put Sobotka through to make it 2–1.

Now it was the turn of the Swiss to bombard the opposing goal, but the resources of Planicka and his defenders frustrated them till at last their inside-left, Trello Abegglen of that famous football-playing family, equalised. At this the Czechs revived once more, and seven minutes from time Nejedly – 'pure as

Italy v. Austria. Peter Platzer dives at the feet of Italy's forwards.

Bohemian crystal' as the French writer Jean Eskenazi once called him – won the tie.

The semi-finals Italy v. Austria

The semi-finals now brought together Italy and Austria in Milan, and Germany and the Czechs in Rome. By all rights, the Italians should have been tired, the Austrians favoured, but Hugo Meisl would have none of it. Italy, he said, had better reserves than Austria, were better prepared and would be better supported. Perhaps his pessimism would have been confounded again had not Horwarth, the lively catalyst, been injured, his place going to Schall; and had it not been for a deluge creating just the heavy surface which the Vienna school found anathema.

Zischek and Sindelar – sternly guarded by Monti – were particularly disadvantaged in the heavy conditions, but Smistik had a magnificent game at centre-half. The only goal was scored by the Argentinian right-winger Guaita after eighteen minutes, in a clever move that followed a corner. Later, he missed another chance to score, and Austria, who looked much more tired than the surprisingly lively Italians, did not have a shot at goal until the forty-second minute. Ferraris was in dominant form, which was as well for Italy when the Austrians turned on pressure for a quarter of an hour after the interval. In the last minute, with Italy again calling the tune, Zischek picked up a clearance by his

The semi-final between Italy and Austria in Milan. Guaita beats Platzer for the winning goal.

goalkeeper, Peter Platzer, and tore through Italy's defence while the crowd watched, silent and aghast. But he shot wide, and Italy had reached the Final.

Czechoslovakia v. Germany

So did the Czechs, who beat Germany in Rome, showing clearly that the W formation, like patriotism, was not enough. They frolicked round the muscular, well-organised but uninspired Germans like Lilliputians round a Gulliver, while a curious weakness of the Germans was poor finishing. Rahn, Seeler and Muller were far away. The Germans, moreover, began the game most cautiously, both inside-forwards, rather than just one, lying deep; Hohmann, their talented inside-right, was seriously missed.

The crowd, including Mussolini in his yachting cap, was neutral and restrained as the Czechs gladly took up the initiative the Germans gave them. After twenty-one minutes Junek, the right-winger, concluded an attack which swept all the way across the forward-line with a shot which Kress could only beat out. Nejedly scored; and Czechoslovakia became a little complacent.

The second half, however, saw them regain their grip, and victory seemed inevitable – when Planicka made one of those errors which remind one of Disraeli's epigram that the defects of great men are the consolation of dunces. He simply stood and watched as a long shot by Noack, Germany's inside-left, sailed over him into goal. 1–1.

Germany, thus reprieved, pressed fiercely, and Ctyroky almost put through his own goal. Ten minutes after the equaliser, however, the forceful Puc belted a free kick from just outside the area against the bar. Krcil, the left-half, sent it back into the net. Germany collapsed, and Nejedly, taking Cambal's pass, dribbled fluently through to add the third.

Three days before the Final, Germany consoled themselves with victory in the third place match in Naples against a dejected Austria. Both teams made several changes, and Germany scored after only twenty-four seconds; another save-rebound-shoot affair, scored by Lehner. Conen got a second, Horwarth, fit again, made it 1–2, and for a while Austria made the Germans look ploddingly inadequate. But Lehner eventually scored again for Germany, and the only goal of the second half came from the Austrian left-back Seszta's thirty-yard free kick. Play became rough, but Germany survived.

The Final   Italy v. Czechoslovakia

Rome had been curiously phlegmatic about the tournament, and even for the Final there were surprising gaps on the terraces. The

Vittorio Pozzo and the winning Italian team. Left to right, back row: Combi (captain), Monti, Ferraris IV, Allemandi, Guaita, Ferrari; front row: Schiavio, Meazza, Monzeglio, Bertolini, Orsi.

Czechs, living at delightful Frascati and very much the underdogs, were showered with gifts: sausages, ham, a silver talisman one player was urged to sew on his shirt, seventeen hundred telegrams of good wishes. Two special trains and three motor coaches of supporters set off from Prague. It was perhaps a pity the game was not played in the north, for the Stadio Torino, with its pitch of less than regulation size, its less than 'capacity' crowd, was hardly an ideal arena.

It was known that Italy had the stamina and the power, not to mention home advantage and support, but the Czechs had wonderful skill and subtlety. The cliché of rapier against bludgeon was not wholly unfair; and how nearly the rapier prevailed!

The Czechs, indeed, began with some splendid, characteristically short-passing 'Danubian school' football, with Cambal, the centre-half, everywhere, Puc a great trial to the Italian right flank, Svoboda a clever inside-right. Planicka, though fate would be cruel to him again, looked authoritative in goal, ably abetted by his right-back, Zenisek. Pozzo felt that both teams were keyed up, not least his goalkeeper, Combi, and that the game was a disappointing one in consequence.

The World Cup Final, held in Rome. Giampiero Combi is beaten by Puc: the Czechs lead 1–0.

There was no goal till twenty minutes from the end. Then Puc, who had been off the field with cramp, returned to take a corner. When the ball finally came back to him, he struck a long shot to Combi's right, the goalkeeper dived late – and Italy were one down. How near the Czechs then came to making the game sure! Sobotka missed a fine chance, Svoboda banged a shot against the post. The Italian attack was stuttering: Schiavio looked tired, Guaita moved into the middle to confuse matters.

Things looked black for Italy till eight minutes from the end, when a goal dropped out of the blue. Raimondo Orsi, the Argentinian left-winger, received the ball from Guaita, ran through the Czech defence, feinted with his left foot and shot with his right. The ball, swerving crazily, brushed Planicka's desperate fingers and curled freakishly into the net. Next day, Orsi tried twenty times to repeat the shot for the benefit of photographers, with no goalkeeper in goal; and failed!

So there was extra time. Pozzo decided he wanted Schiavio and Guaita to keep switching, but such was the tumult of the ecstatic Italian fans – one had earlier seized a Czech journalist's hair through the safety netting – that he was unable to make himself heard. At last – he was a great coacher from the touchline – he rushed around the pitch and managed to tell Guaita. The second time the switch was made it produced a goal.

Ninety-seven minutes had been played when a limping Meazza got the ball on the right wing, where the Czechs had tended to neglect him. He crossed to Guaita, who made ground and in turn found Schiavio. He, with a final effort, beat Ctyroky and shot past Planicka. When asked afterwards what strength he had called on, he said wryly, 'The strength of desperation'.

Italy had not only won the World Cup; they had made a profit of a million lire in the process. The more sceptical wondered if they would have won anywhere else. Four years later, they would get their answer.

The Italian and Czech teams give the fascist salute.

Italy 1934

First round

Italy 7, United States 1 (HT 3/0)
Czechoslovakia 2, Romania 1 (HT 0/1)
Germany 5, Belgium 2 (HT 1/2)
Austria 3, France 2 (HT 1/1, 1/1) after extra time
Spain 3, Brazil 1 (HT 3/1)
Switzerland 3, Holland 2 (HT 2/1)
Sweden 3, Argentina 2 (HT 1/1)
Hungary 4, Egypt 2 (HT 2/1)

Second round

Germany 2, Sweden 1 (HT 1/0)
Austria 2, Hungary 1 (HT 1/0)
Italy 1, Spain 1 (HT 1/0, 1/1) after extra time
Italy 1, Spain 0 (HT 1/0) Replay
Czechoslovakia 3, Switzerland 2 (HT 1/1)

Semi-finals

Rome

Czechoslovakia 3	**Germany 1**
Planicka (capt.); Burger, Ctyroky; Kostalek, Cambal, Krcil; Junek, Svoboda, Sobotka, Nejedly, Puc.	Kress; Haringer, Busch; Zielinski, Szepan (capt.), Bender; Lehner, Siffling, Conen, Noack, Kobierski.

SCORERS
Nejedly (2), Krcil for Czechoslovakia
Noack for Germany
HT 1/0

Milan

Italy 1	**Austria 0**
Combi (capt.); Monzeglio, Allemandi; Ferraris IV, Monti, Bertolini; Guaita, Meazza, Schiavio, Ferrari, Orsi.	Platzer; Cisar, Seszta; Wagner, Smistik (capt.), Urbanek; Zischek, Bican, Sindelar, Schall, Viertel.

SCORER
Guaita for Italy
HT 1/0

Third place match

Naples

Germany 3	**Austria 2**
Jakob; Janes, Busch; Zielinski, Muenzenberg, Bender; Lehner, Siffling, Conen, Szepan (capt.), Heidemann.	Platzer; Cisar, Seszta, Wagner, Smistik (capt.), Urbanek; Zischek, Braun, Bican, Horwath, Viertel.

SCORERS
Lehner (2), Conen for Germany
Seszta for Austria
HT 3/1

Final

Rome

Italy 2	**Czechoslovakia 1**
(after extra time) Combi (capt.); Monzeglio, Allemandi; Ferraris IV, Monti, Bertolini; Guaita, Meazza, Schiavio, Ferrari, Orsi.	Planicka (capt.); Zenisek, Ctyroky; Kostalek, Cambal, Krcil; Junek, Svoboda, Sobotka, Nejedly, Puc.

SCORERS
Orsi, Schiavio for Italy
Puc for Czechoslovakia
HT 0/0

FRANCE 1938

Background to France

By 1938 and the third World Cup, Europe was in turmoil. The *anschluss* had swallowed up Austria, whose best players had been greedily snatched by the German national team, while Spain was in the throes of civil war. From South America, meanwhile, Uruguay, still piqued by the refusals of 1930 and troubled by a continuing crisis of professionalism, declined to come to France; as did Argentina. The Argentinians were still sulking because France's candidature for the World Cup had been preferred to their own at FIFA's 1936 Congress at the Opera Kroll, Berlin. After coquetting with the organisers for months, they at length decided to stay at home; a decision which provoked a riot outside their federation's offices in Buenos Aires that the police had to quell.

Italy's team, in the intervening years, had almost completely changed. Monzeglio would lose his place after the opening World Cup game against Norway, leaving only the two inside-forwards, Peppino Meazza and Gioanin Ferrari, as survivors of 1934. There was, however, new blood in abundance, above all a marvellous young centre-forward called Silvio Piola, originally from the Pro Vercelli club, tall, well made, thrustful, a superb combination of power, speed and skill. His debut for Italy had been made in 1935, with a couple of goals; two years before that Major Frank Buckley, the legendary Wolves manager, had seen him play in Nice and predicted, 'Piola will shortly be the best centre-forward in Europe.'

There was a remarkable new goalkeeper in Aldo Olivieri, and two backs, Foni and Rava, who had been bought by Juventus and had played in the supposedly amateur team which won the 1936 Olympic tournament. Foni was elegant, Rava robust; he had been sent off during that Olympiad. Another member of the Olympic team, the left-half Locatelli, was also in the World Cup party, while there were excellent, fast new wingers in Amadeo Biavati of Bologna and Triestina's Gino Colaussi.

The *azzurri*, beaten only once since 1935, in Prague, still eschewed the third back game, still favoured a muscular, roving centre-half. Monti had gone, but in the burly, forceful Urugu-ayan Andreolo, Pozzo had found another 'successor' to Charlie Roberts. It was a formidable team, and in later years, when Pozzo compared it to their 1934 team, he wrote: 'The Rome team was perhaps stronger, more combative, on the individual plane; the Paris side was better together as a team, collectively, in understanding and amalgam.' The 1938 team, he thought, would have beaten England, as the 1934 team notoriously failed to do – had they played on a neutral ground, 'and not in the mud of London or Manchester'.

With Austria out – England declined to take their place – the Hungarians and Czechs looked the most formidable rivals. *Paris-*

The Italian team badge.

Soir gave the most percipient forecast: Italy to win, Hungary the best outsiders, Brazil the unknown quantity.

Brazil, indeed, were much fancied; and vastly enthusiastic, by contrast with the South American dissidents. They were the first team to arrive and the last to leave, bringing with them a galaxy of brilliant players, but succumbing finally through the sin of presumptuousness, and engaging in a deplorable 'battle of Bordeaux' which foreshadowed the 'battle of Berne' sixteen years later.

Hungary had George Sarosi, at the height of his form, leading their attack again – though he had made his name at and occasionally reverted to centre-half. He had once scored five against Austria in Vienna. In the past nine months, Hungary had thrashed the Czechs 8–3 (seven to Sarosi!), beaten Austria 5–3, and scored eleven against Greece. Zsengeller, a gifted twenty-two-year-old inside-forward, now lined up beside Sarosi, who had turned down a 400,000 lire offer from Inter's Hungarian coach, Feldman, to play in Milan.

Germany had been badly beaten 6–3 in Berlin the previous May by England's touring team – which had then lost to Switzerland but had beaten France. By now they had replaced their manager-selector, Otto Nerz, with little Sepp Herberger, a former Mannheim inside-forward who would remain in office, indestructibly and impressively, till 1962. An immensely shrewd, vigorous, personable manager, a practical psychologist and a cunning tactician, Herberger now could do little more than pull the shattered pieces of his team together. He reinforced it with four Austrian internationals.

The two posters produced for the 1938 World Cup.

The tournament included – for the first and only time to date – the Cubans, Poles and Dutch East Indies, while the Swedes, Romanians and Swiss were again present. The Czechs, runners-up in 1934, still had Planicka in goal, the classic Nejedly at inside-left and Kostalek at right-half. Otherwise they, like Italy, had rebuilt. Once more, despite distances and early eliminations, the competition was to follow a knock-out pattern.

The first round

Italy were very nearly knocked out at once: in Marseilles, by the Norwegians, who had given their Olympic team an arduous run for their money. Perhaps the players were disconcerted by the torrent of insults poured on them before the start, when they gave the Fascist salute, by anti-Fascist refugees in the crowd. Pozzo, typically, made the players hold the salute until the noise abated, when he dropped his arm. Then, with a cry of 'Team, attention! Salute!' he saluted again, once more keeping his right arm aloft till the renewed tumult waned. By this time, the Frenchmen in the crowd were in any case getting bored with the performance, the tumult died – and Pozzo again dropped his arm. The show could go on.

After the match, Pozzo related, he was approached outside the stadium by one of these Italians who asked whether there were any Venetians in the team. 'Serantoni,' Pozzo said. 'Good,' said the man, while Pozzo stoically reflected that the expatriates were really not so hostile – 'or they could have shot at us'.

The Norwegians, in their fashion, certainly shot at them, above all the blond Brunyldsen, a mighty centre-forward whom Pozzo later called 'a cruel thorn in my crown of roses', and who would have won the game for his team were it not for an astonishing one-handed save by Olivieri as Pozzo froze behind the goal.

Norway could scarcely have made a worse beginning on the new Marseilles Stadium, nor retrieved the situation more determinedly. Playing with six of the team which had lost only 2–1 to Italy in the Olympic semi-final, they were a goal down in only the second minute. Piola found Ferrari, whose shot was dropped by the Norwegian goalkeeper. Ferraris II, the left-winger, shot the ball home. R. Johansen, the Norwegian right-back, now indicated Piola to his centre-half, Eriksen, who nodded and dropped back to dedicate himself successfully to the big centre-forward, Henriksen, the little right-half, taking his place in midfield. The pendulum swung.

Brunyldsen, huge and ubiquitous, now began to set dreadful problems for the Italian defence. He was well abetted by his fast, direct left-winger, Brustad – whom Pozzo, though he chose him later for Europe against England, always felt to have a grudge against him, and Kwammen, a composed inside-right. Three times post and bar were hit, and finally Brustad, in the second half, received from Brunyldsen, cut inside Monzeglio, and equalised. Soon afterwards, Brustad had the ball in the net again, to be given offside; and just before time, Olivieri made his famous save from Brunyldsen.

Five minutes into extra time, Piola at last evaded the Norwegian defence, when Paserati shot. Again H. Johansen could only block, and the centre-forward scored. Italy had survived their hardest match of the tournament.

The Brazilians, who had taken up secluded quarters in the forests of Alsace, telling questioners they would begin their training 'at twenty-six o'clock', were drawn against Poland, in Strasbourg. The game turned out to be an extraordinary one, with extra time, eleven goals, and infinite swings of the pendulum. Brazil had the classic, coloured full-back, Domingos Da Guia and the wonderfully elastic black centre-forward, Leonidas, scorer of four goals; the Poles had their blond inside-left Willimowski, himself the scorer of four.

The Brazilian team on board the ship bringing them to Europe.

Fast, agile, tireless, fearless, a deadly exponent of the overhead, bicycle kick, Leonidas was with Da Guia and another fine full-back, Dr Nariz, the highest-paid player in Brazil. He could shoot from any angle, and it was said that throughout this World Cup not one of his shots was off target. Who knows what would have happened had Brazil not committed the sublime folly of omitting him from their semi-final against Italy; truly a *folie de grandeur*?

At Strasbourg it was wet and muddy, but Leonidas was as dangerous as ever. In the second half, he once took off his boots and threw them dramatically to his trainer, but the Swedish referee, Eklind, made him put them on again.

Surprisingly, the Brazilians chose no fewer than six debutants in their team, but by half-time Leonidas already had a hat trick, and his team were leading, 3–1. After this, the Polish halfbacks took hold of the game, and it was Willimowski who ran riot. He scored twice, forcing extra time.

Willimowski got another in the supplementary period, but goals by Leonidas and Romeo, a coruscating inside-right, took Brazil narrowly through; doubtless to the satisfaction of the celebrated variety artiste, Mistinguette. She had sent a telegram of good wishes to the left-back Machados, whose name was the same as that of her current Brazilian dancing partner.

In Paris, at the Parc des Princes, it took a replay before the brave Swiss put out the Germans. For the first game Sepp Herberger, making his debut as team manager, chose seven Germans and four Austrians, one of whom was alleged to have betrayed the half-Jewish Sindelar to the Nazis and provoked his

Germany against Switzerland, playing in Paris.

suicide. At all events, the team did not run smoothly. In the first half, Gauchel gave Germany the lead, but Trello Abegglen, a popular figure in France after much success with Sochaux, headed in Wallaschek's centre. The second half and extra time produced no more goals.

Five days later – World Cups moved at a more leisurely pace in those days – the Swiss fielded an unchanged team. The Germans now picked three Austrians. Pesser, the Austrian left-winger, was out – sent off by John Langenus during extra time in the first match for kicking Minelli on the knee, and laudably suspended by the Germans themselves for two games.

There were now six goals. Germany were actually 2–0 up by half-time, Hahnemann, their Austrian centre-forward, and Loertscher, with an unfortunate own goal, having scored. Wallaschek made it 2–1, and when Aebi, the Swiss left-winger, temporarily went off injured, his team increased rather than relaxed their pressure. Aebi came back, Bickel equalised, and the splendid Abegglen scored twice more to give Switzerland victory.

In Toulouse, Cuba, who were only there because Mexico had withdrawn, astonished the Romanians, who still had three members of their 1930 team. The result was an exciting 3–3 draw and the Cubans, unimpressed by fervent praise for their fine goal-keeper, Carvajales, dropped him from the replay. Undaunted, Carvajales called a Press conference of his own at which he promised that Cuba would win the replay: 'The Romanian game has no more secrets for us. We shall score twice, they will only score once. *Adios, caballeros.*' He proved right, though some, including the linesman and Final referee, Georges Capdeville, thought the Cuban winner was offside.

Stalemates, indeed, proliferated. There was another at Le Havre between Czechs and Dutch; this was, however, resolved in extra time, when the loss through injury of van der Veen finally proved too much for Holland. Their team had a forty-year-old left-back in Caldenhove, and an eighteen-year-old left-winger in Berthus de Harder, who would be a star with Bordeaux after the war. The Czechs got three in extra time, Nejedly scoring the third, but the Dutch severely missed their leading goal scorer, Bakhuijs.

France, the hosts, were another team with plenty of experienced World Cup men. Thépot – who, with Delfour and Aston, had been 'chaired' by the crowd at the Gare de Lyon on his return from the 1934 World Cup – had gone. But a superb new goalkeeper had emerged in Laurent di Lorto, who had played brilliantly against the Italians earlier that season at the Parc des Princes. Delfour and Aston were still there; so was Etienne Mattler. Alfred Aston, indeed, was recalled to the right wing when Roger Courtois dropped out ill, and had a magnifi-

Brazil v. Czechoslovakia: Hercules of Brazil heads the ball while Leonidas and Lopez move forward during the first match in Bordeaux.

The German goalkeeper, Raftl, in action against Switzerland.

cent game against Belgium at Colombes. So did Jean Bastien of Marseilles, a young right-half making his debut in place of the injured Bourbotte.

France scored against their old foes in forty seconds when Badjou, Belgium's surprisingly recalled 1930 World Cup keeper, could only parry Jean Nicolas' shot, and Veinante, yet another 1930 veteran, shot home. After ten minutes Nicolas slipped through for a second, but Isemborghs scored for Belgium in a breakaway, and it was twenty-five minutes into the second half before France made the game sure, Aston taking out two defenders and making a second goal for Nicolas.

At Reims, Hungary brushed aside the Dutch East Indies 6–0, Sarosi and Zsengeller scoring a couple each.

The second round

Now Italy, the holders, met their French hosts in Paris. Pozzo brought in Foni for Monzeglio, and Amedeo Biavati and Gino Colaussi on the wings, but he kept Serantoni, who had had a dreadful game in Marseilles. His confidence was rewarded, for Serantoni played with robust aplomb for the rest of the World Cup, an inspiring figure to the team.

Played at the enlarged Colombes Stadium before 58,000 fans, the match at first found both teams uneasy, remembering perhaps the 0–0 draw of the previous December. It was Piola who turned the tide, playing with a force and versatility which led the veteran French player and journalist, Gabriel Hanot, to say that of all European centre-forwards, only Six of Belgium, killed in the Great War, had been his peer. Piola not only threatened the French goal, he distributed the ball superbly with head and both feet, and moved cleverly to the flanks, lithe and explosive. When his opponent, the naturalised Austrian Gusti Jordan, was presumptuous enough to leave him in the second half, it proved disastrous.

Colaussi put Italy ahead after only six minutes, swerving round Bastien and sending over a cross-ball which made its way through Di Lorto's hands and into the net. But within less than a minute Delfour found Veinante with a delightful pass, praised by Pozzo as the best of the tournament. Aston cunningly let the centre run, and Oscar Heisserer, the Alsatian inside-right, equalised.

In the second half, Piola settled matters. When Jordan and Diagne unwisely went upfield together, Biavati robbed Diagne and sent a long deep pass to Piola, who ran on to score. Next, Piola sent Colaussi down the left, a long crossfield ball found Biavati, the right-winger drew Mattler and flicked it to Piola, who headed it in.

'I am no magician,' a modest if delighted Pozzo told the

Press. 'I content myself with guiding the players with good sense. Their conscience and discipline does the rest.' General Vaccaro, loyal President of the Federation, characteristically close to his side, was more euphoric.

The Swedes, managed by Joseph Nagy, a Hungarian, smartly and uniformly dressed in grey hats and jackets, marine blue shirts and trousers, flying in all over 7000 miles, now annihilated the weary and inept Cubans by 8–0. Torre Keller, captain and inside-right, a survivor of the 1924 Olympic team and now aged thirty-five, made and scored a goal, while Gustav Wetterstroem, the 'bombardier of Norkopping', forerunner of the great Gunnar Nordahl, scored four, his flaxen hair flying.

At 5–0 the French journalist, Emmanuel Gambardella, shut his typewriter. 'Up to five goals,' he announced, 'is journalism. After that, it becomes statistics.'

At Bordeaux, where Brazil played the Czechs, there was carnage. The only pleasant gesture came before the match in the shape of a telegram for the Brazilians: 'All with you sincerely, Polish friends of Strasbourg.'

The game was an example of the sheer anarchy which would go on costing Brazil World Cups till 1958, when their exuberant natural talent was at last harnessed to discipline and strategy. The final toll was one broken leg – alas, the dazzling Nejedly's – one broken right arm, Planicka's, a bad stomach injury for Kostalek, lesser injuries for Peracio and Leonidas, and three expulsions, for Machados and Zeze of Brazil, and Riha, the Czech outside-right.

Soon after the start Zeze, Brazil's right-half, inexplicably and brutally kicked Nejedly, to be sent off by Hertzka, the Hungarian

Brazil v. Sweden: Roberto of Brazil shoots for a goal in the third place match at Bordeaux.

Brazil v. Poland at Strasbourg: Leonidas, Brazil's centre-forward, takes on the Polish defence.

referee. Despite this, Brazil scored after half an hour through Leonidas. A minute from half-time, off went Riha and Machados for exchanging punches.

Fifteen minutes after the interval, Domingos Da Guia, so elegant yet so unpredictable, so opposed to what he called 'shock football' yet at times so violent, handled the ball and Nejedly, then still in one piece, scored the penalty. Walter, Brazil's accomplished goalkeeper, was incensed; he had been promised 30,000 francs if he did not concede a goal to the Czechs. It was afterwards decided that for this purpose penalties should not count, but Walter was beaten again in the replay, and still lost his money. There were no goals in extra time, and Brazil's impertinent appeal against the result of the match was rejected.

The replay, a strange study in group psychology, was as proper and placid as the first match was violent. Georges Capdeville of France succeeded Hertzka as referee; the atmosphere might also have been helped by the fact that the Czechs chose six new players and the Brazilians nine.

Brazil's new left-back was the protean Dr Nariz, a specialist in muscular surgery employed both by Botafogo, his club, and by the municipality of Rio. He was keenly anxious to study for a year in Europe, and many countries pursued him, Hungaria of Budapest seeming to be favourites. Alas, he fell heavily on his arm in this replay, double-fractured his wrist, and dropped out of the World Cup. Physician heal thyself, indeed. . . .

43

Another most gifted newcomer was the inside-forward Tim, later destined to become an immensely successful manager in Brazil and Argentina. His ball jugglery and agility rivalled that of Leonidas; his dribbling was spectacular.

So confident, meanwhile, were the Brazilians of victory that the main party left for Marseilles, and the semi-final against Italy, before the game began! They were taken aback when Kopecky – a fine, attacking left-half, moved to inside-left to replace the irreplaceable Nejedly – scored. In the second half, however, Brazil got into their stride, played much exquisite football, and should have had many more than the two goals they scored. Leonidas, splendid again, equalised after an hour, beating Planicka's deputy, Burkert. What looked like a good goal by Senecky was not awarded when Walter, Brazil's keeper, seemed to pull the ball back from behind his goal line, and Roberto was thus able to volley the winner. Leonidas later praised Ferdinand Daucik, the Czech left-back, subsequently a famous manager in Spain, as the player who impressed him most in the competition.

The semi-finals Italy v. Brazil

Now, however, Brazil's self-assurance would undo them. Pozzo, having settled his *azzurri* at Aix, visited Brazilian headquarters to point out to them that they had booked every seat on the aeroplane to Paris the day after the semi-final. (Brazil and their entourage at World Cups always resemble a small but exuberant army.) 'What of it?' asked the Brazilians. 'Only', said Pozzo, 'that if you lose, you will have to go back to Bordeaux to play the third-place match, while we go to Paris for the Final. 'But we shan't lose,' said the Brazilians, wide-eyed. 'We shall win in Marseilles.'

'*Già stabilito?*' said Pozzo – 'Quite sure?'

'Quite sure,' repeated the Brazilians, who then proceeded, in their astonishing hubris, to omit both Leonidas and Tim from their side. Their manager, Pimenta, explained that he was 'keeping them for the Final'. Pozzo, returning to Aix, told his players what had transpired. 'Very well,' they said, 'we shall show them on the field.'

From Rio came a cable from Luis Aranha, President of the Brazilian Federation, promising each Brazilian player a house and a share in the receipts of the Final in case of victory. Eight changes were made, the revenants including Zeze and Machados, the man sent off in Bordeaux, who would later, but only later, be punished.

It would be a sad, bad day for the Olympian Domingos Da Guia, whose son, Ademir Da Guia, would himself play for Brazil some thirty years later. Piola, big and physical, was just the kind of player to unsettle and annoy him, while to make mat-

The Final – the Italian and Hungarian teams line up for the national anthems before the kick-off.

ters worse the fleet Colaussi streaked past him to score the first goal. For Domingos the game plainly reduced itself to a personal duel with Piola, and when, after fourteen minutes, Piola went past him again, he chopped him down. Piola made a histrionic meal of it; up came the cool Meazza, captain of the side, to convert the penalty – an instant before his ripped shorts fell down.

That was the end of Brazil, whose two best chances went to and were missed by Peracio, standing in for Leonidas. Their one goal came, meaninglessly, from Romeo after eighty-seven minutes, at a time when the *azzurri* had relaxed. So Italy took the train, not the plane, back to Paris, cheerfully reconciled to the fact that there were bunks only for four or five of them. Pozzo allotted these to the most weary of the players.

Hungary v. Sweden

Sweden, christened 'the team of steel', now played Hungary at Colombes on the eightieth birthday of their monarch, Gustav v. It was of no help. Hungary, undeterred when Nyberg scored in a mere thirty-five seconds, majestically walked over them. By half-time Zsengeller had scored twice, Titkos once, and the Hungarians were so dominant that the second half was a formality. Sarosi headed a fourth, Zsengeller got the fifth; there could have been ten. A large blackbird perched in the Hungarian part of the field and stayed there undisturbed for much of the second half, till a rare Swedish attack scared it away. 'An excellent training match for the Hungarians', remarked Rudi Hiden, now keeping goal for the Racing Club de Paris.

Three days before the Final, Sweden, without the veteran draughts-playing Keller, still held a 2–1 lead against Brazil at half-time in the third-place match at Bordeaux. In the second half Leonidas, appropriately captain for the day, scored twice, bringing his personal total to eight, the highest of the tournament. Patesko missed a penalty and Brazil won, 4–2. 'The Swedes are a team of gentlemen,' observed Brandao, Brazil's centre-half, trenchantly, 'who play the ball and not the man.'

'Instinctive footballers,' Pozzo called the Brazilians, 'who could be really formidable if they developed some idea of co-ordination.' He would never forget the business of the Marseilles–Paris aeroplane, with its salutary moral.

The Final – presentation of the Hungarian team.

The Final Italy v. Hungary

On June 19, fifteen days after the opening match, Italy defended their Cup against Hungary at Colombes. Pozzo had chosen a pleasant retreat in St Germain-en-Laye, where all passed placidly; the team was composed and confident. Pozzo, who had actually pocketed a telegram to one of his 1936 Olympic team, announcing the death of his father, till after a match, now had no need for such authoritarian ruses. On the eve of the Final the reserve goalkeeper, Masetti of Roma, entertained the team splendidly with jokes and imitations, while at dinner the places at table were numbered, carefully and superstitiously, with their usual 1 to 11.

The Hungarians were at Vesinst. One man who must have been relieved they had got so far was Dr Dietz, their selector, who announced before their quarter-final against the Swiss at Lille: 'If we don't win, I'll walk back to Hungary.'

'*Verba volant, scripta manent,*' replied the cultivated George Sarosi – 'We'll have that in writing.' So the document was drawn up and signed, but two goals by Zsengeller comfortably won a dull match against a Swiss team without Minelli and Aebi, obviously wearied by their exertions against Germany.

It was agreed that Sarosi himself had still to show his true form; but if he showed it in the Final that would be good enough. On the other hand, his one failing was a lack of devil, a distaste for physical contact, which was hardly a quality to bring success against the ever-robust Italians. Still, half a dozen of the Hungarians had World Cup experience from 1934, Zsengeller had been scoring freely, and the level of individual skill was as always exceptionally high. The players were however, inclined, to be static; nor had they the tremendous finishing power of their successors in the fifties. In the event, it was Italy's greater drive and commitment which would prevail.

To Pozzo's horror, the Italian team coach arrived at Colombes three-quarters of an hour before schedule. There was always, he subsequently lamented, some 'big wheel' sitting in the bus, clapping his hands and crying, '*Presto, presto!*' His solution was simple and immediate. Rather than have his players fret in their dressing-room – even though they had told him with delight that it was the one which had always been 'lucky' for them – he told the coach driver to go straight back to the hotel; with the loyal Vaccaro's approval.

Another surprise awaited him when he came out on to the pitch. A distinguished two-man bodyguard appeared on either side of him; Seeldrayers of Belgium and the FIFA delegate from Uruguay. 'Come with us,' they told him, 'you'll be fine,' and led him to a seat well away from the touchline. There, they insisted, he must stay, with no coaching of his players during the match. It was a dire problem, but Pozzo was equal to it. At half-time he explained to his players what had happened, and got round it by getting Luisin Burlando, the team coach, to sprawl at his feet while he himself would meditate aloud in dialect. Burlando, thus briefed, would leap up periodically to pass these instructions to the players. Once he was nearly arrested by a *gendarme*, but otherwise the strategy succeeded.

The Final: the captains, Meazza of Italy and Sarosi of Hungary, shake hands. The referee is Capdeville of France.

The Final in Paris, between
Italy and Hungary: Rava of
Italy heads clear.

So did the Italian team. After six minutes they broke away from a Hungarian corner. Serantoni cleared to the deep-lying Biavati, who raced almost the length of the field, employing his celebrated foot-over-the-ball feint, before finding Meazza, from whom the ball went swiftly on for Colaussi to dash in and score. There was a sweep and scope about the move which was beyond the powers of the Hungarians.

In less than a minute, however, Sarosi had touched Sas's cross to the unmarked Titkos, and it was 1–1.

But Meazza and Ferrari, Italy's inside-forwards, were still being given far too much leeway, and after fifteen minutes Meazza nonchalantly made the chance for Piola to restore Italy's lead. From this point, the more dynamic, modern Italians never lost their hold. Ten minutes from half-time the balding Ferrari, with an imperious gesture, pointed out the unmarked Colaussi to Meazza. Straight to the winger went the ball, and Colaussi sped past Polger to get his second goal.

Meazza, Italy's captain, receives the trophy.

Twenty minutes into the second half, after a goalmouth mêlée, Sarosi unexpectedly reduced the lead, but Vincze, Locatelli and Sarosi himself were well mastered by the Italian defence, and only the left-winger Titkos gave any real trouble. Meazza and Ferrari quickly recovered their grip on midfield, Colaussi, the master of Polgar, was given plenty of the ball, and the Hungarian right flank tottered.

It was from the Italian right, however, that the last goal came, ten minutes from the end, Biavati interpassing with Piola and finally back-heeling him a pass which the centre-forward smashed into goal.

Benito Mussolini receives the victorious team after their triumph.

Italy, most deservedly, had kept the Cup. At the end of the game Meazza wept; Monzeglio, the reluctant reserve, wept; Biavata put his head in his hands; Andreolo went round embracing everybody; and Pozzo stood uncaring while water poured from the trainer's bucket into his shoes.

There would be no more World Cups for a dozen years.

France 1938

First round

Switzerland 1, Germany 1 (HT 1/1, 1/1) after extra time
Switzerland 4, Germany 2 (HT 0/2) replay
Cuba 3, Romania 3 (HT 0/1, 3/3) after extra time
Cuba 2, Romania 1 (HT 0/1) replay
Hungary 6, Dutch East Indies 0 (HT 4/0)
France 3, Belgium 1 (HT 2/1)
Czechoslovakia 3, Holland 0 (HT 0/0, 0/0) after extra time
Brazil 6, Poland 5 (HT 3/1, 4/4) after extra time
Italy 2, Norway 1 (HT 1/0, 1/1) after extra time

Second round

Sweden 8, Cuba 0 (HT 4/0)
Hungary 2, Switzerland 0 (HT 1/0)
Italy 3, France 1 (HT 1/1)
Brazil 1, Czechoslovakia 1 (HT 1/1, 1/1) after extra time
Brazil 2, Czechoslovakia 1 (HT 0/1) replay

Semi-finals

Marseilles

Italy 2	**Brazil 1**
Olivieri; Foni, Rava; Serantoni, Andreolo, Locatelli; Biavati, Meazza (capt.), Piola, Ferrari, Colaussi.	Walter; Domingas, Da Guia, Machados; Zeze, Martin (capt.), Alfonsinho; Lopez, Luisinho, Peracio, Romeo, Patesko.

SCORERS
Colaussi, Meazza (penalty) for Italy
Romeo for Brazil
HT 2/0

Paris

Hungary 5	**Sweden 1**
Szabo: Koranyi, Biro; Szalay, Turai, Lazar; Sas, Szengeller, Sarosi (capt.), Toldi, Titkos.	Abrahamson; Eriksson, Kjellgren; Almgren, Jacobsson, Svanstroem, Wetterstroem, Keller (capt.), Andersson, H., Jonasson, Nyberg.

SCORERS
Szengeller (3), Titkos, Sarosi for Hungary
Nyberg for Sweden
HT 3/1

Third place match

Bordeaux

Brazil 4	**Sweden 2**
Batatoes; Domingas Da Guia, Machados; Zeze, Brandao, Alfonsinho; Roberto, Romeo, Leonidas (capt.), Peracio, Patesko.	Abrahamson; Eriksson, Nilssen; Almgren, Linderholm, Svanstroem (capt.), Berssen, Andersson, H., Jonasson, Andersson, A., Nyberg.

SCORERS
Romeo, Leonidas (2), Peracio for Brazil
Jonasson, Nyberg for Sweden
HT 1/2

Final

Paris

Italy 4	**Hungary 2**
Olivieri; Foni, Rava, Serantoni, Andreolo, Locatelli; Biavati, Meazza (capt.), Piola, Ferrari, Colaussi.	Szabo; Polgar, Biro; Szalay, Szucs, Lazar; Sas, Vincze, Sarosi (capt.), Szengeller, Titkos.

SCORERS
Colaussi (2), Piola (2) for Italy
Titkos, Sarosi for Hungary
HT 3/1

BRAZIL 1950

Background to Rio

The 1950 World Cup, now known officially as the Jules Rimet Trophy, was dubiously organised, ludicrously unbalanced, and produced one of the finest climaxes, as well as one of the greatest shocks, of any World Cup yet.

Hurdling the world war, it took place for the second time in South America, and for the second time there were defections and withdrawals. England at last competed.

Brazil had approached the competition with great ambitions, buoyant zeal and intensive effort – even if this was not quite intensive enough to complete in time the building of the immense three-tiered Maracanà Stadium by the banks of the little Maracanà river. This colossal edifice, with room for 200,000 spectators – the largest in the world – was still in the process of completion when the teams arrived, just as the Centenario Stadium of Montevideo had been twenty years before. The very soldiers were called in, in a desperate attempt to finish it in time. FIFA, alarmed by what they had heard, had sent out Italy's Ottorino Barassi to press for greater urgency, but on the day of the Final itself, when 200,000 people did in fact throng the Maracanà, its approaches still resembled a vast builder's yard.

Enthusiasm for the game in Brazil, already huge before a war in which they had been only tangentially concerned, was by now fanatical. For the poor, it was the way out of the dreadful slums of the *favelhas* which tumbled down the hills of Rio, of the remote hovels of a vast state-like Minas Gerais. Black players had long since transformed and dominated Brazilian football. Their extraordinary reflexes, at once balletic and gymnastic, their conception of the game, so radically new, so explosively effective, at one point in the tournament caused a Roman newspaper to cry: *'Come resistere?'* – How to resist? Mulattos, quadroons, octoroons; these, too, figured coruscatingly in Brazilian football. Technique was almost an end in itself. On the hard sand pitches above Copacabana beach, where football was played far into the warm nights, small marvels of virtuosity took place. Jackie Milburn, the Newcastle and England forward, told of the day when a Rio urchin stopped outside the team's hotel, peeled and ate an orange, then juggled effortlessly with the peel till he got tired of the game and went away. Milburn himself, rushing outside, could keep it going only eleven times.

The four British Associations had returned to FIFA in 1946, and the World Cup Committee had indulgently designated the British Championship a qualifying zone – for *two* teams. Scotland rewarded their courtesy by sullenly and indefensibly announcing that unless they won the British title they would not compete. All thus turned on their traditional meeting with England at Hampden Park in April. England won streakily with a goal by Chelsea's Roy Bentley. Bauld's shot hit the English bar,

The publicity poster for the 1950 World Cup.

IV CAMPEONAT
MUNDIAL D
FUTEBO
·TAÇA JULES RIMET·

JUNHO DE 1950
BRASIL

and the Scottish FA refused to change its mind. Billy Wright, the England captain, pleaded with the Scottish captain, George Young, to appeal, insisting that Scotland's presence in Brazil would make a great difference to England, but Young got nowhere.

Not that Scotland were the only team to withdraw. The Argentinians, having squabbled with the Brazilian Federation, repeated their peevish behaviour of 1938 and sourly pulled out of a tournament that this time took place on their doorstep. Czechoslovakia, too, who took a long time after the war to regain their powers, opted out in a flurry of spiteful criticism.

The case of France was rather more complex. They did not qualify, for Yugoslavia won their group, but when Turkey refused to come, after beating Syria 7–0 to gain a place, the French were invited. After all, the idea of the World Cup had been nurtured in Paris, where Jules Rimet had kept the trophy under his bed throughout the war; even if no less a pioneer than Henri Delaunay had resigned from the World Cup committee in protest against the decision to play the tournament in pools rather than on the previous knock-out basis which had been intended.

Delaunay, as we shall see, did have a point.

France at first agreed to come, then sent an experimental team to Belgium which was whipped 4–1, lost at home to Scotland, and had second thoughts. These were exacerbated when they heard what their programme would be. Drawn in the same group as Uruguay and Bolivia, they would have to play one game at Porto Alegre, the next two thousand miles away at Recife. They sent a cable threatening to stay at home if the arrangements were not changed. The Brazilian Federation refused and, to their immense chagrin, France withdrew. Brazil pointed out that in 1938 they had willingly played in four French towns with only a couple of days between each match; an argument which, on analysis, was perhaps as disingenuous as that of France.

There is no doubt that the arrangement of the tournament greatly and grossly favoured Brazil, who played every one of their six matches but the second in Rio, while the other teams were obliged to traipse exhaustingly around the whole of this huge country. The idea seems to have escaped everybody that if there were groups, these should logically be centred on one place. Moreover the muggy, humid, debilitating climate of Rio was certainly a handicap to visiting teams.

Since Portugal refused to take Scotland's place, the World Cup was left, as in 1930, with a miserable complement of only thirteen teams; leaving the Uruguayans with merely feeble Bolivia to beat. It was extraordinary that another team could not have been moved into their pool from one of the two pools which had four; the more so as the groups had no geographical basis.

The Uruguayan badge.

There were other, distinguished, absentees. Germany were still excluded from FIFA as a result of the war. Austria, beaten 3–0 by Sweden in the first round of the 1948 Olympiad, had limply decided that their team was too young; though it gave them the lie by beating Italy on Prater just before the competition started. By 1954, it would be too old.

Hungary, like Russia, was for the moment lurking behind the Iron Curtain.

The contenders Italy

Italy, the holders of the Cup, would compete even though the terrible disaster of the Superga air crash in May 1949 had largely destroyed their chances. That day the aeroplane carrying the brilliant Torino team, returning from a friendly in Lisbon on their way to a fifth consecutive Championship, crashed into the wall of a hillside monastery. Every player was killed, including eight of the current Italian national side. Among them were the splendid captain and inside-left Valentino Mazzola, whose son would be a star in the 1970 World Cup Final, Maroso, a classically elegant left-back, and a spectacular goalkeeper in Bacigalupo.

Pozzo had gone that very year, disappointed by the flight to *sistema*, the third back game, from his beloved *metodo* tactics, and disgusted by the galloping commercialisation of Italian football. In his place reigned Ferruccio Novo, the President of Torino; and, surprisingly, a Tuscan journalist, Aldo Bardelli. Bardelli, together with a number of the Italian players, refused to travel by air, and the protracted sea voyage played havoc with the condition of a team which had insufficient time to get fit again. Moreover, Bardelli and Novo quarrelled like cat and dog, and before the competition even began Bardelli had been relieved of his powers. There was talent in the team, but the auguries were bad.

Sweden

Italy played in the same group as Paraguay and Sweden. The Swedish team had been pillaged by Italian clubs after its fine Olympic victory in 1948, when four of the splendid forward-line had decamped. The team manager, an ebullient little Yorkshireman called George Raynor, had put together, with astonishing speed, a new side good enough to qualify for Brazil. A splendid guerrilla-general of a tactician – whose 1953 Swedish team, depleted again, was good enough to draw 2–2 with Hungary in Budapest mere weeks before they thrashed England at Wembley – Raynor was also much loved by his men. He had been a moderate outside-right with clubs like Rotherham and Aldershot, but the war had dramatically changed his career. Posted as a physical training instructor to the Staff College at Baghdad, he had organised an international football team with such rapid success that Stanley Rous, the progressive and internationally-minded Secretary of the English FA, had taken notice. Like good fairies, the FA whisked him in 1946 from reserve team trainer of Aldershot to the team managership of Sweden.

With his coaches' conventions – 'a stewpot of brains' – his camps for 'tomorrow's men' and his devoted coaching of individual players, he made Sweden into a real power. Hans Jeppson, the imminent scourge of the Italians, was one of his protégés; Raynor had marked him early on as a potential international centre-forward and had spent hours in pressure-training on his kicking.

Sweden, having arrived in Rio, played and beat a leading club, with their two little inside-forwards, Palmer and Skoglund, having the time of their lives. When they went to Raynor afterwards for praise, they found themselves castigated. They had indulged themselves, he said, and slowed the game. The lesson was heeded.

'Nacka' Skoglund, a Stockholmer, only just twenty years old, had emerged propitiously just in time for the World Cup. He joined AIK Stockholm from a Third Division club, playing splendidly on their tour of England; little, very blond, he was a delightful ball player with a very good left foot. Kalle Palmer, whose shooting, unexpectedly strong for one so slight, had toppled Eire in Dublin, complemented him well.

Yugoslavia v. Mexico. Carbajal, Mexico's indestructible goalkeeper, beaten by a shot at Porto Alegre.

Spain v. Sweden in São Paulo. The teams stand to attention, Spain on the left, before the match which Sweden won 3–1 to take third place.

England

England's team manager, the first they had ever appointed on a full-time contract, was a very different figure. Walter Winterbottom, who took office in 1946, was a Lancashire man from Oldham; a tall, pleasant, pedagogic figure who had paid his way through Carnegie College of Physical Education by playing centre-half for Manchester United, and had reached high rank in the Royal Air Force during the war.

Fluent and dedicated, he combined with his managership the job of director of coaching, which he pursued with almost religious application, never disguising the significant fact that he considered it the more important of his tasks. Perhaps it was, for he and his followers ultimately changed the reactionary face of British football, but this was not really an attitude to go with winning World Cups. The hardened England professionals at first received Winterbottom with immense scepticism, insisting, as Stanley Matthews did in print, that an international player should be let alone to play his own game. In fact one of the chief charges against Winterbottom is precisely that he did *not* impose and apply sufficiently stringent tactics. But with all his virtues, he was never a players' man, could never bridge the gap left by his complete lack of experience of club management. Moreover, as a team manager he was responsible to a bumbling selection committee of club directors, and in a position paralleling that of a permanent civil servant who stays in office while governments fall. Sir Stanley Rous was unquestionably his mentor, and there was something a little hierarchical about the situation, a sort of officers-and-men, gentlemen-and-players, aspect which would change radically with the appointment of Alf Ramsey.

The England team he brought to Brazil was among the favourites, and was full of talent. True, it had been badly hurt by the defection of its centre-half of the last five years, Neil Franklin of Stoke City. Disingenuously asking permission to miss the World Cup because his wife was having a baby, he had suddenly taken off to Bogotà, and signed for a club called Santa Fé. Colombia was then outside FIFA, and the massive haemorrhage of star players from Buenos Aires, Rossi and di Stefano among them, may have been the real reason why Argentina would not come to Brazil. So Franklin was lost to England; and his career petered out in sad anticlimax, for the streets of grubby Bogotà were not paved with emeralds. He quickly came home, was suspended, joined Hull City, and gently sank from sight.

Still, there were Wright and Ramsey, Finney and Mortensen, Mannion and Matthews. Yes, Matthews; held in deep suspicion by the English selectors as too brilliant, too agelessly indestructible an outside-right to trust. He had been playing for England since 1934, was now thirty-five years old and as embarrassingly effective as ever. The marvellous swerve which, as

The England team in the first match against Chile. Left to right, back row: Aston, Mannion, Ramsey, Hughes, Wright, Williams; front row: Mullen, Bentley, Dickinson, Mortensen and Finney.

he said, 'came out of him under pressure', was intact. Tom Finney, a wonderful two-footed winger in his own right, had provided the excuse for dropping him, but when Finney was chosen on the left and Matthews on the right there had been ten goals in Lisbon, four in Turin. Now, grudgingly and belatedly, Matthews was recalled from the Football Association eleven's tour of North America, where they had played and beaten the USA World Cup eleven despite an exhausting train journey.

Bert Williams, the Wolverhampton goalkeeper, blond and resilient, was a splendid athlete who had ably succeeded the famous Frank Swift. The previous November, in the afternoon gloom of Tottenham, he had defied a brilliant Italian attack which must otherwise have scored several goals. Instead, England had a lucky 2–0 win. Alf Ramsey, the sturdy, creative, but sometimes vulnerable Spurs right-back, had been playing that day: 'the General', who would one day succeed Winterbottom. As for Billy Wright, their fair-haired wing-half and captain, whose face fitted so well and whose boyishly loyal personality made him a perfect third man in the chain of command which devolved from Rous to Winterbottom. He had scored the second English goal. Ultimately winner of 105 international caps, he was not a great player but he was a very fine one, above all in defence, where he would eventually settle down as a centre-half despite his lack of height. He was perhaps a little unlucky, as an indifferent passer of the ball, to play before the days of the 'back four', when, with his biting tackle, he would have made an ideal second stopper.

The inside-forwards, Stanley Mortensen and Wilf Mannion, were both possibly a little past their peak, but still players of exceptional quality. Mortensen, a north-easterner who had turned himself from a slow player into a thrillingly fast one and had survived an aeroplane crash during the war, was a fearless and prolific scorer and Matthews' partner at Blackpool. Mannion, from Middlesbrough, spanned the war with his career; a quick, inventive player who had been the best man on the field when Britain beat 'The Rest of Europe' team 6–1 in Glasgow three years earlier in the match which celebrated Britain's return to FIFA. At centre-half the big, young Laurie Hughes of Liverpool succeeded Franklin.

The other teams in the group were Spain, with fine wingers in Basora and Gainza; Chile, with George Robledo of Newcastle to lead them; and the United States.

Brazil

The new, saturnine, moustached coach of the Brazilian team, Flavio Costa, who was said to earn £1,000 a month, clearly meant there to be no repetition of 1938 and its vagaries. His team was cloistered for four months in a house just outside Rio with veranda and swimming pool, lavishly furnished from top to bottom with the gifts of Rio firms. Married men were forbidden to see their wives, bedtime was ten o'clock sharp and before it each player had to swallow a vitamin drink.

Riccardo Carapellesi, Italy's outside-left, and Carlo Parola, the centre-half.

The opening games

The competition was given a spectacular start at the Maracanà, where the traffic jam was such that hundreds of motorists had to leave their cars and walk to the stadium. Many entrances were still not ready, others were blocked by the crowds, swarming over rubble and smashed scaffolding. When Brazil came on to the field in their white shirts with blue facings they were greeted by a twenty-one gun salute and a cacophony of fireworks let off by the crowd. Toy balloons floated into the air, Brazilian troops released 5,000 pigeons and a cascade of leaflets dropped from an aeroplane on to the pitch. The Mexicans, with a sharp sense either of self-preservation or of *comme il faut*, did not enter this maelstrom till fifteen minutes later.

The game itself was a dull one, in which Brazil scored four goals while scarcely forcing themselves at all. The powerful black Baltazar was Brazil's centre-forward for the moment, with the graceful, incisive Ademir and Jair on either side of him, and these three divided the goals, Ademir getting two. Jair, an astonishing ball player, was said to take an almost sadistic delight in beating his man. The team did not play the third back game; instead it favoured a method of defence known as the Diagonal, whereby Danilo, the accomplished centre-half, was effectively a midfield rover in the traditional manner while Bigode, nominally left-half, was the equivalent of an overlapping left-back. It was a splendid system as long as you were on top but, as Uruguay would show, it left dangerous gaps when you were defending.

In São Paulo Sweden toppled Italy. The Italians were accomplices of their own defeat, for Novo picked an almost perversely unbalanced team. True, he was without the vivacious Benito ('Poison') Lorenzi, his best inside-forward, who was injured, but to replace him with a veteran left-half in Aldo Campatelli, a pre-war survivor playing out of position, was ludicrous.

Several players who had recently helped Italy B thrash England B 5–0 in Milan were hopefully drafted into a team which no longer had a pattern. It was especially foolish to omit the clever and versatile Amadeo Amadei of Inter from the attack. Gino Cappello, that tall, beaky, gifted centre-forward, forever involved in the wheelings and dealings of the Italian end of season, led the line, as he had in Milan, but big Knud Nordahl, brother of Gunnar and Bertil, subdued him. The celebrated Carlo Parola, Italy's tall, elegant centre-half, proved anything but master of the fair-haired Jeppson, who ran him ragged. Since Sentimenti IV, in goal, had a poor day though he might have stopped two of Sweden's three, the defence was porous indeed.

Italy began well enough in front of an Italo-Brazilian crowd which was loudly behind them. Riccardo Carapellese, their clever outside-left and captain, gave them the lead after seven minutes, but by half-time Jeppson and Sune Andersson, the right-half, had scored, Jeppson got another midway through the second half. Muccinelli, the little Italian right-winger, replied and Carapellese hit the bar, but Italy were beaten. Their 're-venge' was oblique but comprehensive; eight of that Swedish side would join Italian clubs.

Now Sweden had only to draw with Paraguay at Curitiba, which they did. Italy, in São Paulo, beat Paraguay 2–0, but it was to no avail. Pool III was Sweden's.

In Pool II, England and Spain began with unexceptional victories. At the Maracanà England found breathing difficult but beat Chile 2–0, with goals from Mortensen in the first half and Mannion in the second. Soon after this Robledo, Chile's half-Yorkshire centre-forward recalled for the World Cup, drove a free kick against the post to be admonished by an Englishman: 'Steady, George; you're not playing for Newcastle now, you know!'

England omitted Matthews, playing Finney on the right and Jimmy Mullen, the tall, fast Wolves winger, a prodigy before the war, on the left. The attack was led by Roy Bentley, a Bristolian. He was perhaps a little too far ahead of his time for the team's good, for when playing for Chelsea he rejoiced in wandering and falling deep. England, used to a Dean or a Lawton – who had played his last international a couple of years before – were not quite geared to such subtleties.

Spain won 3–0 at Curitiba against the United States, who were captained from right-half by Eddie McIlvenny, a Scot who only eighteen months earlier had been given a free transfer by Wrexham, of the Football League's Third Division; and emigrated. Maca, the left-back, was a Belgian; Larry Gaetjens, the centre-forward, a Haitian who would disappear sadly and mysteriously in that sinister island some twenty years later.

Four of the 1948 Olympic team, which playing with a roving centre-half had lost 9–0 to Italy, were present. Now they had a good stopper in Colombo, and they astonished Spain when their clever inside-forward, John Souza, scored after seventeen minutes, a lead they held gallantly till the last ten minutes. Then Spain scored twice in two minutes through the dashing Basora, and the robust centre-forward, Zarra, so powerful in the air, made it 3–1.

Bill Jeffrey, the dedicated Scot who managed the American team, had every reason to feel proud of it. He had emigrated to

Antonio Ramellets, Spain's brilliant reserve goalkeeper, saves during the match against England in Rio.

the United States thirty years earlier, played for a railway works team and was then persuaded to join Penn State College as coach after playing against them. It was a temporary appointment which had lasted ever since. Combining his coaching with teaching in the machine shop, he had produced an unending series of successful teams; but none as remarkable as this World Cup side.

In Pool IV Uruguay had nothing to do but beat Bolivia, which they did 9–0 at Recife. Four goals were by Juan Schiaffino, a tall, pale, slender inside-left of great elusiveness and consummate strategic skill. Schiaffino and the right-wing pair, Alcide (Chico) Ghiggia and Julio Perez, had been members of the previous year's 'amateur' team which took part in the South American Championship, during yet another of Uruguay's endemic strikes. It was indeed an ill wind. . . . 'Amateur' Uruguay had lost 5–1 to Brazil, but did discover three stars. Perez was little behind Schiaffino in craft, while the hunched, thin, moustached, sunken-cheeked Ghiggia, a personification of the anti-athlete, had an acceleration, a control at speed and a right-foot shot that made him formidable.

Earlier that year, Brazil and Uruguay had already played three matches in the Rio Branco Cup, so close as to give little indication of what might now transpire. Uruguay had won 4–3 in São Paulo, lost 3–2 and 1–0 in Rio. Playing with the huge, dominating Obdulio Varela as their attacking centre-half – a player celebrated since his debut and three goals against Brazil in 1940 as an inside-left – Uruguay remained famous for their spirit. Their wing-halves were still attackers on the flanks; the left-half, the little negro Rodrigues Andrade, a doughty competitor, was the nephew of the illustrious José of the 1930 team. There was a dashing centre-forward in Oscar Miguez, who scored twice against Bolivia; an elastic goalkeeper in Roque Maspoli.

Switzerland v. Mexico at Porto Alegre. The Swiss clear and attack.

Spain v. England: Ramellets saves from Jackie Milburn as Tom Finney runs in.

England v. U.S.A.

For their ill-starred second match against the United States, the formality that turned out a fiasco, England travelled to Belo Horizonte. Though the little stadium, with its bumpy surface and inadequate changing facilities, was primitive – the great 100,000-stadium of today lay far in the future – England seemed otherwise to be in clover. The mountain air, by contrast with that of Rio, was invigorating, and the party stayed happily as guests of the Morro Velho gold mine, English-owned and employing 2,000 British workers. Mr Arthur Drewry, acting as sole selector, clearly had two possibilities: to regard the match as a practice run for the team which had beaten Chile, or to rest them and make use of his reserves. He chose the first alternative; and who could blame him? Subsequent criticism, the argument that he should have picked Matthews, was pure wisdom after the event. Even Bill Jeffrey admitted that the United States had no chance. Several of his players stayed up into the small hours the night before.

But for England the game would turn into the waking equivalent of an anxiety dream, in which it was impossible to do the one essential thing, the thing which should have been so farcically easy – score goals.

The day was heavy with cloud, through which the sun broke only fitfully. The American players cheerfully asked an English journalist if he had brought a cribbage board to keep the score. The England attack quickly set up camp in the American half, hit the post, shot over the bar, and all in all they seemed to be comfortably adjusting their sights. In the meantime the excellence of Borghi in goal and the resilience of the half-back line of McIlvenny, Colombo and Bahr, kept them at bay.

Then, eight minutes from half-time, the incredible happened. Bahr shot from the left, Williams seemed to have the ball covered, when in went Gaetjens with his head to deflect it out of his reach. Did he head it, or did it hit him? There were supporters of both views, but the question was irrelevant; the goal was valid. England, keeping the ball too close, shooting wide or not at all, scored none, while the clever distribution of John Souza saw to it that the defence could not relax. Once, from Ramsey's typically immaculate free kick, Mullen's header seemed to have crossed the line before it was kicked clear, but England – with Mortensen now at centre, Finney at inside-right – gained only a corner.

At the final whistle, newspapers burned on the terraces, a funeral pyre for England, and spectators rushed on to the pitch to carry the brave American team out shoulder-high.

Gaetjens, scorer of the American goal which beat England, is carried triumphantly off the field at Belo Horizonte.

61

The Pool winners

England went back to Rio, to try their last throw against Spain. Reports had told them that the Spanish backs played square and were vulnerable to the through pass. Milburn, the perfect centre-forward to exploit this, with his marvellous sprinting was preferred to Bentley, Matthews was brought in on the right and Finney moved to the left. After fourteen minutes, Milburn headed Finney's centre past the otherwise unbeatable Spanish reserve goalkeeper Ramallets, but the goal was disallowed for offside by Italy's Signor Galeati. Newsreel photographs would show a Spanish defender putting Milburn onside, but as it was Zarra headed in Basora's centre for the winner, five minutes after half-time. So Spain won Pool III.

In Pool I there was a closer finish than had been expected. The Brazilians were pushed very hard by a Yugoslav team light years ahead of the 1930 World Cup side. Above all it possessed the essential for a W formation team, a magnificent 'quadrilateral' of wing-halves and inside-forwards: Zlatko Cjaicowski I and Djajic; Rajko Mitic and Stefan Bobek. In the 1948 Olympic tournament they had reached the Final before losing 3–1 to powerful Sweden.

They had no trouble in mopping up the Swiss 3–0 in Belo Horizonte, Tomasevic scoring twice from centre; and the Mexicans 4–1 at Porto Alegre, where Cjaicowski's younger brother got two from left-wing. But these were long journeys they were making and, worse still, just before they were due to take the field in their decisive match against Brazil in Rio, Mitic cut his head on a girder.

It was decisive because Brazil, against all expectations, had slipped, dropping a point to Switzerland at São Paulo, which meant that a draw would see Yugoslavia through.

The Swiss, playing their recently adopted *verrou* formation, the forerunner of *catenaccio*, had made only three changes from the team defeated by Yugoslavia, but it was enough to work wonders. Antenen, later a distinguished outside-right, moved from inside-right to centre; Bickel, the veteran skipper, to the right-wing, while in Jacky Fatton they had a fast, insidious left-winger. The Brazilians – faint echoes here of the 1938 semi-final – had picked something of a political team to please São Paulo, between which city and Rio their football was at that time polarised. The half-back line was completely changed to *paulistas*, of whom the strong, immaculate right-half Carlos Bauer would keep his place, Jair was hurt and Alfredo, a wing-half, played outside-right, with Maneca moving inside.

Against the rugged Swiss *verrou*, with the blond Neury a great barrier in the middle, it wasn't good enough. True, Alfredo put Brazil ahead, but Fatton met one of Bickel's strong, accurate crosses to equalise. Baltazar scored a spectacular goal to

The Swiss score against Brazil in São Paulo. Jean Tamini runs in from the right to beat Barbosa, the Brazilian goalkeeper.

Brazil v. Yugoslavia: Zizinho joyfully carries the ball out of the net after scoring Brazil's decisive second goal.

restore Brazil's advantage before half-time, but two minutes from the end, after the *verrou* had absorbed much punishment, Switzerland broke, for Tamini to make it 2–2.

For the Yugoslav match, Flavio Costa now chose the remarkable Zizinho-Ademir-Jair inside-forward trio, and chose Chico for the left-wing. Brazil came out without Mitic, waited while the Mayor of Rio exhorted the teams, then turned straight round and went back to the dressing-rooms. They were pursued by Mervyn Griffiths of Wales, the referee, who ordered them back and refused to postpone the kick-off while Mitic was treated. So the unlucky Slavs began reluctantly and anxiously with ten men, and had lost a goal traumatically within three minutes, when Ademir received from Bauer and scored. When Rajko Mitic – team manager of their fine 1968 side – finally came on, wearing a huge white bandage, his subtle skills and clever probing, his fine understanding with Bobek, transformed his team, and by half-time Brazil looked a troubled side. Perhaps if Cjaicowski II had taken a marvellous chance to equalise, things might have been different, but he missed it. Within minutes Bauer had found Zizinho, who dribbled his sinuous, irresistible way through Yugoslavia's defence to make it 2–0.

The following day, Uruguay and Spain came through; these three and Sweden would make up the final pool.

The idea of having a final pool was a strange one which has never since been adopted. The trouble with a World Cup is that it is precisely that; a *cup* competition, greatly restricted in duration, in which luck and injuries have little time to level out, however you arrange things. Sometimes, as in the three pre-war World Cups, the three won by Brazil, and perhaps that won in 1966 by England, the strongest team prevails. But on other occasions, as in 1950 and again in 1954, there were dramatic upheavals.

Jair, Brazil's inside-left.

The final pool, then, was nicely balanced between two South American teams, who played an attacking centre-half and had done the minimum of travelling, and two European teams playing out of season after much travelling, with a stopper centre-half. The Brazilians might be favourites, as the home team, but the Swiss and Yugoslavs had shown them fallible, the Swedes and Spaniards looked redoubtable, and the Uruguayans had always had their number.

Whereupon, in their first two matches, the Brazilians simply tore the Swedes and Spaniards, with their supposedly more modern, third back defences, into tiny tatters, playing the football of one's dreams. Sweden went down 7–1, Spain crashed 6–1, yet the Uruguayans found both teams very tough nuts to crack.

Final Pool matches Brazil v. Sweden; Brazil v. Spain

Sweden were Brazil's first victims. George Raynor knew very well the extent of the task; knew, too, that his frail young inside-forwards, Kalle Palmer and Lennart (Nacka) Skoglund, were tired and unlikely to stand the pace. 'With two stronger inside-forwards,' he would say, no doubt regretting Gren and Lied-holm (with Milan) and Garvis Carlsson (with Atletico Madrid), of his Olympic side, 'Sweden would have done much better. Give Palmer the ball, and he can split any defence. But both he and Skoglund were physically very weak.'

For all that, his plan was to seek an early goal – the goal he and Sweden would get in the 1958 World Cup Final – and 'We had two chances before they even moved.' But both were missed, and in the nineteenth minute a hopeful shot by Ademir beat Svensson, after which – the deluge.

Brazil now played the football of the future, an almost sur-realist game, tactically unexceptional but technically superb, in which ball players of genius, while abrogating none of their own right to virtuosity and spectacle, found an exhilarating *modus vivendi*.

Zizinho, Brazil's inside-right.

Before half-time, Ademir had scored his second, while Chico added the third. The second half was sheer exhibition: Ademir brought his total to four, Chico his to two, while Maneca's goal made seven. All Sweden could muster was a penalty by Sune Andersson, their right-half.

Spain were next on the chopping block, tired after their fine, close match against Uruguay. Brazil thrashed them, with Eiza-guirre back in goal for splendid Ramallets, 6–1; 3–0 at half-time. Jair and Chico scored a couple each, Zizinho one, Parra an own goal, Ademir none at all.

That meant four points to Brazil, while Uruguay had with difficulty amassed three; a draw would thus give Brazil a Cup which seemed as good as theirs.

Uruguay v. Spain; Uruguay v. Sweden; Spain v. Sweden

On July 9, while Brazil were annihilating Sweden, Uruguay were just holding out in a dramatic match against Spain in São Paulo. It was a rough game, full of the Spanish temper, but kept under control and saved as an admirable match by the refereeing of Mervyn Griffiths.

Uruguay, whose swift, skilled forwards always troubled the rather heavy, third back Spanish defence, took the lead through Ghiggia. But with Igoa and Molowny a fine, foraging pair of inside-forwards in the best W formation manner, Basora setting Andrade problems on the wing, Spain were 2–1 ahead by half-time; both goals Basora's. Meanwhile, the two Gonzalvos and the gymnastic Ramallets were keeping Uruguay's attack at bay.

Ademir, Brazil's centre-forward.

In the second half, the inspiring Varela drove the Uruguayans forward, just as he would against Brazil, and eighteen minutes from the end he himself thundered into the Spanish penalty area to equalise.

In their second game, once more at São Paulo, Uruguay were lucky to get the better of Sweden, who also held a 2–1 lead against them at half-time. The determining factor was probably the weariness of Skoglund, who made little contribution; nor were Sweden helped when a bad foul by Matthias Gonzales put Johnsson, their right-winger, off the field for an extended period.

Though the Uruguayans were both immeasurably fresher and technically much superior to the Swedes, they never dominated them. Kalle Palmer even gave his team the lead after five minutes for Ghiggia to equalise, but Sundqvist, the fast Swedish left-winger – who, like Ghiggia, would play for Roma – made it 2–1. Sweden, however, had shot their bolt, and two goals in the second half by Miguez, the Uruguayan centre-forward, gave them a bare 3–2 win.

For their last match, against Spain, Raynor switched his team's wingers, brought in Rydell for Skoglund, while Bror Mellberg, already standing in for Jeppson, moved to inside-right. The result, again in São Paulo, was a splendid 3–1 win over Spain, who themselves made four changes: including the omission of Molowny, Gainza and Igoa from the attack.

Sweden had a somewhat difficult opening period but then controlled the game, Raynor's plan to use sweeping wing-to-

The Maracanà Stadium in Rio. Military bands play before the start of the deciding match between Brazil and Uruguay.

wing passes working admirably. After the first goal, scored by Johnsson, two Spanish defenders argued bitterly in midfield, and were still arguing when the ball was on the centre spot for kick-off. Mellberg got a second, to make it 2–0 at half-time, little Palmer a third for 3–0, and only seven minutes from the end did Zarra reply for Spain. It was odd that Palmer, who admittedly delayed his passage to Italy, should have so little success there while Skoglund, at Inter, had so much.

Brazil v. Uruguay

If you are going to have a cup at all, you had better have a Cup Final. The odd thing was that in 1950, though no provision was made for one, the Brazil-Uruguay match which decided things was such a thriller, such a glorious climax, that no official Final could have done its job better. Indeed, people still talk about it, erroneously if understandably, as the Final.

Though Flavio Costa showed anything but over-confidence, the mood in Brazil before the decisive match with Uruguay was one of bounding euphoria. How could they lose? How, indeed, could they do anything but win? The intricate, galvanic combination of their inside-forward trio, Zizinho, Ademir and Jair, was devastating. *Come resistere?* One move, which Raynor had particularly admired, was especially unusual and effective. To vary the normal method of attack – short passes alternating with deeper, sharply-angled balls to the wings, sometimes over twenty

Alcide Ghiggia, No. 7, scores the goal which beat Brazil and won the World Cup for Uruguay. Bigode of Brazil clutches his head in dismay.

yards – Ademir would pass back to the dominating Bauer. Bauer would wait, foot on the ball, while Zizinho in his relaxed, loping way would trot back like an obedient dog to take it from him.

'The Uruguayan team,' warned Costa presciently, 'has always disturbed the slumbers of Brazilian footballers. I'm afraid that my players will take the field on Sunday as though they already had the Championship shield sewn on their jerseys. It isn't an exhibition game. It is a match like any other, only harder than the others.'

Colonel Volpe of the Uruguayan delegation remained sturdily sanguine, reminding those who spoke to him that Uruguay had already beaten Brazil once that year.

Vittorio Pozzo, present this time not as a combatant but as a journalist, was staggered by the address made by the Governor of the state of Rio at the Maracanà, immediately before the game. It was an oration as presumptuous, as perfectly calculated to enrage and incite the opposition, as the Brazilians' behaviour twelve years before over the plane from Marseilles to Paris.

'You Brazilians, whom I consider victors of the tournament . . . you players who in less than a few hours will be acclaimed champions by millions of your compatriots . . . you who have no equals in the terrestrial hemisphere . . . you who are so superior to every other competitor . . . you whom I already salute as conquerors.' The Uruguayans, long before the eulogy had ended, were clearly fretting.

Curiously casual in their light blue shirts, the black shorts nonchalantly tied with white tape, they already contrasted unfavourably with the Brazilians, crisp in their white shirts and shorts which would after this game be superstitiously abandoned forever in favour of yellow and green. Mr George Reader, the Southampton schoolmaster who, though now too 'old' to be allowed to referee Football League games, would handle this one perfectly, called Augusto and Varela to the centre; the teams lined up; and Brazil attacked.

With most of the immense crowd roaring them forward, they beat against a Uruguayan defence in which, for the moment, the huge Varela played a wholly destructive part. If he was marvellously resilient, the little, black Andrade was no less stalwart, while Maspoli performed acrobatic prodigies in goal. Time and again Zizinho, Ademir and Jair, that terrifying trio, worked their sinuous way through the blue walls of Uruguay's defence. Time and again, a last-ditch tackle by Andrade or Varela, an interception by the flying Maspoli, frustrated them. In the sixteenth minute there was a tremendous mêlée in the Uruguayan area, but Andrade strode into the middle of it and cleared. Seven minutes later Jair let fly a tremendous shot, only for Maspoli to leap across his goal and deflect it for a corner. There was another massed onslaught on the Uruguayan goal, this time thwarted at last by

Maspoli, Uruguay's goalkeeper, clasps the ball at the feet of Brazil's centre-forward, Ademir. Matthias Gonzales stands guard.

Brazil 7, Sweden I in Rio. The
Swedish captain, Nilsson (left),
shakes hands with Augusto of
Brazil before the game.

Brazil's team lined up before the kick-off of the decisive match against Uruguay.

Varela, glad to kick upfield.

The respite was short. Soon Friaca was taking Brazil's third corner of the match and shooting when the ball came back to him out of the vortex, only for Maspoli to hurl himself among the lunging legs and turn it for another corner. Next minute Ademir, deadliest shot of the competition, was left alone in front of goal; the shot was powerful and well placed, but again Maspoli somehow reached it.

Giuseppe Moro, Italy's goalkeeper against Paraguay, was wont to say that a great 'keeper could turn a game in two ways: first by inspiring his own team, and second by demoralising the opposition. It was just about now that Uruguay, shaking themselves like a great dog, began at last to come into the game. Barbosa, the agile black Brazilian goalkeeper who had virtually been watching the game, now found himself in sudden, desperate movement as Ghiggia and Miguez broke to make a chance for Schiaffino, whose raking shot forced Barbosa to leap mightily.

Brazil retaliated at once, forcing another corner, at which Jair banged a shot against the post. Now Maspoli performed new heroics, saving from Ademir, diving wonderfully to a low shot by Zizinho.

The last seven minutes of the half saw a relaxing of the

Brazilian pressure, a time out of war for Uruguay's defence. Three times their attack got away for a shot. Barbosa saved, without great difficulty, from Miguez, then Schiaffino, like a pale sleepwalker roused suddenly to vigorous action, dribbled brilliantly through Brazil's defence to finish with a searing shot. Barbosa saved this, too. Then, more significantly still, Varela deserted his post in defence at last, to cap another attack with a drive which Barbosa had to turn for a corner. There were substantial straws in the wind by half-time.

But they were forgotten two minutes after the restart when the Uruguayan citadel fell at last. Ademir and Zizinho, working the ball quickly and cleverly, drew Uruguay's defence left, switched it right, and there was Friaca, running in to shoot in full stride – and score.

The goal had come too late to demoralise Uruguay. They had held out long enough, ultimately launched sufficient attacks, to be quite sure the Brazilians were mortal. Their response to the blow was not to crumble but to hit back vigorously, and while the crowd was distracted by the grim sight of a corpse being taken away on a stretcher, the Uruguayan forwards set about Brazil's defence. After two raids had been beaten off, Schiaffino's typically precise through pass sent Perez away for a rocketing shot which Barbosa reached only with his fingertips. Now Varela had definitively committed himself to attack. Brazil's wingers, thus given more space, enjoyed it briefly, Andrade having to recover superbly to tackle the galloping Friaca. But Ademir, waving his arms urgently to encourage his colleagues, seemed to realise something was amiss.

Barbosa, the Brazilian goalkeeper.

After twenty minutes Uruguay struck again; and scored a goal which had long been in the wind. Varela trundled the ball into the Brazilian half before sending little Ghiggia flying down the right, where he was now the master of inadequately covered Bigode. The winger's centre reached a totally unmarked Schiaffino who, after four strides, let fly a shot Barbosa had no hope of saving.

Brazil kicked off; but the virtue, the *brio*, had gone out of them. It was Varela who bestrode the field, nonchalant and indomitable, masterfully breaking up and launching attacks, the old-school centre-half *par excellence*.

After thirty-four minutes of the half Ghiggia received a pass and found Perez, who shook off Jair, made ground, and returned the ball to Ghiggia. Once more Brazil's left flank was turned. Ghiggia ran on to the ball, shot – and it was in the net again. Uruguay led, 2–1.

Moments later, by some trick of the sun, Maspoli's goal was bathed in light, as if to symbolise the victory. In the last minute even Augusto, Brazil's captain and right-back, was in the Uruguayan penalty area, but there was no breaching that defence. Mr Reader, consummate master of the occasion, blew his whistle; and the World Cup, after twenty years, had returned to Montevideo.

There, three fans died of heart attacks during the broadcast of the match, and three more died in the subsequent rejoicing.

'We knew,' said Varela, unquestioned hero of the day, 'that we were technically and individually inferior to the Brazilians. After the victories won by them against Sweden and Spain, we gave up our plans to use a third-back method of defence and relied on the old tactics. With a few modifications borrowed from the third-back game, we succeeded in erecting a cage, from which the Brazilian forwards were rarely able to escape. How many times did Ademir manage to get away from me? When he did, there was always Andrade or Tejera to cover up. Our plan was to see that every Brazilian forward must beat at least two defenders before being able to shoot. We accomplished this thanks to the acceleration, the speed, the timing of Andrade, who seemed to be everywhere and who brought off some remarkable recoveries. Without him, our counter-measures would inevitably have failed.'

Andrade himself confessed: 'Our team is a strange one. It is capable of anything. Against Brazil we did not keep back one drop of sweat, but what else could we have done?'

What, indeed?

Uruguay, winners of the 1950 World Cup, before the match against Brazil. Left to right, back row (players): Varela, Tejera, Gambetta, Gonzales, Maspoli, Andrade; front row: Ghiggia, Perez, Miguez, Schiaffino, Moran.

Pools I, II, III, IV

Brazil 4, Mexico 0 (HT 1/0)
Yugoslavia 3, Switzerland 0 (HT 3/0)
Yugoslavia 4, Mexico 1 (HT 2/0)
Brazil 2, Switzerland 2 (HT 2/1)
Brazil 2, Yugoslavia 0 (HT 1/0)
Switzerland 2, Mexico 1 (HT 2/0)

	P	W	D	L	F	A	Pts
Brazil	3	2	1	0	8	2	5
Yugoslavia	3	2	0	1	7	3	4
Switzerland	3	1	1	1	4	6	3
Mexico	3	0	0	3	2	10	0

Spain 3, United States 1 (HT 0/1)
England 2, Chile 0 (HT 1/0)
United States 1, England 0 (HT 1/0)
Spain 2, Chile 0 (HT 2/0)
Spain 1, England 0 (HT 0/0)
Chile 5, United States 2 (HT 2/0)

	P	W	D	L	F	A	Pts
Spain	3	3	0	0	6	1	6
England	3	1	0	2	2	2	2
Chile	3	1	0	2	5	6	2
United States	3	1	0	2	4	8	2

Sweden 3, Italy 2 (HT 2/1)
Sweden 2, Paraguay 2 (HT 2/1)
Italy 2, Paraguay 0 (HT 1/0)

	P	W	D	L	F	A	Pts
Sweden	2	1	1	0	5	4	3
Italy	2	1	0	1	4	3	2
Paraguay	2	0	1	1	2	4	1

Uruguay 8, Bolivia 0 (HT 4/0)

	P	W	D	L	F	A	Pts
Uruguay	1	1	0	0	8	0	2
Bolivia	1	0	0	1	0	8	0

Final pool matches

São Paulo

Uruguay 2
Maspoli; Gonzales, M., Tejera; Gonzales, W., Varela (capt.), Andrade; Ghiggia, Perez, Miguez, Schiaffino, Vidal.

Spain 2
Ramallets; Alonzo, Gonzalvo II; Gonzalvo III, Parra, Puchades; Basora, Igoa, Zarra, Molowny, Gainza.

SCORERS
Ghiggia, Varela for Uruguay
Basora (2) for Spain
HT 1/2

Rio

Brazil 7
Barbosa; Augusto (capt.), Juvenal; Bauer, Danilo, Bigode; Maneca, Zizinho, Ademir, Jair, Chico.

Sweden 1
Svensson; Samuelsson, Nilsson, E., Andersson, Nordahl, K., Gard; Sundqvist, Palmer, Jeppson, Skoglund, Nilsson, S.

SCORERS
Ademir (4), Chico (2), Maneca for Brazil
Andersson (penalty) for Sweden
HT 3/0

São Paulo

Uruguay 3
Paz; Gonzales, M., Tejera; Gambetta, Varela (capt.), Andrade; Ghiggia, Perez, Miguez, Schiaffino, Vidal.

Sweden 2
Svensson; Samuelsson, Nilsson, E.; Andersson, Johansson, Gard; Johnsson, Palmer, Melberg, Skoglund, Sundqvist.

SCORERS
Ghiggia, Miguez (2) for Uruguay
Palmer, Sundqvist for Sweden
HT 1/2

Rio

Brazil 6
Barbosa; Augusto (capt.), Juvenal; Bauer, Danilo, Bigode; Friaca, Zizinho, Ademir, Jair, Chico.

Spain 1
Eizaguirre; Alonzo, Gonzalvo II; Gonzalvo III, Parra, Puchades; Basora, Igoa, Zarra, Panizo, Gainza.

SCORERS
Jair (2), Chico (2), Zizinho, Parra (own goal) for Brazil
Igoa for Spain
HT 3/0

São Paulo

Sweden 3
Svensson; Samuelsson, Nilsson, E., Andersson, Johansson, Gard; Sundqvist, Mellberg, Rydell, Palmer, Johnsson.

Spain 1
Eizaguirre; Asensi, Alonzo; Silva, Parra, Puchades; Basora, Fernandez, Zarra, Panizo, Juncosa.

SCORERS
Johansson, Mellberg, Palmer for Sweden
Zarra for Spain
HT 2/0

Rio

Uruguay 2
Maspoli; Gonzales, M., Tejera; Gambetta, Varela (capt.), Andrade; Ghiggia, Perez, Miguez, Schiaffino, Moran.

Brazil 1
Barbosa; Augusto (capt.), Juvenal; Bauer, Danilo, Bigode; Friaça, Zizinho, Ademir, Jair, Chico.

SCORERS
Schiaffino, Ghiggia for Uruguay
Friaça for Brazil
HT 0/0

Final positions

	P	W	D	L	F	A	Pts
Uruguay	3	2	1	0	7	5	5
Brazil	3	2	0	1	14	4	4
Sweden	3	1	0	2	6	11	2
Spain	3	0	1	2	4	11	1

SWITZERLAND 1954

Background to Switzerland

If the result of the 1950 World Cup was a shock, that of the 1954 World Cup was a cataclysm. Never had there been so hot, so inevitable, a favourite as Hungary; the team which had brought new dimensions and horizons to the game. They had thrashed England 6–3 at Wembley the previous November, the first foreign team ever to beat them on English soil, and for good measure they had humiliated them again in Budapest as recently as May by winning 7–1.

For the past few years, since they had ended a long sojourn behind the Iron Curtain by coming out to win the 1952 Helsinki Olympic title, they had been, quite simply, unbeatable. They had squared the circle, solved football's equivalent of the riddle of the Sphinx: how to reconcile the traditional skills, the supreme technique, of Continental football with the strength and shooting power of the British.

Since Poland had scratched, the Hungarians had not even been obliged to win a match to qualify. They were grouped with the West Germans – now readmitted to the World Cup, still under the shrewd command of little Sepp Herberger – and the Turks.

The World Cup Committee, in its doubtful wisdom, had devised a new eliminating scheme whose complexity was rivalled only by its illogicality. Instead of putting a total of four countries in four groups and getting each group to play the others, it seeded two teams in each group and kept them apart, each being thus obliged to play only the two unseeded teams. Since equality

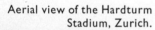
Aerial view of the Hardturm Stadium, Zurich.

on points became highly probable it was laid down, first, that teams level at full-time would play extra time, and second, that if at the end of the group two teams were still level, they would play-off. It was this tortuous, fatuous arrangement which produced the ultimate anomaly of Germany winning the Final against a Hungarian team that had previously beaten them 8–3.

Switzerland itself was a curious choice for the staging of a World Cup, and in the event the task was too great. Though the crowds were encouragingly large, thanks no doubt to Switzerland's accessibility, organisation was haphazard and the excesses of the Swiss police sometimes unpleasant.

The contenders Germany

At the start, Germany were not much fancied. Their team had qualified with some ease against Norway and the Saar, and was built round players from Kaiserslautern. Above all there was the thirty-three-year-old captain and inside-forward, Fritz Walter, a former paratrooper who refused ever to fly because he had seen his friend – himself an Austrian international – killed by his side on an aeroplane.

The German team badge.

Walter was an admirable player, an interesting blend of the Teuton and the Latin, not quite presaging the extraordinary, more spectacular Netzer, but certainly a very skilled ball player, a fine, economical, strategist, with an excellent shot besides. Otmar Walter, his brother, played at centre-forward, while Horst Eckel, the versatile right-half, was another Kaiserslautern man.

Uruguay

Uruguay, the Cup holders, had another strong team, though now were no longer an unknown quantity. There were a couple of splendid new wingers in Julio Abbadie, succeeding the frail Alcide Ghiggia, and Carlo Borges, while even the excellent Julio Perez had been surpassed and replaced, at inside-right, by Xavier Ambrois. Of the 1950 defence, poor Matthias Gonzales was gone, having been brutally attacked with a knife by a Uruguayan fan after Paraguay had beaten Uruguay at home. But the massive Varela was still there, fourteen years after his first cap, as were Andrade, Maspoli, Miguez and the incomparable Schiaffino.

The Uruguayans were seeded in Pool III with Austria, Scotland and the Czechs making up the number. The Czechs, who had qualified against Bulgaria and Romania, were still far from regaining their pre-war stature.

Austria

Austria – such seemed to be their fate in World Cups – were marginally over the crest. Three years before, they had had what was probably the best team in Europe, playing the old *metodo* game, pivoting in the classical way around a marvellous, attacking centre-half in Ernst Ocwirk, who was still their captain. Ocwirk, tall, muscular and dark, the possessor of a wonderfully strong and accurate left foot and impeccable technique, was ironically a supporter of the third back game. Now he had had his wish fulfilled; Austria, though Hugo Meisl would have turned in his grave, had espoused it at last. Uruguay still hadn't, but Brazil had.

Other distinguished members of the Austrian team were Walter Zeman, a stylish goalkeeper who, alas, would crack badly in the semi-final; Ernst Stojaspal, a blond, graceful inside-left; the Koerner brothers on the wings; and the stocky, elegant Gerhard Hanappi, a footballer of immense versatility who had played in positions varying from right-back to centre-forward. With Ocwirk, he was one of the best European players of his epoch.

Scotland

Scotland, having finished second to England in a British championship which doubled as a World Cup qualifying group, this time deigned to compete. They also broke with custom by appointing Andrew Beattie, their former celebrated left-back and manager of Huddersfield Town, as team manager. Unfortunately, the players themselves were a poor lot. A 4–2 defeat at Hampden by England had caused panic. George Young and Sammy Cox, the vastly experienced Rangers backs, had been abruptly jettisoned just as England, after defeat by Hungary, had thrown out the seasoned Ramsey and Eckersley. Lawrie Reilly, the lively Hibernian forward, was ill, and there was no obvious goalkeeper, the job going to Fred Martin of Aberdeen. Willie Fernie, the Celtic inside-right, was a player of undoubted technical gifts but most doubtful consistency; his club colleague, Neil Mochan, was a centre-forward who had returned to Scotland after failing in English football; the reverse of the career of the little outside-right, McKenzie. He had been allowed to join Bournemouth, made a name in the English Third Division, and returned triumphantly to Scotland.

Tommy Docherty, the fair-haired, powerful Preston North End wing-half, was a footballer of bite and intelligence, deeply interested in foreign football, who would afterwards praise Schiaffino as the finest inside-forward he had ever met. But even in prospect the general impression was one of honest mediocrity.

England

England, who were grouped with Belgium and Switzerland, with Italy the other seeded team, were in something of a state of shock. Their thrashing in Budapest had largely been thanks to Hungary's brilliance, though inept selection and tactical naiveté had also played a part.

Worried by the memory of their 6–3 thrashing, worried again by a 1–0 defeat in Belgrade *en route* to Budapest, their selectors chose a ridiculous team in which two men – Peter Harris, outside-right, and Bedford Jezzard, centre-forward – were winning their first caps. These players were deployed by Walter Winterbottom with total ingenuousness, showing again that those reactionaries like the peerless Matthews, who accused him of 'not letting players go out and play their own game', were quite deceived.

The World Cup poster, 1954.

Matthews himself, now aged thirty-nine, and still good enough to shame the selectors with his untarnished excellence, had again been grudgingly recalled to the colours at the last moment. There was no successor at centre-half to Neil Franklin, after four uneasy years; if the backs had been defenestrated, Gil Merrick, the goalkeeper against Hungary in both disastrous games, had been retained. Having conceded thirteen goals in them, he was somewhat in the plight of a fighter pilot who has twice crashed and twice been sent up again.

Tom Finney was still about; Nat Lofthouse, the squat, strong Bolton centre-forward, with bags of courage and a fierce left foot in addition to his ability in the air, would lead the line. Ivor Broadis, a Londoner who had begun with Spurs and then made a name as the clever player-manager of Carlisle before joining Sunderland and other leading clubs, was at inside-forward; a neat prompter with a good shot. Once again the captain was Billy Wright, who would gain new fame in a new position.

Brazil, Yugoslavia and France

Brazil, with Pinheiro as a third back and Zeze Moreira as their sternly dedicated manager, came without their marvellous 1950 trio, Zizinho, Ademir and Jair. Of these only Zizinho was a possible choice, but he had been rigorously passed over in favour of less exotic players. One of these was the black Didì, master of the swerving free kick. Baltazar, another negro, was back again at centre-forward, and there was a formidable new outside-right in Julinho, a strongly-built, moustached and melancholy figure, with fabled control and finishing power.

At full-back the two Santoses – stalwart, black Djalma and tall, strong, stylish Nilton – would play, while Bauer, a hero of 1950, would captain the team from wing-half. Yugoslavia and feeble Mexico would make up the pool, the fourth team being France.

The Yugoslavs, who had given Brazil such a run for their money in Rio, had taken full points in a qualifying group with Israel and Greece, but scored a mere four goals. They had developed a spectacular new goalkeeper called Vladimir Beara, who had once briefly studied ballet, and had all the associated attributes. Zlatko Cjaicowski was captain again, Mitic and Bobek resumed at inside-forward, while there was a resourceful new left-half in Boskov and a superb left-winger in the versatile Branko Zebec.

The French team had a talented half-back line in Penverne, Jonquet and Marcel, the young, emerging Raymond Kopa at outside-right, Jean Vincent on the left wing. They too had taken maximum qualifying points, against Eire and Luxembourg.

Italy

Italy arrived, once more in this post-Pozzo era – his name was still chanted in the stadiums as an evocation and a plea – in some turmoil. All had gone right, now all had suddenly been going wrong.

Lajor Czeizler, an elderly, *rusé* Hungarian, had built his qualifying team on the so called *blocco viola*; that is, on the Fiorentina defence. This had not pleased the Milanese fans, who had whistled the team loudly when it scored a plodding win over the shivering Egyptians in a snowstorm at San Siro, 5–1, after it had been anxiously 1–1. Then Fiorentina had shipped water, Internazionale of Milan had won the League, and Czeizler had in the process quite abandoned his previous attacking principles, recalling the vulpine, veteran Capello and making the slim Carlo Galli of Roma his centre-forward. Though Italian football had not yet succumbed to the dreadful dead hand of *catenaccio*, with its manic defensive posture, pressures were enormous, economics arcane.

Still, there was Benito 'Poison' Lorenzi, the Tuscan with the forked tongue, whose control, imagination and finishing power had been so valuable to Inter. There was the handsome, blond, olive-skinned, blue-eyed *jeune premier* Giampiero Boniperti of Juventus, whom the Agnelli – of Fiat – would later make into a millionaire and who, captaining club and country, would later become Juventus' very President. Giorgio Ghezzi, nicknamed 'Kamikhaze', was a brave and elastic goalkeeper; and surely Switzerland and Belgium formed no great obstacle?

Unfortunately Czeizler, despite his outward appearance of middle European aplomb and sophistication, simply lost control in Switzerland, picking ridiculous teams – or allowing them to be picked for him – and letting discipline go to the winds. By the

Lajor Cziezler, Italy's team manager, chatting with his centre-forward, Benito Lorenzi, before sending the team to bed. Things did not remain so tranquil.

time the team was ensconced in its picturesque *ritiro* outside Basel for the play-off, anarchy reigned.

One Italian critic later wrote that it was as though the ghosts of Novo, Bardelli and all the other recent failed team managers stood at Czeizler's elbow, gibbering into his ear the misbegotten schemes which had caused their downfall.

Hungary

Puskas, Kocsis, Hidegkuti, Bozsik; these were the names, the men, around whom the extraordinary Hungarian team was built. Ferenc Puskas, nicknamed the 'Galloping Major' in England for his army rank, was the captain, the star of stars, a squat little Budapest urchin-figure, plastered hair parted down the middle, with superb control, supreme strategy, and above all a left-footed shot which was unrivalled in the world, dangerous from any distance up to thirty-five yards. Sandor Kocsis – 'Golden Head' – a smaller and more delicate player than Puskas, was just as formidable when the ball was in the air; another accomplishment in which foreign footballers could previously never match the British, with their Lawtons, Deans and Loft-houses.

Nandor Hidegkuti had perfected a quite new concept of centre-forward play. Don Revie and Manchester City would later adopt it in what was called the Revie Plan, but they went only half the way. Hidegkuti's secret was that he not only lay

The Hungarian international side against Brazil, before the Battle of Berne. Left to right: Bozsik, Grosics, Lorant, Hidegkuti, Zakarias, Buzansky, Lantos, M. Toth, J. Toth, Czibor, Kocsis.

deep much of the time, allowing Kocsis and Puskas to work as a double spearhead and to ply them with clever passes; he was also deadly when he broke upfield, to make use of his own tremendous right-foot shot. At Wembley that November day, when the Hungarians dazzled and overwhelmed a far from negligible England team, it was Hidegkuti who had been chief destroyer. He it was, in the first ninety seconds, who with a prodigious feint put Harry Johnston on the wrong foot, creating just enough space to fire the ball home through the English wall. Later, he would score two more.

In midfield – a term which then still lay in the future – Hidegkuti had the vigorous assistance of the team's right-half, Josef Bozsik, a driving, attacking player, with strength, confidence and, of course, superb control; his side's chief dynamo.

On the wings there were excellent players, little behind these three, in Budai II on the right, and the fast and incisive Zoltan Czibor on the left.

Gyula Grosics, the goalkeeper, was a player of particular importance, not only because he was an excellent and supple performer beneath the bar, good with crosses, but because he was so ready to tear out of his penalty area to kick clear as an extra back.

Though nobody applied the term at the time, it can be seen with hindsight that Hungary's tactics were an early version of 4-2-4. Zakarias, the left-half, was always tucked in beside his burly centre-half Lorant, leaving Bozsik to roam the area of midfield. The tendency of Hidegkuti to go up as well as back, however, was a major variant.

The Hungarian backs, Buzansky and Lantos, were big, muscular players who did not stand on ceremony. The tendency was to say that Hungary's attack carried its defence, but if the record were analysed the 'goals against' were relatively few.

Teamwork was guaranteed by the Iron Curtain habit of simply swooping on the best talent in the country, like so many scouts for a harem, putting the players in uniform and calling them soldiers. They then played in the so-called 'army team' – Honved, in the case of Hungary, all of whose major stars belonged to it with the exception of Hidegkuti. His team was Voros Logobo (Red Banner), which would change back its name to MTK after the 1956 revolution, for one of the sops given the Hungarian people was a reversion to the *status quo* in club football.

Over this remarkable team presided the Deputy Minister of Sport, Gustav Sebes, and under him a coach, Gyula Mandi. Training was varied and inventive, as we were told almost *ad nauseam*, for Hungary's success made pupils of us all – *Learn to Play the Hungarian Way* was a popular book in England. The players were encouraged to practise athletics, even mountaineering. Needless to say there was great emphasis on training with

Hungary v. South Korea in Zurich. Hong, the Korean goalkeeper, challenged by Kocsis.

the ball – still, amazingly, a rare thing in bizarrely conservative Britain – and 'match situations' were re-created in practice.

It seemed as if, having harnessed finishing power to their new Sarosis, Orths and Konrads, Hungary had produced a type of super-footballer, had found a way of preparation which was ideal. Even their discipline, though severe, seemed effective. Grosics was once suspended for a year for smuggling and thrown out of Honved. Kocsis was obliged, not long before the World Cup, publicly to confess the errors of his ways; though he did so almost plaintively, implying that he might have been warned.

Yet when the smoke cleared, when Puskas and Kocsis decamped a couple of years later, it became perfectly clear that all we had been seeing was an illustration of Walter Winterbottom's dictum that every great team is built round a core of great players. While Kocsis and company were present, every man looked a giant, Sebes was a wizard, Mandi an inspired manager. When they went, the fabulous structure of Hungarian football proved to be nothing of the sort; the lean years began.

The opening matches

The Hungarians began by scoring seventeen goals in their first two games. Ultimately more significant was the fact that in the second, against West Germany, they lost Puskas, kicked by the big, blond German centre-half, Werner Liebrich. In retrospect, it was the kick that won the World Cup. Puskas would later vow it was deliberate. Observers felt that the tackle was at least harsh.

Hungary found no great difficulty in scoring nine goals against South Korea in Zurich. The fearful civil war in Korea had not long ended, and it was a little surprising to find the South Koreans there at all. They had beaten Japan; for whom, ironically, their trainer, Kim Yong Shik, had played in the 1936 Berlin Olympiad when a Japanese team made up largely of Koreans had beaten Sweden.

There was to be no beating Hungary, though Gustav Sebes made a pleasant gesture, defusing a potentially charged political atmosphere by greeting South Korea's delegation in the dressing-room. Kocsis and Puskas scored five between them and Lantos, the burly left-back, belted a free kick through the Korean wall.

West Germany, having easily beaten Turkey 4–1 in Berne, virtually threw away the Hungarian match in Basel; perhaps the most cunning card even Sepp Herberger has ever played. The Turks, whom they knew they would thus meet again, and surely beat again, in a play-off, were lucky to be there at all. Opposed to Spain in a play-off for the qualifying group in Rome, they found the Spaniards without their key forward, Ladislao Kubala, a Hungarian who had also represented Hungary and Czechoslo-

83

vakia. A cable had been received in Rome, purportedly from FIFA, forbidding Kubala to play. FIFA later denied having sent it, the match was drawn, and a blind Italian boy drew lots in Turkey's favour.

All the German forwards but Fritz Walter scored for Germany, the first goal going to Berni Klodt, for the moment their right-winger. In the wings lurked the brawny, dark-haired Helmut Rahn, belatedly recalled in the nick of time from Montevideo, where he had played superbly for his club, Rot Weiss Essen, when they beat Penarol – who had offered him a prodigious contract.

West Germany v. Turkey: Posipal, the West German defender, being helped off the field by Turek and Eckel.

The team annihilated 8–3 by Hungary at Basel was not quite the scratch side some later called it. For one thing, it included Rahn himself, scorer of the third German goal; an augury to which few can have paid attention. For another, it introduced at centre-half Liebrich, who would regain his place in the quarter-final. But it cannot be pretended that Germany played flat out. Even with Puskas off the field for an hour with his injured ankle, it was a Hungarian picnic; especially for Kocsis, who scored four. The Germans then made seven changes of personnel and thrashed Turkey 7–1 in Zurich, with Morlock, the strongly-built inside-right, scoring three. Clearly their Hungarian experience had left no trauma.

England began with a curious game against Belgium in Basel; one awash with goals. The Belgians had eliminated Sweden,

England v. Belgium at Basel. Nat Lofthouse, on the ground, heads a spectacular goal for England.

hopelessly denuded of their stars by Italian clubs, and had beaten Yugoslavia in Zagreb. They had two admirable centre-forwards in Anderlecht's great-hearted Jef Mermans, who now played on the right wing, and Rik Coppens, the well-sprung Beerschot leader, famous for the skill he showed with his back to the goal.

This game, like many others, was televised. Television would now become a potent reality in the World Cup; not always, as we shall see, for the better. The beginnings, in 1954, were modestly substantial; by 1970 the television audience for the Final had built up to a stupendous 800 million.

For the English television audience at least, the game was a disappointment, even though there was consolation in the splendour of Matthews, adding yet another glorious performance to the many he had given for his country. Until he pulled a muscle during extra time, he was the soul of the English attack; nor was he restricted to his usual beat on the right wing, waiting for the ball to be played to his feet, as he preferred it. Instead, he was all over the field, sinuously beating opponents, cleverly making openings, a complete forward and footballer whose suggestions were all too often spurned.

The English team, lamented *The Times*, were 'like those rare children of light who can pass through any experience protected by a sheath of impenetrable innocence'. The blond, versatile Pol Anoul shot Belgium into the lead from the irrepressible Coppens' pass after only five minutes. England responded with three goals. After twenty-five minutes an admirable through pass from Billy Wright sent Broadis through to equalise. Nat Lofthouse, with a spectacular diving header, gave them the lead and in the second half, after Taylor of Manchester United should have had a penalty, Broadis made it 3–1 with a deflected shot.

West Germany score one of their seven goals against Turkey in Zurich. The Turkish goalkeeper and captain was Turgay.

85

The match looked signed, sealed and delivered; but then the English defence, in which Luton's Sid Owen was a shaky centre-half and Merrick a porous goalkeeper, collapsed twice, allowing first Anoul and then Coppens to make it 3–3. Another remarkable burst by Matthews, finishing this time with the untypical crescendo of a fine shot, almost restored the lead, but Gernaey seized the ball under the crossbar.

So there was extra time, and a very quick goal for England; a dummy by Taylor, a square pass by Broadis, a strong, high shot by Lofthouse. The crowd, steadily pro-British throughout the series, seemed relieved; but then Jimmy Dickinson, the quiet, consistent Portsmouth left-half, headed Dries' long free kick into his own goal. 4–4. Billy Wright, significantly, spent the closing minutes at centre-half, with Owen limping on a wing with cramp. Wright would stay there for five distinguished years.

The previous day, a Scottish team showing plenty of fight had lost 1–0 to Austria in Zurich. The defence played strongly and well; the forwards might have had two goals: once when Ernst Happel flung Mochan to the ground in the penalty area – but the kick was given outside it – and once in the very last minute. Willie Ormond, the clever Hibernian left-winger, crossed the ball, Alan Brown back-heeled, Neil Mochan shot through a crowd of players. The ball struck Happel, and as

Third place match between Uruguay and Austria. A tense scene in front of the Uruguayan goal, as Probst tries to score.

Uruguay 7, Scotland 0 at Basel. Miguez, the Uruguayan centre-forward, heads over the bar, beating Martin, Scotland's goalkeeper.

Schmied, Austria's goalkeeper, plunged, it hit his hand, rolled up his arm: he finally seized it just the right side of the line.

So the goal which Probst had coolly scored, taking a return pass from Alfred Koerner to beat Martin after thirty-three minutes, won the game.

What Scotland had lacked in finesse they had largely made up in spirit, but now came disaster. Andy Beattie resigned. He would go, he said, immediately after the second game, which was to take place in Basel against the champions, Uruguay. The implication was that the Scottish officials, having gone as far as appointing a team manager, could not bring themselves far enough to let him manage. The immediate consequences would be atrocious.

Uruguay had not begun well. In Berne, they had beaten the Czechs 2–0 on an unfamiliar, muddy pitch, presenting Abbadie, Borges and Ambrois in attack, and the powerful, fair-haired José Santamaria as stopper. So far, indeed, did he sometimes fall behind the rest of his defence that he virtually became a sweeper. 'This defence,' wrote a sanguine British journalist, 'would be a sitting target for an up-to-standard English attack.' He went on to mourn the days of Raich Carter and Wilf Mannion, and also criticised the quality of Uruguay's shooting.

It was true that the champions did not score till Miguez headed in Ambrois' centre twenty minutes from time, Schiaffino adding a second with a thundering free kick; one of those shots which belied the slenderness of his limbs.

'Whoever wins the World Cup,' remarked the Czech players sourly, 'it won't be Uruguay.'

The game was confidently refereed by a Yorkshireman, Arthur Ellis, who reflected subsequently on the nature of the Uruguayans' boots. In doing so, he suggested just how primitive the habits of British football remained; though shorts were gradually becoming a little shorter. 'To save weight,' wrote Ellis, 'their clothes are no heavier in fact than a bikini: by comparison, the English equipment is like an overcoat! The Uruguayan football boots are almost featherweight, cut low round the ankles, made of the softest box calf, and with very light studded soles. The toe-caps are not stiffened with steel, but are padded on the inside with soft rubber to protect the toes.'

In Basel, the Uruguayans simply cut the Scots to pieces; ridiculed them, toyed with them, humiliated them. The 'vulnerable' defence contained Scotland's plodding forwards without difficulty, while Scotland's own defenders, in the words of an English critic, 'stood around like Highland cattle'.

'They will die in the sun,' predicted Vittorio Pozzo before the kick-off – and, metaphorically at least, he was right. Schiaffino quite simply bestrode the field, his swerve and footwork baffling Scotland's defence, his passes splitting it time and again. To such delectable promptings Abbadie and Borges responded with glee, running the Scottish backs ragged. Obdulio Varela, huge-thighed and ubiquitous, made nonsense of the fact that, at thirty-nine, he was a few months older even than Stanley Matthews. Rodriguez Andrade, on the right flank now, distributed the ball immaculately and controlled it effortlessly. Again one was told that the defensive system 'left gaps', though a more obvious inference was that the system as a whole was flexible, and would open or close, oyster-like, according to the circumstances.

Not one of Uruguay's seven goals was headed. Borges and Miguez scored in the first half, while in the second Borges and Abbadie got a couple each, Miguez another. The last of all, ten minutes from time, saw Abbadie dribble round both Scottish backs and then Martin, the goalkeeper. With their glorious technique, their bewildering changes of pace – an ability they shared with the Hungarians – Uruguay had taken Scotland back to school. Most ironically, it was in Scotland itself that such football had been conceived.

Italy, meanwhile, were having vertiginous ups and downs. Their first game, held in Lausanne, was narrowly lost to Switzerland when it might have been won, and Czeizler must have mourned Eduardo Ricagni, the Argentinian star; his burst of speed, his shot. Not that Ricagni's initial choice for Italy had been without its absurdity. Scarcely, it seemed, had he arrived from Argentina to play for Juventus the previous autumn, than he was playing for Italy, too. Later, the honeymoon over, the Juventus players had begun to blame him for doing nothing but score goals; a contretemps which had, in part, led Czeizler to drop him.

The Swiss, who had drawn 3–3 with Uruguay a month before the tournament, had less of the play, but prevailed through enthusiasm, while the erratic refereeing of Brazil's Viana led to chaos. 'An English or Scottish referee,' wrote the doyen of French critics, Gabriel Hanot, 'would have given two or three penalties in the first half against the Swiss, and would have sent the two Italian backs Vincenzi and Giacomazzi off in the second.' Galli and Boniperti were dumped or obstructed time and time again without let or hindrance, till the Italians decided on lynch-law, Fatton being kicked in the stomach and Flueckiger in the back.

Twenty-four minutes into the second half, when Benito Lorenzi scored a goal which would have made it 2–1 for Italy but was given by Viana as offside, there was pandemonium. 'Goal disallowed,' said the official Press communiqué. 'The whole Italian team attacks the referee, who has to flee. The game continues later.'

The goal looked a perfectly good one to most people, and there were those who thought Viana's decision influenced by the

Switzerland v. Italy. Parlier, the Swiss goalkeeper, catches a high centre, challenged by Pandolfini.

way Lorenzi had been chiding him throughout the game. After a limpid movement, Galli drove Pandolfini's pass against a post, and Lorenzi finished the job; only for the goal to be denied.

One then, as the *Corriere della Sera* put it, 'witnessed one of those scenes which often occur on our grounds, the players swarming round the referee, some tearing their hair, some eating the grass in their desperation. Boniperti was the fiercest towards Viana, who in his turn vigorously shoved the *azzurri* away until the little storm had blown over.'

So, some twelve minutes from time, when Giacomazzi missed a pass by Jacky Fatton, Hugi was able to beat Ghezzi for the winner.

The Italians now made three changes and, on the familiar territory of Lugano, thrashed a wearied Belgian team 4–1, to force a play-off with Switzerland. One of the three new men was Gino Cappello, who struck one shot against the crossbar and lent weight to the attack, in spite of being slightly off form. It was a little surprising he should be there at all for, apart from his age and lack of stamina, he had two years earlier been suspended for life after striking a referee in a summer friendly. Immense pressure was brought on the referee to mitigate his charges, the suspension was reduced to a single year, and Cappello had resumed playing for Bologna at the start of the season.

The star of the Italian attack, however, was the vivacious Lorenzi, switched to the centre from the right wing after thirty-five minutes. This time when he scored, in the second half, the goal was allowed, and he might have had several more, in a dazzling performance.

Switzerland, meanwhile, lost 2–0 to a far from exceptional English team on a boiling hot afternoon in Berne. England made a number of changes, the most significant of which was the moving of Billy Wright to centre-half, where he had a dominating game. Matthews and Lofthouse were unfit, so the Wolverhampton left-wing pair of Dennis Wilshaw and the veteran Jimmy Mullen, in his fifteenth year as a professional, played. Tommy Taylor, who would die so wretchedly at Munich four years later, led the attack, while Bill McGarry (Huddersfield) was successfully capped at right-half. Merrick, encouragingly but, as it proved, deceptively, had a much better game in goal.

The most distinguished feature of the match were the goals scored by Wolves' left wing. Mullen, receiving Taylor's flick three minutes from half-time, went round Parlier, the goalkeeper, for the first. Midway through the second half, Dennis Wilshaw calmly and cleverly evaded Eggimann, Bocquet and Neury, before beating Parlier, too. So much, it seemed, for the Swiss *catenaccio*; Italy must surely win the play-off in Basel.

But in their castellar retreat the Italians were in a state of turmoil and anarchy. 'Open acts of indiscipline' were spoken of, and

90

when Czeizler announced his team it was a weird one. Cappello was out, Galli was out and Segato, the Fiorentina left-half, an essentially defensive player, was at inside-left. The formation never began to get together. What is more, within the opening minutes more than half the Italian team was in such a parlous condition that it could scarcely walk, let alone run, as a horrified commentator pointed out. 'It was not a defeat,' observed the *Corriere della Sera*, 'it was a disaster. . . . We left the stadium in a state of authentic prostration, unable to look the Swiss in the face.'

At half-time the Italians were but one goal behind – scored by Josef Hugi after thirteen minutes. But a couple of minutes into the second half the lively Ballaman headed in a corner he himself had forced, and Italy cracked. Though Nesti did head a goal some twenty minutes later, the Swiss were constantly on top, Hugi and Jacky Fatton adding goals in the last five minutes. Switzerland were triumphantly through to the quarter-finals against Austria.

Having squeezed through against Scotland, the Austrians had had no trouble with the Czechs, whom they despatched 5–0 in Zurich; two for Stojaspal, three to Probst, all but one in the first half.

The best of all these group games was unquestionably that drawn 1–1 by Brazil and Yugoslavia in the exquisite setting of

Delighted supporters chair the Swiss team after their 4–1 victory in the play-off against Italy.

Lausanne's Olympic Stadium, with Lake Geneva lambently below and the misted Savoy Alps above. The teams provided football of a purity worthy of the setting, though it was a pity that the tournament's silly rules should automatically oblige them to play extra time when there was no question of a deadlock on points.

Yugoslavia were an impressive blend of youth and experience, their 1950 stars now being supported by such players as Bernard Vukas, the wiry, blond centre-forward, and Milos Milutinovic, a fair-haired, skilful outside-right. Zeze Moreira had justified the 'new order' in Brazilian football on the grounds that 1950's was a fair-weather attack, capable of scoring goals only when it did not matter; yet now his team played some beguiling football.

At first, the supple Vladimir Beara had much to do in goal, but then Yugoslavia, strong in their formidable 'quadrilateral', took hold of the midfield and might have scored, were their finishing only better. The Brazilians entertained with the wizardries of Didì and the tight, fast dribbling of Julinho, his face as impassive as an Aztec god's, his right foot a mighty hammer.

Three minutes from half-time, Vukas and Mitic made an opening for Branko Zebec which the left-winger exploited. From that point, Brazil controlled the game. Didì hit a post, Julinho put in three deadly shots and at last Didì, with a cannonade on the turn, got the equaliser. Neither team over-exerted itself in extra time.

The draw meant that France were eliminated. Narrowly defeated by Yugoslavia in their opening game, they had a most impoverished 3–2 win over Mexico, secured with a late penalty by Raymond Kopa, which prompted several enraged Mexicans to attack the referee.

France v. Yugoslavia. Beara, Yugoslavia's goalkeeper, turns a shot over the bar.

The quarter-finals Brazil v. Hungary (Battle of Berne)

The quarter-finals pitted Hungary against Brazil at Berne, in a match which was destined to become notorious; England against Uruguay in Basel; Germany against Yugoslavia, in Geneva; Austria against Switzerland, in Lausanne.

The Battle of Berne, as it has come to be known, has in retrospect been blamed chiefly on Brazil. Theirs were the first and greater excesses on the field, theirs the shameful, brutal invasion of the Hungarian dressing-room after the game. Yet there was provocation. The World Cup Disciplinary Committee would, Pilate-like, wash its hands of the horrid affair; Brazil and Hungary themselves would lamentably refuse to punish their players. Indeed, when Arthur Ellis, the game's one hero, later asked the expelled Josef Bozsik whether he had been suspended, Bozsik haughtily replied: 'In Hungary, we don't suspend Deputies.'

What remains a matter for contention is the exact part played in the fracas by the injured Ferenc Puskas, who watched the match from the touchline. At the end of the game, according to the *Corriere della Sera*, he 'struck the Brazilian centre-half Pinheiro in the face with a bottle as he was entering the dressing-rooms, causing a wound eight centimetres long.' The same report quoted Ernst Thommen, the Swiss President of the World Cup Committee, as saying that he had seen Puskas' attack on Pinheiro, that he had been present at the battle in the dressing-rooms which followed, and that he would be making a full report. Subsequently, however, doubt was cast on Puskas' alleged aggression; though there is no doubt that Pinheiro left the stadium heavily bandaged. Some accounts later made the assailant 'a spectator'; but which?

The match was seen, initially, as the 'real' final, and with hindsight there does seem to be a certain wry appropriateness

The Battle of Berne: Brazil v. Hungary. Bauer, No. 6, the Brazilian captain, tries to restore calm while a Swiss policeman subdues a spectator attempting to attack Brazil's Pinheiro.

Brazil v. Hungary at Berne. A penalty for Brazil, as Indio sprawls in the area.

about this, for if Brazil were the 'real' World Cup winners of 1950, then Hungary, by the same token, would become the 'real' champions of 1954.

In the event, it was only the superb refereeing of Arthur Ellis that enabled the match to be completed at all; and even then he was obliged to send off three players. In England his refereeing was eulogised, in Brazil it was excoriated – but neutral critics agreed that it deserved the warmest praise. An Italian journalist called it 'magisterial', adding that if it was severe, then 'severity was legitimate and necessary'.

Without Puskas – at least *on* the field – Hungary moved Czibor to inside-left, and used the Toths on the wings. Brazil made three changes in attack, keeping only their formidable right-wing pair of Didì and Julinho. Within eight minutes, under pelting rain, they found themselves two goals down; the Hungarians had made their familiar galloping start.

Hidegkuti's was the first goal, coming after only three minutes. He drove the ball home after Castilho had blocked shots by Czibor and Kocsis, having his shorts ripped off him in the process. Then he was involved in the second goal, moving Toth II's pass on to Kocsis for the inside-right to drive in his shot leaving Brazil's defence bemused. At this point the Hungarians seemed altogether too quick in thought and pace for the Brazilians. But some of the virtue now went out of them, and Brazil's abundantly gifted, if tempestuous, team came more and more into the game. Their apologists later maintained that the burly Hungarian defenders maddened them with a series of commonplace but irritating fouls. At the same time, those who proceeded from here to discern weaknesses, possible vulnerabilities, in Hungary's team, were surely out of order; for how could they be properly assessed without Puskas? What was perfectly plain was that Brazil had not assimilated the third back method of defence; which, indeed, would be abandoned by 1958.

After seventeen minutes a move between Didì and Indio was brusquely ended when Buzansky felled Indio. Djalma Santos thumped in the penalty. By half-time the Brazilians were giving quite as good as they got, Julinho was marauding on the right wing; and Toth I, his Hungarian equivalent, was a limping passenger.

The second half was soon besmirched with sly fouls, deliberate obstructions which in turn bore fruit in another penalty. Pinheiro handled Czibor's pass to Kocsis, and this time it was the turn of Lantos to score from the spot with tremendous power.

Just as powerful, however, was the ferocious, right-footed shot with which the brilliant Julinho beat Grosics, after an amazing undulating dribble, to make it 2–3. Twenty-four minutes were left, the game was open, the moral climate abysmal.

Souvenir of the Battle of Berne. Two Uruguay officials, Gustav Sebes, deputy Minister of Sport, and Isvan Krajczowitz, adorned with sticking plaster, attend a FIFA meeting to discuss the incidents of the previous day.

England v. Uruguay. Billy Wright of England shakes hands with Varela of Uruguay.

England v. Uruguay. Maspoli, the Uruguay goalkeeper, punches clear.

Six minutes more, and two great players, Bozsik and Nilton Santos, came squalidly to blows and were both sent off, Bozsik having reacted to Santos' harsh tackle. Twice Julinho got away again, once to shoot wide and then to give Didì a ball which he struck against the bar.

The Brazilians were now on top, but their very insistence left them open, Hungary breaking in the forty-fourth minute of the half for Czibor to dash down the right and cross, and Kocsis to head past Castilho. It must have been especially gratifying to Czibor, who at one point had been chased about the field by an incensed and threatening Djalma Santos.

There was still time for Humberto Tozzi, the young Brazilian inside-left, to kick Lorant and be expelled in his turn, though he fell weeping on his knees to plead with Arthur Ellis. Then the violent match was over, giving way to worse violence still in the dressing-rooms, where bottles and football boots were swung and Gustav Sebes had his cheek cut open. Perhaps it should be recorded that Castilho had tried to calm his colleagues, that Kocsis and Hidegkuti stayed steadfastly aloof – but these were small comforts. To the Battle of Bordeaux now had to be added the Battle of Berne.

Uruguay v. England

The game between Uruguay and England produced the same score but none of the same brutality. Though there were several injuries, mostly to Uruguayans, the match was a clean and memorable one, in which Matthews, for England, and Schiaffino, for Uruguay, were superb.

Though the cupholders were unquestionably the better, more gifted team, and won despite the fact that Varela, Abbadie and Andrade pulled muscles, they were much helped by Merrick's feeble goalkeeping. He should certainly have saved two of the goals; he might well have saved three, a fact particularly galling to an English defence inspired by Billy Wright to resist splendidly.

In attack, Matthews was the driving force, again playing not merely on the wing but often in the middle, at inside-right or left. With Varela, till he was injured, having yet another of his dominating, omnicompetent games for Uruguay, it was a fine, hot afternoon for thirty-nine-year-olds.

Uruguay opened the score with a lovely goal, after only five minutes. The masterly Schiaffino sold the dummy to McGarry, who never dominated him, and unleashed Borges. The outside-left raced away, crossed a long diagonal ball to Abbadie and, with England's defence entranced, raced in to convert the return pass.

England rode the punch well and equalised eleven minutes later, when Matthews turned the defence with a clever ball behind Varela, Wilshaw ran on to it and gave Lofthouse a reverse pass to score. For twenty bright minutes England called the tune, but now one saw the flexibility of the Uruguayan methods; saw that the allegedly 'open' defence could be manned, when necessary, by seven or eight players. Lofthouse had a fine shot beaten out by Maspoli; Wilshaw shot just wide when a goal seemed sure. A sly shove was largely responsible.

Two minutes from the interval, Uruguay delivered a counter-punch — to the solar plexus. Varela shot from near the edge of the area, and Merrick allowed the ball to pass across him — and home. It was bad enough that England should go in at half-time a goal down when they could have been a goal up. It was still worse to fall a second goal behind almost immediately afterwards; and a dubious goal, at that. Varela picked the ball up for a free kick and was allowed, inexcusably, to drop kick it. Schiaffino ran through a bewildered English defence to score.

With three players limping, it was inevitable that Uruguay should find the second half difficult, but with Schiaffino now playing splendidly in Varela's position they kept the lead. After sixty-seven minutes Maspoli got his hand to a shot by Tom Finney, and the ball bounced into the net to make it 2–3. Matthews hit the post and had one shot punched by Maspoli for a corner, but the last word was Uruguay's.

With thirteen minutes left, Miguez found Ambrois, who scored with a shot which Merrick should have saved, just as he should have saved Schiaffino's. England were out; but at least, by comparison with the Scots, they had gone out with honour.

Austria v. Switzerland

At Lausanne that same Saturday, Austria and Switzerland produced one of the highest-scoring World Cup matches there has ever been; twelve goals, seven of them to Austria.

It was an astounding match in which the Swiss, roared on by their crowd, scored three in the first twenty minutes; only for the defiant Austrians to reply with three in three minutes, five in seven minutes, building a 5–4 lead by half-time — and missing a penalty into the bargain!

The strange score was partly to be accounted for by an uncharacteristically poor display by Roger Bocquet, the Swiss captain; behind which lurked a sad tale.

Bocquet, in fact, had been suffering for some time from a tumour. His doctor had earnestly advised him not to play, but Bocquet, perhaps his country's most celebrated player of the era, replied, 'Afterwards, I shall be going into hospital for an operation, and I don't know whether I shall survive.'

Play, therefore, he did, and the intense heat provided the worst possible conditions for his tumour. Several times Karl

Rappan, the Swiss team manager, tried to persuade him to move from his vital position at centre-half, but on each occasion Bocquet told him, 'It's all right, it's all right!'

'We all felt,' said a Swiss Federation official, years afterwards, 'that he was playing in a sort of trance, and didn't know what happened on the field.'

In due course, Bocquet had his operation, which was happily successful; though it left him with a fearful scar, and the need to wear dark glasses, in consequence.

Austria, who so comprehensively overturned the Swiss *catenaccio* which had mastered Italy, did it in a most un-Viennese manner: with sizzling long shots after runs by the Koerners down the wings. At 5–3 to Austria, Ballaman replied for the Swiss. 'All goals scored against Switzerland owing to the sun,' announced the official, unblushing Press *communiqué* at half-time, though it was true that Parlier, the Swiss 'keeper, had a touch of sunstroke. But even with the sun at their backs the Swiss could not recover. In the second half the forceful Theo Wagner ran through for his third goal and Austria's sixth. Though Hanappi put the dynamic Hugi's shot past his goalkeeper for Switzerland's fifth, Probst dribbled through for the most spectacular goal of all. 7–5. It had been a magnificent game for Ernst Ocwirk, and for two forwards who did not score: Stojaspal of Austria and the dark Roger Vonlanthen of Switzerland.

West Germany v. Yugoslavia

In Geneva the following day the West Germans sprang their first great surprise of the tournament. They beat Yugoslavia. The manner of their success won them few admirers, with the possible exception of the cool Kohlmeyer who, with Turek beaten, cleared no fewer than three shots off the line – from Zebec, Cjaicowski and Bobek. But there were equivocations about both German goals, and the Yugoslavs were badly handicapped by injuries to Vukas and Beara; the first hurt early in the second half, the second towards the end. The Yugoslavs had the finesse, but not the finish. The Germans had muscle, stamina, immense determination. Moreover, after ten minutes they were presented with a goal.

Ivan Horvat, the tall Yugoslav centre-half, was possibly the best in the tournament; a Titan in this match, too. But running back with Schaefer towards a ball headed on by Morlock, he headed it in his turn, without observing that Beara had come off his line. 1–0 to Germany. Their second goal came four minutes from the end when Schaefer put through Rahn – offside, in the opinion of some critics – who ran on, on, on before beating a Vladimir Beara unable now to move. It was absurd, wrote an Italian critic, that a team like Germany should be in the semi-final when a team like Brazil was out, but this was irremediably what could happen in Cup competitions.

Germany would now play Austria, their victims in the third-place match of 1934, their companions in the World Cup of 1938. The Uruguayans, who had enraged their fellow hotel guests by perpetually and loudly playing a record which proclaimed their virtues, would meet Hungary. They promised there would be no violence; the Brazilians, they said, had lost their heads.

The semi-finals Hungary v. Uruguay

Uruguay kept their word at Lausanne, sharing one of the classic matches of World Cup history resembling the holocaust of Berne only in its score. Either team might have won, for the game went into extra time. Moreover, it lacked a key player in each side, for if Puskas did not play for Hungary, Varela could not play for Uruguay. Each side, moreover, had to change its outside-right – Abbadie being forced to give way to Souto, while Budai replaced the injured Toth I, whose brother was succeeded by Palotas. This enabled Czibor, in turn, to go back to the left wing. Miguez, another absentee, was succeeded as Uruguay's centre-forward by Hohberg, though Schiaffino nominally played there. Hungary were favoured, but Uruguay had never yet been beaten in a World Cup.

The rain beat down throughout the match but made no

Uruguay v. Hungary: a classic semi-final. Hungary's Nandor Hidegkuti dives for an enterprising header. The Uruguayan goalkeeper is Maspoli.

difference to its quality. Charlie Buchan, veteran English journalist and once a famous inside-forward, called it 'one of the greatest games I have ever seen', while Billy Wright, the England captain, said it was 'as near perfection as we will ever see'.

The Uruguayans were slightly faster and more energetic than they had previously been; but after a quarter of an hour

Hungary went ahead. Kocsis headed a pass by Hidegkuti to Czibor, and the left-winger volleyed the ball past Maspoli. Just after half-time, Hungary doubled their lead when Buzansky intercepted a poor clearance by Carballo, Varela's deputy. He sent Budai and Bozsik flying away, and when Budai crossed Hidegkuti flung himself at the ball to head it in.

Uruguay seemed beaten beyond hope, but their marvellous morale, not to mention their skill, brought them back into the game. Schiaffino began to work his spells, nicely supported by Juan Hohberg, a naturalised Argentinian who would manage their World Cup team of 1970. Lorant had to clear on the line, Schiaffino had a couple of near misses, and then at last, fifteen minutes from the end, Schiaffino gave Hohberg the chance to beat Grosics. Three minutes from the end Schiaffino and Hohberg did it again, Hohberg being so violently felicitated by his team mates that they knocked him out.

His goal necessitated extra time, and soon after it had started Schiaffino put him through yet again, this time for a shot which smacked the post.

Poor Uruguay; it was not to be their night. In the second extra period, the peerless Andrade was hurt in a tackle and, desperate to get back into the game, was still having treatment behind the goal when right in front of him Budai centred for Kocsis to soar and head past Maspoli.

Seven minutes from the end Kocsis headed another memorable goal, and Hungary had won 4–2. 'We beat the best team we have ever met,' said their manager, Gyula Mandi.

Uruguay v. Hungary: in spite of Maspoli's dive, Czibor's shot scores the first goal in the semi-final.

Uruguay v. Hungary. Juan Hohberg, Uruguay's centre-forward is revived on the touchline with smelling salts, overwhelmed after scoring his side's two goals.

West Germany v. Austria

At Basel a crowd of 58,000 saw the Austrians fall to pieces like a burning house. They had been expected to win quite easily; their technique was far ahead of the Germans', and they had scored a cascade of goals against the Swiss. In the meantime, Sepp Herberger had worked hard at training Toni Turek, whom he felt should have made Kohlmeyer's saves on the line superfluous. Austria, for their part, made the cardinal mistake of dropping Schmied and restoring the famous Walter Zeman – a goalkeeper previously omitted precisely because he had lost form.

It proved a disastrous error, for Zeman, once so polished and authoritative, played like a man who had lost his nerve, running about his area like a chicken with its head cut off, utterly confused by crosses. Two of the goals, indeed, came from centres, two more from corners; a damning commentary on Austria's defence in the air. The other two were from penalty kicks.

The Germans now showed that they were a great deal more than mere destroyers, a mincing machine for other people's talent. Their football was sweepingly effective, splendidly incisive, with Fritz Walter the supreme strategist, scorer of two penalties to boot, and Helmut Rahn as powerfully effective a right-winger, in his muscular way, as the exotic Julinho.

During the first half there was little sign of what awaited poor Austria in the second. For twenty minutes their team did pretty things, relaxed and elegant, but on the half-hour Max Morlock sent Fritz Walter away, and Hans Schaefer flicked in his well-judged centre. At half-time it was still 1–0.

In the third minute of the second half an equally exact corner kick by Fritz Walter was headed in by Morlock, and though four minutes later Germany gave Austria a chance, Turek dropping the ball for Probst to score, the die was cast. The German attack, with only Rahn keeping his position firmly, the others switching at speed, overran the Austrians. Fritz Walter scored the third and fifth goals from the spot, each time sending the unfortunate Zeman the wrong way, while his brother Otmar headed the other two – one from Fritz's corner, one from Schaefer's cross – after Fritz had sent him down the right. In turning from the old *metodo* to the third back game, Austria seemed to have gained no more defensive solidity than Brazil.

They consoled themselves a little by beating Uruguay 3–1 in the third-place match at Zurich, Ocwirk dominating the game, but it was scarcely one in which the Uruguayans gave their all.

The Final West Germany v. Hungary

The great question before the Final was whether Puskas would play. He would, said the reports. He wouldn't. He was hoping to. There was no chance. There was a fifty-fifty chance; a specialist had said so. The ankle was better. It would never recover in time. The Germans had offered him special treatment; and been rejected. 'Now it is certain Puskas will not play,' wrote the *Evening Standard*, the Friday before the Final. 'After the briefest possible test here (Solothurn) today, it was realised there was no chance of his being fit.' Electric treatment had failed, the Germans' underwater massage had been spurned. 'The Hungarians feel badly about the way Puskas received this injury. They say it was the result of a bad foul by Werner Liebrich, the new German stopper centre-half.'

In the event, however, Puskas *did* play; and it would prove a manifest mistake, a testimony to the captain's own powers of persuasion rather than the good sense of Sebes and Mandi.

Ciro Veratti, the Italian journalist, spoke to Sepp Herberger, the little German manager, and wrote of his 'formidable ascendancy' over his players, his power to make them give almost more than they possessed, to inspire them to miracles of stamina, never allowing their opponents to develop a movement, never halting an instant once they themselves had the ball. Their

In the World Cup Final for 1954 Grosics, Hungary's goalkeeper, clears under pressure.

World Cup Final, 1954: a photographer gloomy in the rain.

World Cup Final, 1954: Max Morlock has scored West Germany's first goal. Buzansky retrieves the ball from Hungary's net.

physical preparation permitted them to play at this pace, so 'the simple and almost rudimentary mechanism of their play never stops'. There had been 30,000 Germans in Basel when they beat Austria. There would be about the same number in Berne for the Final, so they would virtually be playing at home. Living now 'in a climate of exaltation', the Germans hoped to give the lie to everybody. If it happened, 'it would be the greatest upset of the World Championship. But we don't believe it, and we are making ready to hail as champions tomorrow that marvellous goal-scoring machine which is the great Hungarian team.'

Sunday was another rainy day; rain, indeed, drenched the players and most of the 60,000 crowd at the Wankdorf Stadium throughout the match. If Hungary were the favourites, Gustav Sebes had still warned that their 'greatest enemy is not so much physical fatigue as nervous tension. I had never suspected that the World Cup would be such a test of nerves.' Where Germany had skated home against Austria, Hungary's draw had condemned them to two exhausting matches against Brazil and Uruguay. Their 8–3 victory in Basel was clearly no guide.

Restoring Puskas, they also dropped Budai, who had played so well against the Uruguayans but had never been *persona grata* with Puskas. Germany's team was that which beat Austria, with Posipal, centre-half of the Rest of Europe team, still at right-back, Liebrich as stopper.

Once again, Hungary made a devastating, potentially a demoralising, start. Within eight minutes they were two goals up, and there seemed every prospect of another Basel. In the sixth minute, after Germany had three times menaced the Hungarian goal, Hungary counter-attacked. Bozsik sent Kocsis through, his shot hit a German defender in the back, the ball ran to Puskas, and that formidable left foot drove it past Turek.

Within a couple of minutes Kohlmeyer, Germany's saviour against the Yugoslavs, had given Hungary their second goal with the complicity of Turek. His misjudged back pass, suddenly bewitched, sprang out of Turek's grasp and Czibor drove the ball in.

It was enough to unhinge most teams; but not Germany. Within three minutes, shaking off the effects of so depressing a goal, they had struck back. Hans Schaefer crossed, Rahn returned the ball to the centre and this time Bozsik erred, fractionally deflecting it into the path of Morlock. The inside-forward stretched out a telescopic leg, and jabbed it past Grosics.

It was becoming plain that for all the fury of their beginning, Hungary were not running smoothly. Puskas, clearly hampered by his ankle, was unwontedly heavy and slow, and now threw away a chance when he insisted on carrying on alone, losing the ball, when Czibor was free and better placed. Czibor, meanwhile, switched to the right, was obviously not at ease there, and things would go better when he moved to the left after half-time.

So, after sixteen minutes the Germans equalised. Taking the third of three successive corners, Fritz Walter curved an insidious ball which was missed both by his brother's head and by Grosics' hands. It thus reached Helmut Rahn, who drove it thunderously back into goal.

To this the Hungarians responded vigorously, Turek making the first of his many gallant saves from a header by Kocsis, then being saved by a post when beaten by Hidegkuti. Thus reprieved, the Germans attacked in their turn, and banged away at the Hungarian goal for a full three minutes. At half-time, the game was pulsatingly open.

The Hungarians began the second half with a new and furious assault on the German goal, and only Turek denied them. Twice he saved gloriously from Puskas – who on one occasion was alone in front of goal – once Kohlmeyer kicked Toth's shot off the line; once Kocsis' header from Toth's cross skidded off the bar.

World Cup Final, 1954: the West Germans leave the field rejoicing.

The storm weathered, Germany returned to the attack; the Hungarians were now beginning to look weary. Yet twelve minutes from the end of a game so well refereed by Bill Ling, the tall, blond Czibor broke brilliantly away, Turek saved his shot, the ball reached Hidegkuti; and Hidegkuti missed. Five minutes later came the *coup de grâce*.

Leaving Bozsik behind, Hans Schaefer got away down the left wing and crossed. The ball flashed over a crowded, pullulating goalmouth, touched, perhaps, by Otmar Walter's head. For a moment Lantos seemed to have it, then it escaped him, reaching Rahn. The big outside-right controlled it, advanced with it, and seemed, for a moment of pregnant hiatus, to stop and deliberate. Then he drove it past Grosics with his left foot.

Frantically the Hungarians sought to equalise, and two minutes later it seemed they had. Toth, from the right, took Posipal out of the game with an exquisite through pass and Puskas, seeming to judge the moment perfectly, darted through the gap to beat Turek in his old, irresistible style. The Hungarians embraced; but the flag of Mervyn Griffiths, the Welsh linesman, was up. Puskas had been given offside, and to this day the decision is argued.

Hungary had one shot left in their locker. Suddenly Zoltan Czibor was away once more, to let fly a strong, precise shot which Turek elastically reached again to punch clear, while Czibor rolled on the ground in despair.

So, in the drenching rain, it was over, and Jules Rimet, the retiring President of FIFA, gave to Fritz Walter the Cup which had seemed destined for Puskas. In the dressing-rooms, Gustav Sebes spoke of bad luck, and slumped on a bench; Herberger spoke of seriousness and enthusiasm. His team, physically exceptional, morally resilient, tactically straightforward, had won a remarkable triumph.

Even now, so long afterwards, there are arguments about whether under ideal circumstances Hungary would in fact have won. *If* Puskas had not been kicked and injured in the first German match, *if* what looked to many like a good, equalising goal by Puskas had not been disallowed for offside. . . . But the ineradicable fact is that Hungary did *not* win the World Cup, and their place in the history of the game must be rather like that of a very great athlete who has failed to win an Olympic gold medal.

As Gertrude Stein might have said, a cup is a cup is a cup.

Fritz Walter, the West German captain, holds the World Cup after victory over Hungary.

West Germany, winners of the 1954 World Cup. Left to right, back row: Sepp Herberger, Fritz Walter, Helmut Rahn, Jupp Posipal, Horst Eckel, Werner Liebrich, Ottmar Walter, Hans Schaefer, Max Morlock. Kneeling: Karl May, Toni Turek, Werner Kohlmeyer.

Switzerland 1954

Pool I

Yugoslavia 1, France 0 (HT 1/0)
Brazil 5, Mexico 0 (HT 4/0)
France 3, Mexico 2 (HT 1/0)
Brazil 1, Yugoslavia 1 (HT 0/1) after extra time

	P	W	D	L	GOALS F	A	Pts
Brazil	2	1	1	0	6	1	3
Yugoslavia	2	1	1	0	2	1	3
France	2	1	0	1	3	3	2
Mexico	2	0	0	2	2	8	0

Pool II

Hungary 9, Korea 0 (HT 4/0)
Germany 4, Turkey 1 (HT 1/1)
Hungary 8, Germany 3 (HT 3/1)
Turkey 7, Korea 0 (HT 4/0)

	P	W	D	L	GOALS F	A	Pts
Hungary	2	2	0	0	17	3	4
Germany	2	1	0	1	7	9	2
Turkey	2	1	0	1	8	4	2
Korea	2	0	0	2	0	16	0

Play off Germany 7, Turkey 2 (HT 3/1)

Pool III

Austria 1, Scotland 0 (HT 1/0)
Uruguay 2, Czechoslovakia 0 (HT 0/0)
Austria 5, Czechoslovakia 0 (HT 4/0)
Uruguay 7, Scotland 0 (HT 2/0)

	P	W	D	L	GOALS F	A	Pts
Uruguay	2	2	0	0	9	0	4
Austria	2	2	0	0	6	0	4
Czechoslovakia	2	0	0	2	0	7	0
Scotland	2	0	0	2	0	8	0

Pool IV

England 4, Belgium 4 (HT 2/1)
England 2, Switzerland 0 (HT 1/0)
Switzerland 2, Italy 1 (HT 1/1)
Italy 4, Belgium 1 (HT 1/0)

	P	W	D	L	GOALS F	A	Pts
England	2	1	1	0	6	4	3
Italy	2	1	0	1	5	3	2
Switzerland	2	1	0	1	2	3	2
Belgium	2	0	1	1	5	8	1

Play off Switzerland 4, Italy 1 (HT 1/0)

Quarter-finals

Geneva

Germany 2
Turek; Laband,
Kohlmeyer; Eckel,
Liebrich, Mai; Rahn,
Morlock, Walter, O.,
Walter, F. (capt.), Schaefer.

Yugoslavia 0
Beara; Stankovic,
Crnkovic; Cjaicowski, I.,
Horvat, Boskov;
Milutinovic, Mitic (capt.),
Vukas, Bobek, Zebec.

SCORERS
Horvat (own goal), Rahn for Germany
HT 1/0

Berne

Hungary 4
Grosics; Buzansky,
Lantos; Bozsik (capt.),
Lorant, Zakarias; Toth, M.,
Kocsis, Hidegkuti,
Czibor, Toth, J.

Brazil 2
Castilho; Santos, D.,
Santos, N.; Brandaozinho,
Pinheiro (capt.), Bauer;
Julinho, Didi, Indio,
Tozzi, Maurinho.

SCORERS
Hidegkuti (2), Kocsis, Lantos (penalty) for Hungary
Santos, D. (penalty), Julinho for Brazil
HT 2/1

Lausanne

Austria 7
Schmied; Hanappi,
Barschandt; Ocwirk
(capt.), Happel, Koller;
Koerner, R., Wagner,
Stojaspal, Probst,
Koerner, A.

Switzerland 5
Parlier; Neury, Kernen,
Eggimann, Bocquet
(capt.), Casali; Antenen,
Vonlanthen, Hugi,
Ballaman, Fatton.

SCORERS
Koerner, A. (2), Ocwirk, Wagner (3), Probst for Austria
Ballaman (2), Hugi (2), Hanappi (own goal) for
Switzerland
HT 2/4

Basel

Uruguay 4
Maspoli; Santamaria,
Martinez; Andrade,
Varela (capt.), Cruz;
Abbadie, Ambrois,
Miguez, Schiaffino,
Borges.

England 2
Merrick; Staniforth,
Byrne; McGarry, Wright
(capt.), Dickinson;
Matthews, Broadis,
Lofthouse, Wilshaw,
Finney.

SCORERS
Borges, Varela, Schiaffino, Ambrois for Uruguay
Lofthouse, Finney for England
HT 2/1

Semi-finals
Basel

Germany 6
Turek; Posipal, Kohlmeyer; Eckel, Liebrich, Mai; Rahn, Morlock, Walter, O., Walter, F. (capt.), Schaefer.

Austria 1
Zeman; Hanappi, Schleger; Ocwirk (capt.), Happel, Koller; Koerner, R., Wagner, Stojaspal, Probst, Koerner, A.

SCORERS
Schaefer, Morlock, Walter, F. (2 penalties), Walter, O. (2) for Germany
Probst for Austria
HT 1/0

Lausanne

Hungary 4
(after extra time)
Grosics; Buzansky, Lantos; Boszik (capt.), Lorant, Zakarias; Budai, Kocsis, Palotas, Hidegkuti, Czibor.

Uruguay 2
Maspoli; Santamaria, Martinez; Andrade (capt.), Carballo, Cruz; Souto, Ambrois, Schiaffino, Hohberg, Borges.

SCORERS
Czibor, Hidegkuti, Kocsis (2) for Hungary
Hohberg (2) for Uruguay
HT 1/0

Third place match
Zurich

Austria 3
Schmied; Hanappi, Barschandt; Ocwirk (capt.), Kollmann, Koller; Koerner, R., Wagner, Dienst, Stojaspal, Probst.

Uruguay 1
Maspoli; Santamaria, Martinez; Andrade (capt.), Carballo, Cruz; Abbadie, Hohberg, Mendez, Schiaffino, Borges.

SCORERS
Stojaspal (penalty), Cruz (own goal), Ocwirk for Austria
Hohberg for Uruguay
HT 1/1

Final
Berne

Germany 3
Turek; Posipal, Kohlmeyer; Eckel, Liebrich, Mai; Rahn, Morlock, Walter, O., Walter, F., Schaefer.

Hungary 2
Grosics; Buzansky, Lantos; Bozsik, Lorant, Zakarias; Czibor, Kocsis, Hidegkuti, Puskas, Toth, J.

SCORERS
Morlock, Rahn (2) for Germany
Puskas, Czibor for Hungary
HT 2/2

SWEDEN 1958

Played in Sweden, the 1958 World Cup was notable for the emergence of 4-2-4, the explosion of Pelé, the first victory by Brazil, the surprise of France and Fontaine. Though it was won by an immensely distinguished team it was not, overall, a distinguished competition.

The contenders Sweden

For the Swedish team, which ultimately and admirably became runners-up, it was a World Cup of nostalgia. At last the Swedish Federation had decided to allow overtly professional football and overtly professional footballers, a corollary of which was not only that such great players as Gunnar Gren returned to Sweden but also that others were recalled that summer from Italy. George Raynor, meanwhile, came back as team manager after the heartaches and the thousand natural shocks of management in Italy – 'I always thought football was a game for gentlemen,' he sighed wretchedly at one bleak moment in Rome – and Coventry, where things went sadly awry. Niels Liedholm's subsequent description of him as 'a good manager for a happy team', was highly pertinent; and Raynor himself did much with his ebullience and concern to make his team happy.

One of the most beguiling features of the side was that it harked back not merely to 1950 and Sweden's last World Cup in Brazil, but even earlier – to the 1948 Olympic Games. From these, Gren and Liedholm were mighty survivors. Like the powerful and prolific centre-forward Gunnar Nordahl, they had left Sweden for Milan, making up the so-called Grenoli trio, with Nordahl in the middle, 'The Professor' Gren at inside-right, Nils Liedholm at inside-left. Liedholm, indeed, after a long and impressive spell at right-half, had just played splendidly at inside-left for the Milan team which had lost 3–2 to Real Madrid in the European Cup Final in Brussels.

A tall, strong player, at once elegant and forceful, he could play in any of the inside-forward or wing-half positions. Gren, lean and canny, a beautiful passer and striker of the ball, especially with his right foot, had moved on from Milan to Florence and Genoa before returning to his native Gothenburg.

The little, tow-haired Nacka Skoglung was back, too, after eight splendid years with Internazionale of Milan in which he had been transformed from an inside-left into a left-winger, a position which suited his delicate ball skills, pace and left-footed shot. On the right wing, a more recent Italian 'export' was Kurt (Kurre) Hamrin, a sturdy little man, coolly insulated and taciturn, with superb powers of dribbling and acceleration and the ability and courage to strike through the middle as well as from the wing. 'Beautiful,' he once remarked, breaking one of his sustained silences on the way by coach to play for Fiorentina against

World Cup poster for 1958.

Bologna. When his companion said yes, the countryside *was* beautiful, Hamrin replied that he was referring, in fact, to the new *autostrada*. In the earlier stages of the competition, these little wingers would shine refulgently, only to sputter out in the Final.

Yet such was their earlier prowess that Raynor gave only one game to the spectacular left-winger or inside-left, Arne Selmosson, nicknamed in Italy the 'Ray of Moonlight'. He had his cogent tactical reasons. Selmosson, he felt, played at a pace too hectic for his rather seigneurial eleven. 'We're the slowest team in the competition,' he remarked, just after Sweden had defeated Hungary. 'If there was a relay race over a hundred yards, Sweden would finish last. But we'll still reach the Final.' And they did.

At centre-half they recalled, with great success, another Italo-Swede, Julli Gustavsson, a former policeman playing for Atalanta who had been at right-back for the Rest of Europe team which beat Great Britain in Belfast in 1955. Atalanta, indicted by the Italian Federation for alleged corruption, had a vital play-off game against Bari coming up, and at first were reluctant to let Gustavsson go. Eventually they compromised grudgingly, after a tense time when it seemed that he would be unable to play for Sweden in the semi-final, allowing him to go on provided that if he wished to take part in the Final he would pay the massive indemnity of 25,000 crowns! Gustavsson, who had a superbly dominating match against Russia in the quarter-finals, did play the Final.

Sweden 3, Mexico 0: the World Cup opening game. Antonio Carbajal, Mexico's goalkeeper, jumps to a high cross.

The one 'Italian' disappointment was the powerful Bror Mellberg, a goal-scoring forward who was expected to provide finishing power to end what Gren and Liedholm well began, but who quickly disappeared from the team.

Ironically, however, the Swedish Press and public had no initial confidence in their team's chances, despite home advantage and the return of the Italian brigade. Indeed, cautious pessimism, an almost superstitious self-deprecation, was at first the order of the day. As the Swedish team made more and more progress, won one match after another, the patriotic euphoria of this traditionally neutral, peaceable, unchauvinist nation rose to an orgy of patriotism in the semi-final match against West Germany. It was a riveting and somewhat alarming study in national behaviour.

Russia

The Russians were competing for the first time in a World Cup, under the managership of the blond, Cagneyesque figure of Gabriel Katcheline assisted by the huge Mikhail Yakushin, who resembled some craggy hero of the revolutionary war and had taken Moscow Dynamo on its famous tour of Britain and Sweden in 1945. Thereafter the Russians, whose elegant, enterprising football had been excitingly successful, withdrew into splendid isolation till the Olympic tournament of 1952 in Helsinki, where they were put out 3–1 by Yugoslavia after an astonishing, oscillating 5–5 draw. They had just drawn a lively game against England in Moscow, and would now contest the same group in Gothenburg, together with Brazil and Austria.

They had gifted players in Simonian, the mobile little Armenian centre-forward; Lev Yachine, the superb goalkeeper who had succeeded and surpassed 'Tiger' Khomich in the Moscow Dynamo goal; Salnikov, a thoughtful inside-left; and Igor Netto. This blond left-half, captain of the side, who had helped it to win the Olympic title of 1956 in Melbourne, had hurt his left knee and was an uncertain starter; a blow to a Russian team which greatly depended on his lively, attacking play.

The loss would be the greater in that Edouard Streltsov, a thrusting, powerful young centre-forward from Torpedo Moscow, had just been sent to a labour camp for twelve years for alleged rape. In due course his career was to have an extraordinary second chapter when he was amnestied, returned to football and the international team, and was twice voted Footballer of the Year. But he never played in a World Cup.

England v. Russia in Gothenburg. Colin McDonald, watched by a grimacing Billy Wright, cuts out a centre.

West Germany v. Northern Ireland. Harry Gregg, the Irish goalkeeper, beaten by a shot from Uwe Seeler, the West German centre-forward at Malmö.

Northern Ireland, Wales and Scotland

Of the British teams, England were the most fancied, Northern Ireland the most intriguing. It was the first occasion on which all four had qualified for the Finals.

England's chances were severely affected by the disastrous Munich air crash the previous February, when the Manchester United team's Elizabethan, twin-engined aircraft failed to gain sufficient height on a snowy day and hit a building at the end of the runway. The team, which had just drawn a European Cup tie 3–3 in Belgrade, was cruelly afflicted. Among those who died instantly were the captain, England's resourceful left-back Roger Byrne, and Tommy Taylor, their excellent centre-forward, a fine player in the air and a vigorous one on the ground. Duncan Edwards, still only twenty-one years old, a superbly powerful player thought by many to be the finest left-half to have played for his country since the war, died pitifully in hospital after fighting for life with the help of a kidney machine. The experience profoundly disturbed the twenty-year-old Bobby Charlton, whose natural shyness became a persistent melancholy which would remain with him for the next decade. He had played for England on their pre-World Cup tour, done badly in Belgrade, when they lost 5–0 in intense heat to Yugoslavia, and would not play a single World Cup match. This represented a perverse decision by team manager and selectors but, as we shall see, it may have been better for Charlton, in the circumstances, that he did not play.

Northern Ireland had won their way to the finals against all expectation by eliminating Italy – and their cohorts of South Americans. Unlucky to lose 1–0 in Rome, when the tough but tiny Wilbur Cush played successfully at centre-half and Sergio Cervato slyly moved the ball to the right to make a gap through which he could score from a free kick, they finished the job in Belfast. The decisive game should have taken place in January, but Istvan Zsolt, the Hungarian referee and theatre director, was held up in the fog, the Italians refused to accept an Irish referee and what followed was the unfriendliest friendly which can ever have been seen in Belfast.

Juan Schiaffino, star of the previous two World Cups with Uruguay, now playing for Milan and – on tenuous qualification – for Italy, broke Wilbur Cush's shinpad with a kick; Chiapella, the Fiorentina right-half, jumped with both knees into McAdams' back after a challenge on the goalkeeper, and when the final whistle blew on a 2–2 draw the crowd invaded the field. Danny Blanchflower, the Irish captain, allocated each Italian player to an Irish one. Ferrario, the huge centre-half who had jumped feet first at two Irish forwards at a corner, knocked down a couple of invaders, then panicked and cowered on the ground, and the police badly beat up a fan who had come on merely in quest of an autograph. It was a brutal, sombre affair, but Ireland eventually won the real match 2–1 on their merits, with goals by McIlroy and the ill-used Cush. Alcide Ghiggia, another Uruguayan hero of the 1950 World Cup called up by Italy, was sent off, ironically for a trivial offence.

Having fought their way through so bravely to the finals, the Northern Ireland team then had to fight again – against pressure in Ulster to prevent their playing on Sundays, an unavoidable necessity in the World Cup. The Irish Football Association was torn, but eventually sanity prevailed over bigotry.

Northern Ireland's extraordinary improvement and success was the result of the inspired managership of Peter Doherty and the emergence of a nucleus of greatly talented players – notably Gregg, the Blanchflowers, Peacock, McParland, Cush, McIlroy and Bingham. All the team lacked, before the Munich horror, was a good centre-forward; what marvellous use they could have made of the mature Derek Dougan, who was at that time so young and raw! After Munich, they also found themselves without a centre-half, the crash having an appallingly traumatic effect on Jackie Blanchflower, Danny's younger brother, and on their goalkeeper Harry Gregg, who was so severely affected that he had to sleep in the same room as the trainer, Gerry Morgan, in Sweden. There were many nights when Morgan would walk up and down the room with Gregg, whose behaviour at Munich had been gallant in the extreme, for he saved several passengers from the wreckage.

Ferenc Szojka,
Hungary's right-half.

Peter Doherty had himself been a magnificent inside-left with numerous different English clubs, especially Manchester City and Derby County. He had never forgotten the humiliations of being an Irish international player in the pre-war years, when leading English clubs would not release their Irish players and hastily assembled sides were thrown into battle with a minimum of preparation. Now that he was manager he was determined to see that the Irish team would never again be so demoralised and disadvantaged.

Doherty was fortunate in having two splendid lieutenants to implement his policies on the field. Danny Blanchflower, the right-half, and Jimmy McIlroy, the Burnley inside-forward, were two drily witty, technically gifted, tactically sophisticated footballers whose good influence permeated the rest of the team. Before the World Cup, in which Ireland were drawn in a group with the West German holders, the Czechs and the Argentinians, Blanchflower whimsically observed that their plan would be to equalise before the other side had scored.

Billy Bingham, the well-sprung little Sunderland and Luton outside-right, who would form such a fine right wing with Cush in the World Cup and later become team manager himself, attributed the team's success to Doherty's 'pep talks', his double

Ferenc Sipos,
Hungary's centre-half.

centre-forward plan which largely made up for the lack of a sufficient centre-forward, the devoted rehearsal of free kicks, corners and throws-in, and the fact that the minimal changes Doherty made ensured that the team became 'more like a club side'.

This was true of the equally impressive Welsh. Initially Wales were lucky to be going to Sweden at all, for they had been eliminated by the Czechs. When the withdrawal of all Israel's opponents – on political grounds – left them with a free passage to Sweden, FIFA decreed that those countries which had taken second place in their group should be put in a hat, the team drawn out to meet Israel, home and away. Uruguay proudly refused, Wales came out of the hat, won 2–0 home and away, and went to Sweden, their chances improved by Juventus' release of the massive, formidable John Charles to play centre-forward. Charles, who had made his international debut as a seventeen-year-old centre-half, had just finished a wonderfully successful first season in Italy. The Welsh team manager was the lively Jimmy Murphy, who had efficiently taken over Manchester United when Matt Busby was badly hurt in the Munich crash, and there were other famous players in Jack Kelsey, a strong, calm, agile goalkeeper, and the classical inside-left, Ivor All-church.

The Welsh benefited enormously from their sojourn in training camp at Saltsjobaden, where the beer was said to disappear in large quantities though with no detriment to a team which would surpass itself, not least in making Brazil fight all the way. Both Wales and France, who trained at Kopparberg, followed the previous Hungarian habit of scoring large quantities of goals against local teams, victories meaningless in themselves but surprisingly good for morale.

Scotland had done well to eliminate Spain, but they had just been thrashed 4–0 by England at Hampden and would predictably finish bottom of a group which included Paraguay – Uruguay's unexpected conquerors – Yugoslavia and France.

Wales v. Mexico. John Charles, the Welsh centre-forward, dives for a header over Jorge Romo, Mexico's centre-half.

Hungary

The Hungarians, moral victors and actual losers in 1954, were a parody of their great team of the early fifties. Comes the Revolution; in this case, the Hungarian Revolution of 1956. Honved, the army team into which, willy nilly, the authorities had stuffed almost all their best footballers, was touring abroad; and the authorities were properly hoist with their own petard. The incomparable, irreplaceable inside-forwards, Kocsis and Puskas, exiled themselves and eventually, like Kubala before them, found gainful employment in Spanish football. The excellent winger, Zoltan Czibor, expatriated himself, too, and though

Josef Bozsik and Nandor Hidegkuti duly went dutifully home, they were fading veterans by now.

Moreover, it was alleged that there had been a descent by police on the Hungarian players at Budapest airport to confiscate money which they were taking out of the country to buy goods. It may well have been true, for the players seemed very much down in the mouth. Gustav Sebes, who led them in the 1954 World Cup, remarked, 'I have never seen a Hungarian team in such a deplorable physical condition and nervous state.' The myth of Hungarian superiority, their supremacy in tactics, men and training, went to the winds, though the comfortable journalese soubriquet of Magic Magyars would be with us for a few wistful years to come.

France

The French arrived nineteen days before the competition started at Kopparberg under the inspiring and benevolent guidance of Monsieur Paul Nicolas, once an international himself, with their former splendid goalkeeper Alex Thépot among the selectors and Albert Batteux an excellent manager assisted by Jean Snella. No one thought France a serious candidate, which if anything helped them by removing pressure. They had not won a game that year, though the release of little Raymond Kopa by Real Madrid was sure to improve them. Banished to the wing at Real by the dominating Alfredo Di Stefano – who could not, even with Kubala's help, enable Spain to eliminate Scotland – Kopa flourished anew when back in the middle and on the conductor's podium. A superbly balanced player with exquisite control and a splendid eye for the through pass, his partnership with Just Fontaine would be one of the features of the tournament, bringing Fontaine a record thirteen goals.

Fontaine, born in Morocco, had come to Sweden quite reconciled to being a reserve, and even said, 'I'm centre-forward only till Kopa comes'. When René Bliard kicked the ground in training, hurt his ankle and went home – singing Fontaine's praises – his choice was assured. Dark, sturdily built, a fast and determined runner with excellent acceleration and a fine shot, Fontaine was also extremely intelligent in his responses to Kopa's splendid prompting. When French journalists later called their team *le vrai Dauphin* of the 1958 World Cup, it was not mere chauvinism.

West Germany

West Germany, the holders, had stood apart from the moralistic orgy in which Russians, Czechs and Paraguayans had joined. The Russians, as we have seen, had imprisoned Streltsov. For

114

good measure they suspended from the World Cup, for indiscipline, Boris Tatushine, a fast right-winger, and Ogonkov, their left-back. The Paraguayans in their turn suspended for 'professionalism' two of their best forwards, the Jara brothers, while the Czechs disqualified Jiri Hledik, a most gifted, versatile centre-half, who had had the temerity to ask for a transfer.

The two outstanding players of the series, Didì of Brazil and Raymond Kopa of France.

West Germany, however, did not suspend Helmut Rahn. They rehabilitated him. The enormous right-winger, bombardier of the last World Cup Final, had been drinking heavily since then, putting on alarming amounts of weight, even getting himself gaoled for drunken driving. But 'Uncle' Sepp Herberger, who would laugh when Swedish journalists accused him of treating players like numbers, was a pragmatist, not a moralist. Just as Rahn was whisked back in 1954 from South America in time to play in Switzerland, so he was rehabilitated, morally and physically, in time to play admirably in Sweden.

Since their victory in Berne little had gone right for the West Germans. Almost at once their team had been smitten with an epidemic of jaundice, which led to wide but unsubstantiated charges that they had been on drugs. No fewer than seven of the 1954 team had fallen by the wayside: Turek, Kohlmeyer, Liebrich, Mai, Otmar Walter and Morloch. But Fritz Walter was still there to be the chief strategist at the age of thirty-seven, and Hans Schaefer would resume his dialogue with Rahn on the wings. Moreover, there were two exciting additions to the team in the strong young left-half, Horst Szymaniak, and Uwe Seeler, a stalwart, highly mobile and combative centre-forward from Hamburg, who had been capped initially in 1954 at the age of eighteen and would become the very symbol of German football for years to follow.

Argentina

Argentina played in West Germany's group, but their team had been sadly plundered by the Italians. Only a year before, its young 'Angels with Dirty Faces', its *Trio de la Muerte* of Maschio, Angelillo and Sivori, had won it a spectacular South American title in Lima. In swooped the marauding Italian clubs to sign all of them, and the accomplished inside-left Ernesto Grillo for good measure.

Bob Jonquet, whose injury spoiled the French chances in the semi-final, has treatment on the touchline.

It was only by rehabilitating the famous forty-year-old inside-left Angel Labruna of River Plate, that Argentina had managed to scrape through the qualifying rounds, in which they had the shame of losing to obscure Bolivia. Another celebrated veteran in the giant, perambulating centre-half, Nestor Rossi, was in the side, but the omens were poor.

Brazil

Not that Brazil had had an easy passage to Sweden, even if they were the favourites by the time they got there. Their last, all-important qualifying match – against Peru in Rio – had been won only by 1–0, thanks to one of Didì's celebrated *foglia secca* (falling leaf) free kicks; which by 1970's World Cup would be known as banana shots. A similar shot, though from open play, had scored for Brazil against England at Wembley two years earlier, when they lost 4–2 and should have gone down by many more. Yet Didì was very nearly not brought to Sweden, and his place was in doubt until the opening game. First, he was criticised for being, at the age of thirty, too old! Second, he had married a white woman; third, he was supposedly not trying hard enough. 'It would be funny if they left me out,' he remarked with irony, 'after I had paid for their ticket.' He had the remote, brooding aspect of a great negro jazz musician.

Since Brazil's unimpressive European tour of 1956 one very important thing had happened: they had adopted the system of 4-2-4 instead of the third back game which was foreign to them. There is much dispute over who began 4-2-4 in Brazilian football, though many thought the Paraguayan coach, the celebrated Fleiras Solich, brought it to Rio. At all events it was the plump, rumbling, occasionally explosive Vicente Feola, a São Paulo man of Salernitan descent, who introduced it to the national side.

Feola brought to Sweden the best, most thoroughly organised Brazilian side ever to visit Europe. His right-hand man was the large and imperturbable doctor Hilton Gosling, who had covered hundreds of miles in Sweden before he found the ideal place for a training camp among the trees of Hindas outside Gothenburg. The Russians too, had taken up residence there, and sometimes, when they were not fishing, would come lumbering out of the woods like bears to watch the Brazilians joyfully train, with the cacophony of a male voice choir gone berserk. England, alas, had been too late for Hindas, and had unimaginatively put themselves in an hotel bang in the middle of Gothenburg. They attempted to make up for lack of isolation with a sour inaccessibility which utterly contrasted with the familial friendliness of the Welsh and the Irish. 'Isn't it a sin and a shame,' said George Raynor, 'that England had to stay at the Park Avenue?'

The Brazilians not only had Gosling, whom the players treated as father or father-confessor, they also had, with memories of Berne in mind, their own psychologist, an amiable eclectic from São Paulo, grey-sweatered, often unshaven, whose precise methods were a little hard to comprehend. He did not, he said, believe in haranguing the players in groups, yet neither did he believe in talking to them individually, since this made their problem bigger. He believed in getting them to draw pictures of

Semi-final: Brazil v. France Vavà, the Brazilian centre-forward is tackled while in full flight.

Gilmar, Brazil's goalkeeper, weeps with joy after the Final. Nilton Santos looks preoccupied.

a man. The more cerebral players drew sophisticated pictures, the instinctive players drew virtual matchstick-men. The two made good wing partnerships. Forwards must project their aggression, defenders must contain it; a theory which must have taken heavy punishment if he chanced to see such defenders as the terrible Erhardt of West Germany.

Feola, meanwhile, shook his heavy head and said, 'How can he know the ambience?' He was also critical of his nineteen-year-old, blond centre-forward José Altafini, known then by the nickname of Mazzola for his resemblance to the old captain of Italy and father of Sandrino. Altafini had just been transferred for a large fee to Milan – the team, indeed, had played two impressive matches in Italy en route to Sweden. 'He's nineteen,' complained Feola. 'All the publicity about his transfer to Milan; how can it help but go to his head? He doesn't fit in with the team.'

Feola's preference and ultimate choice went to the Vasco da Gama centre-forward Vavà, a sturdy, Aztec figure, while there were two other imponderables. The seventeen-year-old Pelé, already described as the finest player ever produced by Brazil, was injured, while Feola was reluctant to choose the forward the psychologist regarded as the most unsophisticated of all, the outside-right Garrincha.

Garrincha, 'the Little Bird', was all the more dangerous and unpredictable because he had been crippled since childhood; he was a footballer of superb natural gifts, astonishing speed and swerve, but utterly inconsistent. The safe and early choice was Flamengo's Joel – with another Flamengo winger in Zagalo on the left, and their club mate Dida at inside-right, beside Vavà.

The 4-2-4 system solved the old Brazilian problem of pivotal covering in defence by simply putting the left-half alongside the centre-half; just as Hungary had done with Zakarias. Two players foraged and passed in midfield, while two wingers and two central strikers stayed in attack. If you had the extraordinary talent at your command that the Brazilians had, it was a marvellous system. If not, it would present as many difficulties as it solved, especially in midfield.

The Brazilians gave it an extra dimension through the unique and at first much under-rated Mario Lobo Zagalo, whose exceptional lung power gave him phenomenal stamina and who could quite happily patrol the whole length of the touchline. This was most helpful in Sweden; it would prove essential in Chile four years later.

England

England, who were expected to qualify from Gothenburg with Brazil, had compounded the problems created by Munich with their odd choice. They brought only twenty players, though entitled to twenty-two (the Czechs brought only eighteen) and these twenty included neither Stanley Matthews nor Nat Lofthouse, both successes of the 1954 World Cup and both still in imposing form. Matthews, indeed, had run ragged the usually impeccable Brazilian left-back Nilton Santos at Wembley in 1956 – at the age of forty-one – while Lofthouse had just scored both Bolton's goals in the Cup Final.

The loss of Edwards, Byrne and Taylor was thus exacerbated. Any hope of overcoming it was severely compromised by the fact that Fulham and Blackburn Rovers had just been engaged in a fierce, exhausting struggle to emerge from the Second Division which had left its mark on Johnny Haynes, the young Londoner whose superb crossfield and through passing made him the key man in attack, on Bobby Robson, his inside-forward partner at Fulham, and the talented little right-winger, Blackburn's Bryan Douglas. Ronnie Clayton, Blackburn's captain and right-half, gained a place only in the group's play-off.

England v. Austria at Boras. Johnny Haynes on the ball, while Bobby Robson, his Fulham colleague, appeals for a foul.

Group matches

Worse still was to come, for in the opening game in Gothenburg's new Ullevi Stadium where the roof, with its wire suspensions, suggested a monster puppeteer, Tom Finney was hurt. It did not prevent his inspiring the English revival in the last half hour or equalising from a penalty six minutes from time when Douglas was tripped, but his loss was a dreadful blow. Beyond question he was the one forward of world class England possessed, and there was no one now to compensate for the staleness of Haynes, Douglas and Robson, the banal crudities of the huge centre-forward Derek Kevan, the patent inadequacy of his successor Alan A'Court – and Walter Winterbottom's astonishing reluctance to make changes.

It was Salnikov, not Haynes, who was the arch strategist of this interesting match, one in which Russia played much clever football, even without Netto. Voinov and Tsarev, the robust wing-halves, made up for his absence, Krishevski dominated the centre, and it was as well that England's cool new goalkeeper, Colin McDonald of Burnley, was the equal even of Yachine.

After thirteen minutes, however, he could only block a shot by the vivacious left-winger Ilyin, and Simonian, who usually lay deep, was there to score. England's short, square, unimaginative passing was making no progress against a Russian defence whose methods often transgressed the rules.

Ten minutes into the second half the second Russian goal arrived. The English defence, in these pre-overlapping days, stood bemused as Kessarev, the right-back, advanced, crossed beautifully; and Ivanov scored. It was Finney's mastery of Kessarev, however, which began to turn the tide. After sixty-five minutes Billy Wright, an indomitable centre-half and a fine captain, booted a free kick high into the goalmouth. Kevan's fair head rose above the defence, even above Yachine, and headed down into goal.

Brazil, meanwhile, had had no trouble with ponderous Austria at Boras' little ground, Mazzola scoring twice, and Nilton Santos strolling through from left-back to get the third. Their critics, however, were dissatisfied, in particularly accusing Dida, who had done some good running off the ball, of lack of courage. Dida promptly disappeared from the side.

Elsewhere there were various alarms and excursions, though Sweden had opened the ball, unscathed, on the afternoon of June 8 with a 3–0 win in Stockholm over indifferent Mexico. Two of their goals were scored by a tall, talented young centre-forward, Agne Simonsson, while thirty-six-year-old Liedholm, at right-half for the moment, got the other from a penalty.

In Group 1, the astonishing Northern Irish beat Czechoslovakia by Cush's solitary goal at Halmstad, while the holders, West Germany, showed up Argentina's deficiencies at Malmö,

José Altafini, alias Mazzola, Brazil's young centre-forward, treated by Dr Hilton Gosling and the trainer, Americo, during the match against England.

West Germany v. Argentina in Malmö. The captains, Carrizo (Argentina) and Hans Schaefer (West Germany) exchange pennants.

West Germany v. Czechoslovakia: Dolejsi, the Czech goalkeeper, clutches the ball after being charged over his line by Hans Schaefer. The Czechs disputed this goal.

defeating them 3–1. Poor Fritz Walter, who would end the tournament in bed nursing his injuries, was horribly fouled by Rossi towards the end; a foul which many thought deserved to be punished with expulsion.

Not even a goal scored by Argentina's slim and dangerous little outside-right Corbatta in two minutes, cutting past the muscular Juskowiak, could give them the impetus they needed. The Germans were superior in teamwork and stamina, the Argentinians too much inclined to play off the cuff. So Rahn, half an hour after the goal, equalised with a sudden ferocious left-footer from the inside-left position when served by Walter, and five minutes from half-time Seeler, giving and receiving from Schaefer, lunged forward to make it 2–1. Even an injury to Eckel which had him limping on the left wing for most of the second half could not tip the balance, and ten minutes from the end Rahn bent his shot past the veteran Carrizo with the outside of the foot. 3–1.

The Irish, who had trained by running round the upper reaches of the River Lagan and sprinting half-laps at Windsor Park, Belfast, used the young Derek Dougan at centre-forward. The first choice, Billy Simpson of Rangers, had pulled a muscle after a mere five minutes' training in Sweden. Dougan had an awkward first half, but when Billy Bingham was pushed into the middle in the second he made good use of his fine acceleration. Harry Gregg, who had travelled to Sweden by sea, allayed all fears with his performance in goal, Bertie Peacock had an exceptional game at left-half and Wilbur Cush headed the only goal from the rugged Peter McParland's centre. The lack of Jackie Blanchflower had a seriously negative effect on the team, obliging his brother to play a far more defensive game alongside their makeshift centre-half, the full-back Willie Cunningham, but the defence held out well under vigorous pressure in the closing phases.

France got away to a spectacular beginning, annihilating the Paraguayans 7–3 at Norkopping, five of their goals coming in the second half; a rampant Fontaine got three. Paraguay actually scored first through Amarilla, and were level, 2–2, at half-time. Thereafter the superb combination of the French inside-forwards, Kopa, Fontaine and the incisive Roger Piantoni, was simply too much for them.

Scotland, at Vasteras, did a great deal better against Yugoslavia than had feeble England in Belgrade, holding them to a 1–1 draw in a strangely schizophrenic match. Its star was the thirty-five-year-old Hibernian right-half Eddie Turnbull. With Gren, Liedholm, Walter and Turnbull, it was quite a World Cup for veterans. Formally an inside-left, Turnbull had dropped back to the middle line, and now he gave a memorable performance in his first and only World Cup.

Yugoslavia, far superior in technique, began the game as if they were going to treat Scotland as they had England. With the blond, elegant Milos Milutinovic in splendid form at centre-forward and abetted by a new star, the dark little gipsy inside-left Dragoslav Sekularac, and the admirable Boskov at wing-half, they assailed the Scottish goal. At first, wrote one commentator, the Scots seemed like juniors getting a lesson. The right-winger Petakovic gave Tommy Younger, the big, blond Scots goalkeeper, no hope; from Milutinovic's pass Eric Caldow kicked off the line; Younger made a fine save, and somehow no more goals resulted.

In the second half Scotland's immense determination and robust challenge ground down the more fragile Slavs. Petakovic had scarcely hit a post when Turnbull crossed, Beara – in goal – and Krstic confused one another, and Murray headed the equaliser. Though Veselinovic also hit the post, Yugoslavia had lost their command. 'The artists of Belgrade and Zagreb,' wrote the French critic, 'were upset by the artisans of Edinburgh and Glasgow.'

In Group 1 Wales held Hungary to a draw at Sandviken. A Hungarian team whose methods in defence were sometimes violent warmed up for half an hour before the game and scored in four minutes through Josef Bozsik when Kelsey was dazzled by the sun; but one of John Charles' formidable leaps and headers saved the day for Wales, at a corner.

In Gothenburg, England would now play Brazil for the first time in a World Cup. To the amazement of the English Press the only change made in the team which looked so banal against Russia was A'Court for the injured Finney. No change, indeed, would become the tedious motif of the series, as it gradually became clear that Walter Winterbottom dominated his selectors, though nominally at their command. 'I'd pick Charlton,' a selector would say in the lobby of the Park Avenue, and then go into a team selection meeting which would confirm the same side. An almost messianic campaign evolved in favour of Charlton, so that ultimately one could only feel relieved that he had not been chosen, for even a Pelé would have found it hard to satisfy such immense expectations. Charlton's World Cups would come, even if he was so arbitrarily kept out of this one.

What England did for once have in the Brazilian game was intelligent tactics, thanks to the Tottenham Hotspur coach and later manager, Bill Nicholson. Nicholson, having watched the Brazilians, evolved a defensive scheme whereby Don Howe, the tall, cool West Bromwich right-back, would play as a second centre-half beside Billy Wright; Eddie Clamp, the big, dark Wolves half-back, as an attacking full-back; while another Wolves man, the studious Bill Slater, would play 'tight' on Didì.

With Pelé and Garrincha still missing from Brazil's attack,

Semi-final: Sweden v. West Germany. Svensson clears under pressure from the West German captain, Schaefer.

though Vavà now lined up beside Mazzola, the scheme worked remarkably well. Brazil dominated the first half, Didì and the attacking right-half, the bald Dino, dominating midfield, but Vavà hit the bar, Clamp kicked off the line, and Colin McDonald made two spectacular saves from headers by Mazzola.

In the second half, the pattern changed and England might even have won. If some had cast doubt on the English penalty against Russia, claiming that the foul took place outside the box, the England were most unfortunate not to get one when Bellini hauled Kevan down as he thundered after one of Haynes' rare through passes.

By and large, however, the England attack was as grey as it had been against Russia, especially without Finney's eventual brilliance. It was the defence which excelled, Tommy Banks, the robust Bolton left-back whose appearance recalled a Great War private of the trenches, surpassing himself. Once, when Don Howe skied the ball, he brought it down with a delicacy any Brazilian might have envied.

In Boras, goals by Ilyin and Valentin Ivanov gave Russia a 2–0 win over Austria and put England's qualification in doubt.

The Irish, paying for bad intelligence on the Argentinian team, lost 3–1 to it at Halmstad. Told that the Argentinian players were huge and ruthless they were surprised, said Jimmy McIlroy, to find awaiting them in the tunnel 'a lot of little fat men with stomachs, smiling at us and pointing and waving to the girls in the crowd.' Some of those fine, flaxen girls, it was said,

Derek Kevan has headed England's first goal of the tournament against Russia in Gothenburg.

had boldly been scaling the drainpipes of the Argentinians' hotel.

When Peter McParland headed a beautiful goal from Bingham's cross after only three minutes, a second victory seemed in prospect. Instead, the sheer skill of the Argentinians overcame an Irish team which lacked bite in the middle, Coyle's unexpected replacement of Dougan bringing no improvement. This above all was a game in which Danny Blanchflower's subtle talents, his always imaginative use of the ball, were needed not in defence but in midfield, where Rossi and the splendid veteran Labruna dominated. The ingenuousness of the brief Ireland's observer gave Peter Doherty may be gauged from his assertion that 'their right-half seemed to be playing at right-back'. The double-spearhead tactic was of no use against a defence with two stoppers, and there was no equivalent of Sepp Herberger's successful plan which had Schmidt, the inside-left, playing on Rossi, Rahn lying deep to draw the Argentinian left-half upfield, Seeler drifting left and Fritz Walter swinging the ball largely to that wing.

Luck certainly went against the Irish on the half-hour when a ball whipped off the damp turf to hit Cunningham's hand, and a penalty was given from which Corbatta scored. It was not one of Harry Gregg's best days and he was too far out of goal when Menendez scored in the second half. Nor was he quick enough to Corbatta's cross on the third goal.

West Germany at Hälsingborg brought Hans Schaefer in from the wing to inside-left, and it was his controversial goal, scored on the hour, which turned a game they seemed to be losing to the lively Czechs. Two goals down, they made it 1–2 when Schaefer charged the Czech goalkeeper Dolejsi over his line with the ball, and the goal was surprisingly allowed to stand. Helmut Rahn – again – equalised.

An unexpected result was the defeat of France 3–2 by Yugoslavia at Vasteras, despite two more goals for the prolific Just Fontaine. A lack of authority in defence, despite the composed presence at centre-half of the accomplished Bob Jonquet, an inability to get the best out of two excellent wingers in Wisnieski and Jean Vincent, a penalty refused when Fontaine was fouled; all these played a part in France's defeat. So did the opportunism of Veselinovic, who got two of the Yugoslav goals. The winner came three minutes from time when France were besieging Beara's goal. Then Yugoslavia broke away, Roger Marche – France's bald, experienced left-back – erred, and Veselinovic scored his second.

Scotland, seemingly weary after their display against the Yugoslavs, went down 3–2 to Paraguay at Norrkoping where Silvio Parodi, an inside-forward with experience of Italian football, was the dominant player and Bobby Evans an excellent

Boris Kuznetzov, Russia's left-back.

Yuri Voinov, the Russian right-half.

centre-half. Indeed, not one of the British teams won their match in this round, for Wales played very poorly in Stockholm, to be held 1–1 by Mexico. 'Every time you knocked one of them down, he cried,' complained the Manchester United forward Colin Webster, never the most gentle of players, but Kelsey was impressed by their ball control and fitness.

Sweden made heavy weather of winning their evening game in the same stadium against Hungary, a match notable for the tremendous right-footed shooting of Hungary's Lajos Tichy and the deadly finishing of Sweden's Kurre Hamrin.

Hungary dropped Hidegkuti and used Bozsik as deep centre-forward, a position in which he played skilfully but unhappily. Gren and Liedholm were masterly inside-forwards for Sweden, Hamrin and Skoglund tormenting wingers, Skoglund making the first goal when he twice beat his man and then crossed for Hamrin to score.

After ten minutes of the second half Tichy shot mightily against the underside of the crossbar. From the stands it looked a goal but play continued, and half a minute later Hamrin's deflected lob beat Grosics to make it 2–0. Liedholm missed a penalty, one of Tichy's drives ripped home and Sweden had won 2–1. Raynor afterwards explained that he had ordered his heavy defence never to go in for a ball that wasn't at least a 50-50 one. To Skoglund, involved in a fracas with Matray, he would be speaking in the morning – 'We want no circus men in our lot.'

Hungary v. Wales in Stockholm. Hungarian spectators hold black-edged flags in protest against the execution of their former premier, Imri Nagy.

The concluding round of matches brought, above all, the annihilation of Argentina by Czechoslovakia at Hälsingborg, a humiliation which may now be seen as the bleak turning point in Argentinian football. What was especially strange was that the Argentinians should be made to look so slow and obsolete by the Czechs, so often criticised – as they would be even in the 1962 World Cup – for one-pace football.

The Czechs, who confirmed the burly Popluhar at centre-half in his second World Cup match, simply overwhelmed the Argentinians who, said one critic, seemed to be continuing one of the endless head-tennis games they played outside their hotel. Borovicka, who had missed the German game – there were tales of a bitter quarrel in the dressing-room during the Irish match – returned to blend perfectly with the powerful Molnar, while Hovorka was a strong and effective outside-right, making two goals and scoring the last two. Another two went to Zikan, the outside-left, and Argentina's only reply came from a penalty by the inevitable Corbatta. With the exception of him, Menendez and Varacka – who, commentators were quick to point out, was of Czech origin – the team looked slow and unfit.

When it was over poor Guillermo Stabile, team manager and leading scorer of the 1930 World Cup, extended his hand to his Czech counterpart Kolsky, and said, 'You have the finest team I have ever seen. I congratulate you and wish you good luck.'

When the Argentinians arrived at Buenos Aires airport initial disbelief had turned to fury and they were pelted with rubbish. The wound went deep. In future, Argentinian football would shed its old traditions of spectacle and artistry and become more destructive than the most negative.

In Malmö, with thousands of their supporters in attendance, West Germany were held to an exciting 2–2 draw by Northern Ireland, for whom Harry Gregg, superb in goal, and Peter McParland, a deadly opportunist, surpassed themselves.

The Irish players had been astonished when Tommy Casey, a left-half, had been picked as their latest centre-forward, but Casey's enormous determination made it a better choice than it appeared. Within twenty minutes Ireland had gone into the lead when Bingham sent over an oblique centre, Herkenrath, the goalkeeper, challenged by Cush, missed it and McIlroy found McParland, who scored.

With the stalwart Newcastle United backs Dick Keith and the red-haired Alf McMichael dealing well with the German wingers and little Bertie Peacock splendid in midfield, Ireland were more than a match for the holders; even if Rahn did equalise a couple of minutes after their goal. Gregg hurt his ankle but continued to plunge fearlessly among the German boots, Casey had eight stitches put in his right shin but played on, and after an hour Ireland went ahead again. Receiving Bingham's short corner Cush crossed, and again McIlroy served the unforgiving McParland.

With twelve minutes left, Uwe Seeler equalised from over thirty yards, but the closing minutes were all Ireland, banging away at the German goal. At the final whistle Gregg was cheered off the field, and Ireland had forced a play-off in Malmö against the Czechs.

In Gothenburg, Brazil at last let slip the astonishing Pelé and the inimitable Garrincha, routing the Soviets in the process. Though the score was 2–0 it might easily have been doubled or even trebled.

Pelé had been an international for almost a year, a striking inside-forward who came from a poor black family at Tres Coracoes in the heart of the great state of Minas Gerais. As a boy he had been coached by the old Brazilian international forward, de Brito, who brought him to the Santos club where his progress had been phenomenal. Five feet eight inches tall, weighing some ten and a half stone, superbly muscled, he was at this stage a goal-scorer *par excellence*, gymnastically agile and resilient, a tantalising juggler of the ball, a fine right-footed shot with the ability to climb and head like a Lawton. Above all, his temperament was extraordinary, his coolness in the thick of the battle, the most tense and dramatic situations, uncanny.

Three Austrian players, Kollmann, Stotz and Körner, in training.

Brazil's training camp at Hin
The players are Djalma San
Zito and V

His face, which would become so familiar throughout the world over the next decade, never lost its innocence, its boyish appeal. He was no saint; in years to come his policy under provocation was much more the Old Testament one of an eye for an eye than the New Testament's turning the other cheek, but somehow the image remained untarnished, the pristine appeal untouched.

Garrincha came into the team by popular request of the players themselves. A deputation led by Nilton Santos went to Feola and asked for his inclusion. Feola gave way. As the teams stood in line before the kick-off, Nilton Santos murmured to Garrincha that he hoped he would not let them down. Garrincha, in his cheerful simplicity, replied, 'Look at that linesman; he's like Charlie Chaplin' – his way of showing Santos that he was relaxed.

This was the last thing that his unfortunate opponent Kuznetsov could ever be. From the opening minutes, Garrincha's incomparable swerve and acceleration left him helpless. First he beat him to the wide, shot, and hit the left-hand post. Next, Pelé hit the right-hand post. Finally, after three minutes Didì emerged calmly and magisterially from a group of Russian opponents, and with an exquisite pass found Vavà who dashed through to score.

Didì had now found his ideal complement in the Santos right-half Zito, who had replaced Dino. Stronger in defence, much less inclined to carry the ball, an adroit passer who could strike for goal when necessary, Zito would emerge as the best half-back in the tournament.

It was extraordinary that Russia's bemused defence should hold out till thirteen minutes from time when Vavà, after an exchange of passes with Pelé, got the second. At one late, memorable instant, Garrincha had and held the ball against five encircling Russians. Genius had overwhelmed mere effort.

At Boras, in a match played on a lower plane, England laboured to a draw with the ponderous Austrians, who were twice ahead. The British sailor who ironically blew the Last Post when a histrionic Austrian went down might well have been blowing it for England. Haynes, at his best, must have made more of Kevan's dominance of the ageing Happel, Austria's stopper. He himself scored England's first goal after fifty-six minutes and made the second for Kevan. Austria's goals both came from impressive, uncharacteristic long shots, by Koller and Koerner.

In Group II France duly beat Scotland, but they found it hard. Each team changed its goalkeeper. Bill Brown, of Dundee and later of Spurs, won the admiration of Kopa and Fontaine with his agility; Abbes replaced Remetter for France. Kopa volleyed home Fontaine's cross – a brief reciprocation – but Scot-

Raymond Kopa, the outstanding French centre-forward.

Brazil v. France: semi-final in Stockholm. Bob Jonquet, the French centre-half, is helped off the field.

land struck back forcefully. Abbes had to make a fine save from Murray; then, when the Hearts forward was fouled – by Jonquet and the talented right-half Armand Penverne – John Hewie, Charlton Athletic's South African, wastefully hit the penalty against a post.

It was as well for France that in the very last seconds of the half Fontaine, served by Jonquet, should sprint away to make it 2–0. In the second half, when they were much less good, Baird emulated him and the final score was a narrow 2–1.

At Ekilstuna a hero tottered, Vladimir Beara having one of his worst games in goal for Yugoslavia against Paraguay. The score was 3–3, and all three Paraguayan goals could be blamed on the unhappy Beara. Three times the Paraguayans, inspired again by Parodi, equalised against a Yugoslav team which had dropped the graceful Milutinovic; but the Slavs went through.

Play-offs for quarter-finals

Goal average counting for nothing, three of the British teams now entered play-offs – and two got through. It was, most unforeseeably, England who failed, losing 1–0 to Russia in Gothenburg. Almost perversely, having stubbornly refused to make changes, they now, still disdaining Charlton, capped two new forwards: Peter Brabook, the Chelsea right-winger, and Peter Broadbent, the industrious young Wolves inside-right. George Raynor had something to say: 'We'd never blood a player in an international match of that kind. We'd have done all that before. Take Agne Simonsson, our centre-forward. I watched him twelve times before I decided that he was the man we wanted.'

In the tepid Ullevi – tepid till Sweden arrived there – England did not deserve to lose, though Haynes, apparently untouchable, had another grim game. Brabook twice hit a post; Ilyin hit one after sixty-eight minutes, and scored. Sadly for the otherwise faultless McDonald, it was his careless throw which put Russia away.

Decimated Ireland, faced by a Czech team which had swamped Argentina, patched up their team at Malmö and won, as Peter Doherty promised they would.

Norman Uprichard replaced Gregg in goal, and Jackie Scott was capped for the first time in place of the injured Tommy Casey. Uprichard was hurt, Peacock was hurt, Czechoslovakia took the lead, the game went into extra time; and still Ireland won. They owed something to Billy Bingham's inspired bluff when, just before the start of extra time, casting an eye on the exhausted Czechs, he persuaded the equally exhausted Irish to do calisthenics.

Zikan gave the Czechs the lead after nineteen minutes, but on the stroke of half-time the irresistible McParland equalised after Cush had had two shots blocked. Nine minutes into extra time he volleyed home Danny Blanchflower's free kick. Bubernik of Czechoslovakia was sent off. Ireland qualified.

So did Wales, eliminating Hungary at Stockholm; a match in which an opponent was also sent off – Sipos, for brutally kicking Hewitt; also in extra time.

One of Tichy's shots gave Hungary a first half lead; Ivor Allchurch equalised with an astonishing forty-yard volley; Terry Medwin's winner was in its way more remarkable still. He swooped cheekily on Grosics' short goal kick to Sarosi, and scored.

Neither British team survived the quarter-final, though Wales, even without the mighty John Charles, gave Brazil immense trouble in Gothenburg. Perhaps Charles would have exploited the early centre with which Webster, his deputy, did nothing.

Thereafter, it was the iron Welsh defence against the Brazilian attack which found the going harder and harder. Mazzola was back again for Vavà, Garrincha was most cleverly played by Mel Hopkins, Dave Bowen was an inspiriting captain, Stuart Williams and Derek Sullivan a muscular right flank. Behind them, Jack Kelsey held everything. 'Chewing gum,' he modestly explained afterwards. 'Always use it. Put some on my hands. Rub it well in.'

Pelé has often said that the goal with which he cut the Gordian knot after sixty-six minutes was the most important he ever scored. It was also one of the luckiest, for Kelsey had the shot covered before it struck the foot of the impeccable Williams and was deflected past him. There was a pile-up, a very pyramid of yellow-shirted Brazilian bodies in the goalmouth. By this time it had long been plain that Wales themselves were never going to score, but if John Charles was so sorely missed Mel Charles, his younger brother, was the most defiantly reliable of centre-halves.

The weary and depleted Irish team, all the wearier for an ill-planned coach journey, did their best against France but blew up. The two hundred and ten-mile drive to Norkopping the previous day was bad enough preparation; the absence of Gregg and Peacock (with torn ligaments) and the need to play the damaged Casey still a greater handicap. There was just one early moment in which the team might have scored and thus found the morale, the magic energy, they had before. In one of their set-piece throw-ins, Blanchflower threw the ball to Bingham's head and the little winger flicked it on for McIlroy, but he, clear through,

Russian footballers relaxing at Hindas.

Pelé is mobbed by delighted Brazilian players after scoring the only goal of the quarter-final against Wales in Gothenburg.

squared it instead of shooting. That was that. With McParland on this occasion lost in the middle, Wisnieski scored just before half-time and Ireland collapsed. In the second half Fontaine, twice more, and Piantoni added goals.

The quarter-finals

Sweden found a weary Russian team stiff opponents in the first half at Stockholm, where the public's incredulity still kept the crowd down to less than 32,000. In the second half Kurt Hamrin embarked on a one-man siege of the Russian goal. Twice he almost headed in; eventually, after his own run and cross, the ball bobbled loose and head it in he did. He made the second goal for Simonsson from the left-hand goal line two and a half minutes from time.

Jasseron, an experienced French coach, observed of the Swedes that they were a good enough team provided they were not outpaced. Raynor knew it; Brazil would capitalise on it.

At Malmö Helmut Rahn yet again won the match for Germany, racing away from the vulnerable Crnkovic to score after twelve minutes, Krivocuka, Beara's equally unhappy replacement, failing to narrow the angle. It was a match blemished by the ruthlessness of Juskowiak and Erhardt, who was lucky indeed not to give away a penalty when, nine minutes from the end, he not only brought down Milutinovitch – restored and iridescent – but held his leg for good measure. But Alexander Tirnanic, the Yugoslav manager and their right-winger in the 1930 World Cup, said wearily, 'Even if we'd got this penalty, which was a hundred times deserved, I don't know if it would have made any difference. My team couldn't score goals, and it would only have prolonged the affair.'

The semi-finals Sweden v. West Germany

The semi-finals pitted Sweden against West Germany in Gothenburg and Brazil against France in Stockholm. The Gothenburg match provided an extraordinary study in national behaviour, as the Swedes' unfettered chauvinism put even the Germans' in the shade, and very nearly resulted in the game not being played at all.

In the first place, the Swedes outraged all the canons of hospitality by bringing their own cheerleaders right on to the pitch before the match, to incite the crowd. Heaven knows there was reason for believing that the crowd required it, yet it was an outrageous solecism. Stern and blue-blazered, a solemn father-figure with the Swedish flag in hand exhorted the spectators through a microphone to chant and cheer. He then introduced his cheerleaders, who frisked on to the field bearing flags like so

Sweden v. West Germany. Helmut Rahn, Germany's outside-right, challenged by Sweden's Julle Gustavsson.

many jesters. The German cheerleaders, meanwhile, were confined to the running-track.

In the stand, an embittered row was going on between Dr Pecos Bauwens, the Olympian President of the German Football Association, whose own chauvinistic pronouncements after the 1954 World Cup had caused concern in West Germany, and Swedish officials. The Swedes would not provide seats for some of the West German supporters. Dr Bauwens threatened that if they were not forthcoming he would withdraw his team from the match. They were provided.

The game itself was a fascinating one, even though blemished by fouls and at least one major refereeing error. With the tremendous Swedish choruses of *Heja, heja, heja!* thundering over the stadium, the home team dictated the early play. Erhardt had chosen the wrong studs and slipped about parlously on the greasy ground, while Herkenrath looked an uncertain goalkeeper. Nevertheless, it was Germany who broke away for a sensational goal.

Seeler, always busy and thoughtful, went to the left to catch a ball rolling out of play and centred, and Hans Schaefer despatched it past Svensson with a ferocious twenty-five-yard volley.

Sweden's equaliser, after Liedholm and Gren had gradually brought them back into the game, should never have stood. Liedholm blatantly brought the ball under control with his hand before running on with an approving wave from the referee, and Skoglund ultimately scored from a sharp angle. There were only five minutes between the goals.

It was Hamrin, already tormenting Juskowiak, who turned the game early in the second half, though in a somewhat unusual way. In the third minute Herkenrath had to plunge at his feet. In the twelfth he fouled Juskowiak, who was foolish enough to kick him. Hamrin made the most of it, rolling about in apparent agony, though when Juskowiak was sent off, his recovery was quick.

Parling, the large, blond Swedish left-half known as the Iron Stove, was just as worthy to be sent off for a dreadful foul on Fritz Walter sixteen minutes from the end. Walter was carried off for a couple of minutes, and spent the next day in bed. So Sweden, now virtually playing against nine men, finished the job.

Nine minutes from time, when Hamrin's shot was blocked, Gunnar Gren let fly immediately for the top left-hand corner, for one of his rare goals. Finally, Hamrin scored a goal of rare skill and impertinence, first stopping with the ball and walking it towards the right touchline like a man bemused, then coming to galvanic life, dancing past three men and beating Herkenrath. The slowest team in the tournament had reached the Final.

Kurt Hamrin finishes a spectacular run by scoring Sweden's third goal against West Germany in the Gothenburg semi-final.

Pelé, No. 10, scores for Brazil
against France.

Pelé, Brazil's seventeen-year-old
phenomenon.

The French goalkeeper,
Claude Abbes, beaten by
Brazil's fifth goal in Stockholm.

Brazil v. France

So did Brazil, though the promised feast against France never materialised. It would have been fascinating to see how the deep central thrust of Fontaine and Piantoni, fed by Kopa, would have fared against Brazil's uncertain central defence. For thirty-seven minutes, indeed, the marvellous little Kopa caused all sorts of trouble. Didì, Garrincha and Pelé made Vavà a devastating goal in the second minute, but Fontaine had equalised within nine. Then Bob Jonquet was hurt and left the middle, Didì scored within two minutes, and in the second half the fabulous Pelé ran riot with three more goals, Piantoni scoring a late, meaningless second for France.

The Final Sweden v. Brazil

So Sweden would play Brazil, and the Brazilians worried about the effect an atmosphere as torrid as Gothenburg's might have on their emotional players. The World Cup Committee set their minds at rest by sternly forbidding the Swedes to bring cheer-leaders on to the pitch again. Thus deprived of example and in-struction, the crowd at Rasunda was astonishingly quiet.

As an *hors d'oeuvre* Kopa and Fontaine played ducks and drakes at Gothenburg with a weakened Germany – in which the young, blond Karl-Heinz Schnellinger made his second appear-ance of the series, at right-half. Kopa, the son of a Polish miner and a Frenchwoman, who might never have turned professional footballer were it not for a boyhood mining accident, was ir-resistible. Svengali to Fontaine's Trilby, he helped him to four splendid goals and got a penalty himself. France took the third-place match 6–3.

Thus to Stockholm, and a day heavy with rain. George Ray-nor cheerfully forecast that if the Brazilians went a goal down they would 'panic all over the show'. They did go an early goal down; and stayed serene.

Feola made a bold change in defence, suddenly withdrawing his right-back de Sordi to give the powerful black Djalma Santos, a veteran of 1954, his first game in the competition. The two Santoses snuffed out Hamrin and Skoglund with the non-chalance of men extinguishing a candle.

Yet Sweden had a goal in four minutes, a goal worked out by Gren and Liedholm with such facility that many seemed sure to follow. Gren gave Liedholm the ball, Liedholm picked his way precisely past two Brazilian defenders in the penalty box and beat the poised Gilmar with a low, strong shot into the right-hand corner. It was the first time in the tournament that Brazil had been in arrears.

Six minutes later they were level, thanks to the pantherine Garrincha. Receiving from Zito on the right wing, he took the

135

ball up to Parling and Axbom, caught them both off balance with a miraculous swerve and acceleration down the line and cut the ball back hard and fast. In tore Vavà to score.

The game grew wonderfully vivid. Pelé crashed a shot against the post, tireless Zagalo headed out from almost beneath the Brazilian bar. After thirty-two minutes, however, Garrincha again left the Swedish left flank standing, and Vavà again drove in his pass.

Sweden were losing the battle in midfield and were impotent on the wings. Their last hopes died ten minutes after half-time, when Pelé scored a marvellously impertinent goal. Catching a high ball in the thick of the penalty box on his thigh, he hooked it over his head, whirled round and volleyed mightily past Svensson.

Now Zito and Didì were switching play at will, now Djalma Santos was racing up from full-back, now Pelé and Vavà were probing, interpassing. With thirteen minutes left Zagalo went past Boerjesson, then Bergmark, and shot the fourth, and knelt in tears of joy.

Next, with the overjoyed Brazilian fans keeping up a shout of *Samba, samba!*, Liedholm sent Agne Simonsson through the middle, possibly offside, for Sweden's second goal – only for Pelé to reply with Brazil's fifth. Zagalo's was the centre, and Pelé rose to it with majestic elevation and power.

The World Cup was Brazil's at long last, and who could not rejoice with them as they ran, like ecstatic children, round the pitch, holding first their own flag, then the Swedes'? There was no doubt this time that the best, immeasurably the finest, team had won.

Nils Liedholm scores for
Sweden from the penalty spot
against Mexico, whose
goalkeeper is Carbajal.

Brazil's first goal in the World
Cup Final. Garrincha centres
hard and low, Vavà dashes in to
score.

Garrincha, Brazil's remarkable
outside-right, cuts through the
Swedish defence in the Final.

Luis Bellini, Brazil's captain,
flourishes the World Cup.

Pool I

Germany 3, Argentina 1 (HT 2/1)
Ireland 1, Czechoslovakia 0 (HT 1/0)
Germany 2, Czechoslovakia 2 (HT 1/0)
Argentina 3, Ireland 1 (HT 1/1)
Germany 2, Ireland 2 (HT 1/1)
Czechoslovakia 6, Argentina 1 (HT 3/1)

	P	W	D	L	GOALS F	A	Pts
Germany	3	1	2	0	7	5	4
Czechoslovakia	3	1	1	1	8	4	3
Ireland	3	1	1	1	4	5	3
Argentina	3	1	0	2	5	10	2

Pool II

France 7, Paraguay 3 (HT 2/2)
Yugoslavia 1, Scotland 1 (HT 1/0)
Yugoslavia 3, France 2 (HT 1/1)
Paraguay 3, Scotland 2 (HT 2/1)
France 2, Scotland 1 (HT 2/0)
Yugoslavia 3, Paraguay 3 (HT 2/1)

	P	W	D	L	GOALS F	A	Pts
France	3	2	0	1	11	7	4
Yugoslavia	3	1	2	0	7	6	4
Paraguay	3	1	1	1	9	12	3
Scotland	3	0	1	2	4	6	1

Pool III

Sweden 3, Mexico 0 (HT 1/0)
Hungary 1, Wales 1 (HT 1/1)
Wales 1, Mexico 1 (HT 1/1)
Sweden 2, Hungary 1 (HT 1/0)
Sweden 0, Wales 0 (HT 0/0)
Hungary 4, Mexico 0 (HT 1/0)

	P	W	D	L	GOALS F	A	Pts
Sweden	3	2	1	0	5	1	5
Hungary	3	1	1	1	6	3	3
Wales	3	0	3	0	2	2	3
Mexico	3	0	1	2	1	8	1

Play off Wales 2, Hungary 1 (HT 0/1)

Pool IV

England 2, Russia 2 (HT 0/1)
Brazil 3, Austria 0 (HT 1/0)
England 0, Brazil 0 (HT 0/0)
Russia 2, Austria 0 (HT 1/0)
Brazil 2, Russia 0 (HT 1/0)
England 2, Austria 2 (HT 0/1)

	P	W	D	L	GOALS F	A	Pts
Brazil	3	2	1	0	5	0	5
England	3	0	3	0	4	4	3
Russia	3	1	1	1	4	4	3
Austria	3	0	1	2	2	7	1

Play off Russia 1, England 0 (HT 0/0)

Quarter-finals

Norrköping

France 4
Abbes; Kaelbel, Lerond; Penverne, Jonquet, Marcel; Wisnieski, Fontaine, Kopa, Piantoni, Vincent.

Ireland 0
Gregg; Keith, McMichael; Blanchflower, Cunningham, Cush; Bingham, Casey, Scott, McIlroy, McParland.

SCORERS
Wisnieski, Fontaine (2), Piantoni for France
HT 1/0

Malmö

West Germany 1
Herkenrath; Stollenwerk, Juskowiak; Eckel, Erhardt, Szymaniak; Rahn, Walter, Seeler, Schmidt, Schaefer.

Yugoslavia 0
Krivocuka; Sijakovic, Crnkovic; Kristic, Zebec, Boskov; Petakovic, Veselinovic, Milutinovic, Ognjanovic, Rajkov.

SCORER
Rahn for West Germany
HT 1/0

Stockholm

Sweden 2
Svensson; Bergmark, Axbom; Boerjesson, Gustavsson, Parling; Hamrin, Gren, Simonsson, Liedholm, Skoglund.

Russia 0
Yachine; Kessarev, Kuznetsov; Voinov, Krijevski, Tsarev; Ivanov, A., Ivanov, V., Simonian, Salnikov, Ilyin.

SCORERS
Hamrin, Simonsson for Sweden
HT 0/0

Gothenburg

Brazil 1
Gilmar; De Sordi, Santos, N.; Zito, Bellini, Orlando; Garrincha, Didi, Mazzola, Pelé, Zagalo.

Wales 0
Kelsey; Williams, Hopkins; Sullivan, Charles, M., Bowen; Medwin, Hewitt, Webster, Allchurch, Jones.

SCORER
Pelé for Brazil
HT 0/0

Semi-finals

Stockholm

Brazil 5
Gilmar; De Sordi, Santos, N.; Zito, Bellini, Orlando; Garrincha, Didì, Vavà, Pelé, Zagalo.

France 2
Abbes; Kaelbel, Lerond; Penverne, Jonquet, Marcel; Wisnieski, Fontaine, Kopa, Piantoni, Vincent.

SCORERS
Vavà, Didì, Pelé (3) for Brazil
Fontaine, Piantoni for France
HT 2/1

Gothenburg

Sweden 3
Svensson; Bergmark, Axbom; Boerjesson, Gustavsson, Parling; Hamrin, Gren, Simonsson, Liedholm, Skoglund.

West Germany 1
Herkenrath; Stollenwerk, Juskowiak; Eckel, Erhardt, Szymaniak; Rahn, Walter, Seeler, Schaefer, Cieslarczyk.

SCORERS
Skoglund, Gren, Hamrin for Sweden
Schaefer for Germany
HT 1/1

Third place match

Gothenburg

France 6
Abbes; Kaelbel, Lerond; Penverne, Lafont, Marcel; Wisnieski, Douis, Kopa, Fontaine, Vincent.

West Germany 3
Kwiatowski; Stollenwerk, Erhardt; Schnellinger, Wewers, Szymaniak; Rahn, Sturm, Kelbassa, Schaefer, Cieslarczyk.

SCORERS
Fontaine (4), Kopa (penalty), Douis for France
Cieslarezyk, Rahn, Schaefer for Germany
HT 3/1

Final

Stockholm

Brazil 5
Gilmar; Santos, D., Santos, N.; Zito, Bellini, Orlando; Garrincha, Didì, Vavà, Pelé, Zagalo.

Sweden 2
Svensson; Bergmark, Axbom; Boerjesson, Gustavsson, Parling; Hamrin, Gren, Simonsson, Liedholm, Skoglund.

SCORERS
Vavà (2), Pelé (2), Zagalo for Brazil
Liedholm, Simonsson for Sweden
HT 2/1

CHILE 1962

Background to Chile

Brazil retained the 1962 World Cup, held in Chile, showing in the process that they were very much more than a one-man – or one-demigod – team; or rather that if one hero succumbed, another sprang up to take his place. It was the World Cup of Garrincha, the World Cup of 4-3-3. That long, thin, impoverished Chile should put it on at all was remarkable. Earthquakes had devastated the country at the time they were pleading their case, and Carlos Dittborn, the President of the Chilean Football Federation, coined the magnificent *non sequitur*, 'We must have the World Cup *because* we have nothing.'

They got it, quickly building one superb new stadium in Santiago in the snowy lee of a still more superb mountain and another, small but exquisite, on the coast at Viña del Mar, where pelicans sat on the rocks and the sea wrack blew in over the pitch. A third group would play in seedy, broken-down Rancagua in the stadium of the Braden Copper Company, and a fourth thousands of miles to the north, at Arica, near the Peruvian border.

When the Chilean team itself made more progress than had ever been expected, when it suddenly appeared that Chile might win her first international victory since the Pacific War a hundred years before, the capital went wild, the night-time streets were thronged with jubilantly rejoicing fans, with the noise of motor horns tooting the motif of 'Viva Chee-*lay*!'

Chile's National Stadium just before completion in December 1961.

Criticisms of the country, of the organisation, were often unfair. If there was corruption over tickets, at least an official was hauled off to gaol. When there were similar stories, four years later, in England, the dirt was swept quickly under the carpet. If there were tales of overcharging for accommodation, then the police quickly made indictments. The two Italian journalists who indicted Chile as a backward country, and thereby exposed their own team to the calvary of the Battle of Santiago, were not even justified in their criticism. It was a country at once squalid and sophisticated, backward yet subtle. The winter climate was depressing, the smog and smut wept out of the Santiago skies, the unhygienic kitchens caused innumerable casualties; and yet the tournament worked. For the visitor, Chile left more congenial memories than either Sweden or Mexico.

The Brazilian team badge.

Brazil, playing on South American soil, were inevitably the favourites, though illness had obliged Vicente Feola, that rumbling, Buddha-figure, to stand down as manager in favour of Aymore Moreira, brother of 1954's Zeze. Aymore was a white-haired, patient, courteous man who, with Hilton Gosling beside him, had again ensured a climate in which the Brazilians could express their overflowing gifts in peace and with effect. They would play in the Viña del Mar group with the Czechs, Spaniards and Mexicans. As Danny Blanchflower, Ireland's fine captain in 1958 and now a journalist, remarked, it was really quite extraordinary how all the major competitors seemed to know, in advance, just where they would be playing. . . .

The contenders

The Viña group: Brazil, Czechoslovakia, Spain and Mexico
In the four years since they had won the World Cup, the component pieces of the Brazilian team had sprung apart, then strangely and steadily come together again. Two players had gone to Madrid, with sharply varying fortunes; and had come back. Vavà, the centre-forward who scored twice in the Final, was transferred to Atletico Madrid, did well for a few seasons, then returned to play in Brazil; in time to displace Pelé's precocious teenaged colleague at Santos, Coutinho, with whom he had worked many a spectacular one-two.

Didì, the great orchestrator in Sweden, and already a star in Switzerland, had joined Real Madrid, where he found they already had an orchestrator in di Stefano; one, moreover, who did not welcome anyone else on the podium. For a sickening season, Didì had brooded round Madrid scarcely getting a game. Then he, too, had come home, in time to win back his place from the confident young Cinesinho.

Zito, his midfield colleague, challenged by Zequinha, had edged in front of him at the eleventh hour, while an injury precluded any chance of Pepe supplanting Zagalo on the left wing; history repeating itself. Garrincha, that extraordinary child of nature from Pau Grande, was there again; now the father of eight daughters and closely pursued by a Brazilian singer, Elsa Soares, whom he would marry after the World Cup.

There were changes, however, in the central defence. Mauro, a reserve in 1958, took over at centre-half and captain from Bellini. The little black Zozimo, who had toured Europe with Brazil in 1957, succeeded Orlando, who had been playing in Argentina.

The Santoses, though veterans now – Nilton was thirty-six – were irreplaceable at back; the grey-jerseyed Gilmar was as calmly efficient as ever in goal. And of course there was Pelé, as wonderfully gymnastic, as astonishingly inventive, as brave, strong, inimitable and explosive as ever. At twenty-one there was little doubt that he was now the best footballer in the world, surpassing even di Stefano who, with Puskas, had just played for Real Madrid in the European Final won by Benfica. Puskas had scored three, di Stefano had given him many bullets to fire and now, naturalised Argentinian and naturalised Hungarian, here they were under the banner of Spain; their manager a Franco-Argentinian, Helenio Herrera.

At Viña – or rather, just outside it at Quilpue, where Pelé rejoiced to play daringly in goal – Aymore Moreira confessed his fears of Czechoslovakia. 'The Czechs play a very athletic game, hard and vigorous, which will certainly give us trouble. And then I know that they are also good technicians!' He added his belief that 'this World Cup will be terribly rough and violent. Scarcely any goals will be scored.'

The Czechs did not share his faith in themselves; the less so as a sad accident to their new goal-scoring star, Rudolf Kucera – a bad head injury – had put him out of the side. He had done much to win the play-off in Brussels which they had had with Scotland. So unsanguine were they that they twice checked out of their hotel, before the quarter-final and the semi-final, and they did not even bring a qualified masseur. They were known to be a gifted team though a slow one but, as one acute French journalist wrote, their very slowness, their very pessimism, were turned to advantage.

Slowness – when players were at the same time such fine ball-players – meant precision; a packed defence, a sparsely-manned attack, with large areas of space to play in. Pessimism meant lack of pressure, plus a desire to show everybody they had been undervalued. Teamwork was guaranteed by the fact that most of the side played for the Dukla Prague (Army) club; and there was an outstanding left-half in Josef Masopust, a calm, deft player who used the ball cunningly and could score goals, too. In the centre of the defence, Pluskal and the massive, bald

The Chilean poster for the 1962 World Cup.

Popluhar, both World Cup centre-halves in their time, were no mean barrier, while behind them played the bald, elastic goal-keeper Wilhelm Schroiff, whose contribution would, until the Final, be so great.

Spain were managed by Helenio Herrera, the Internazionale manager, who had previously flanked Giannino Ferrari as coach to the Italian side. Controversy over the drugging of Inter players, and Herrera's public delight when Juventus were knocked out of the European Cup, had led to his resignation. Spain – where he had worked for many successful years – now appointed him.

It was a surprising development, which led predictably to a conflict of egos between Herrera and Alfredo di Stefano. Pulling a muscle just before leaving Spain, di Stefano announced he would be coming merely 'as a tourist'. His cheerful father arrived from Buenos Aires with a 'magic' liniment which he urged him to use, but the prevailing view was that no liniment would heal the breach between di Stefano and Herrera.

Still, there was Luis Suarez, a fine, creative inside-forward, once with Herrera at Barcelona and now with him again at Inter. There was the leggy Peirò of Atletico Madrid. There was Martinez from Paraguay, and Puskas from Hungary. The talent was there, if not the team.

The remaining country was Mexico, two of whose players had tried on their arrival in Viña to attack an Australian journalist who had written that they would be there only to live the gay life.

In retrospect, there are good reasons for calling this Zagalo's World Cup as much as Garrincha's. 'One could never sufficiently stress the key role played by Zagalo in the Brazilian victory,' wrote the French journalist Jean-Philippe Réthacker. 'An active and courageous footballer, very perceptive in his passing and positional play, precise and varied in his technique, Zagalo was certainly, with the Czech Masopust, the most intelligent player of the 1962 World Cup.'

Zagalo's story read like some moral fable. Born in the bitterly impoverished north-east of Brazil, he was said by Dr Hilton Gosling to have built up his phenomenal lung capacity by swimming in the rough coastal breakers. His family brought him down to Rio as a boy. Flamengo, the most numerously and fanatically supported club in Brazil, signed him as a young left-winger. Chance catapulted him from third reserve into the first team, but he received no response from the crowd, who were unused to forwards doing good by stealth. They wanted fantasy, flamboyance, and Zagalo gave them stamina, self-sacrifice. It was a long time before he won his battle for acceptance, but win it he did.

Seriousness was the keynote of his game and his personality. In hot, gay Rio, he was the player who spent his evenings quietly

Brazil's new hero, Amarildo, congratulated by his team manager, Aymori Moreira, after scoring both goals against Spain.

with his fiancée, his Sunday mornings in church. Strength of lung and strength of will would transform him into an international star, capable now of labouring in midfield, now of bursting forward to deliver a short, deadly accurate cross, who had never been more important to Brazil than at this moment.

The Rancagua group:
England, Hungary, Bulgaria and Argentina

England, this time, had found a better refuge; or appeared to have done. Thanks to the pro-English tendencies of the young mayor of Coya, they had been able to install themselves in this coveted mountain retreat, high above Rancagua, where the air was pure and perfect, interlopers minimal, and a fine, if parched, green golf course rolled away towards the horizon. The setting appeared idyllic; yet one English player, on the very day of his arrival, said, 'I feel so fed up, I could cry.' Certainly Coya was isolated, and the problem of loneliness, the problem of boredom, is a very real one in such circumstances.

England had Walter Winterbottom in charge, for what would be his fourth and last World Cup. He had just been out-voted for the Football Association's Secretaryship, in which he was expected to succeed his mentor, Sir Stanley Rous, now President of FIFA. He was assisted as coach by the English Footballer of the Year, Burnley's Jimmy Adamson, a tall, lean, humorous Geordie, captain and future manager of his club, who would subsequently turn down Winterbottom's job.

Yet although they had scouted the ground this time, had got the retreat that everybody wanted, there was still something vaguely amateurish and haphazard about the English preparation. What other team, for instance, would include in its practice matches a middle-aged Australian millionaire businessman.

The 1958 side had largely evaporated, with one major exception; the attack was still built round Fulham's inside-left, Johnny Haynes, who was now the captain. 'Why is everything with England number 10?' a Yugoslav coach would demand rhetorically, as his team's aeroplane finally flew out of Santiago. 'Number 10 takes the corners! Number 10 takes the throw-ins! So what do we do? We put a man on number 10! Goodbye, England!'

It was exactly what the Hungarians would do in the first match at Rancagua, when Rakosi dogged Haynes' every move. And indeed, the nemesis of making one man so important was precisely that if he failed, so did the team. Haynes had failed in Gothenburg; he would fail, alas, again in Chile. But since he was captain, the failure would if anything be more costly. A most gifted player with a superb left foot, brisk control and high strategic flair, Chile saw him at his least amenable. There was a thin-skinned petulance about him which seemed to permeate the team, and led to strained relations with the Press. On the other hand, it was not Haynes' fault that the over-hierarchical atmosphere of the England team was so marked that players still tended to give less for England than they gave for their clubs; and they still travelled without a doctor, an omission which might have had fatal results for Peter Swan, the reserve centre-half, in Viña del Mar.

Bryan Douglas, the skilful little Blackburn outside-right, who had scored an important goal in the vital qualifying match against Portugal, also survived from Sweden. As for Bobby Charlton, the blameless cause of such controversy in 1958, he had developed in these years from a goal-scoring inside-forward into an outside-left of classical gifts, marvellous acceleration, a willowy swerve, a prodigious shot not only in his left foot but now in his right.

Then there was Jimmy Greaves, quintessentially Cockney, a 'boy-wonder' still more remarkable than Charlton; an East Ender who at the age of seventeen had walked straight into the Chelsea First Division team on the opening day of the season at Tottenham to embark on a dazzling series of goals. His turn of speed was extraordinary, his confidence more remarkable still, his left foot a hammer, his instinct for being in the right place near goal almost psychic. The previous year he had gone briefly and reluctantly to A.C. Milan, hated the atmosphere and the disciplines, and obliged them to transfer him home; but to Tottenham, not to Chelsea. He was one of the most exciting talents England had thrown up since the war; yet now, when the chips were truly down, he would be as disappointing as Haynes.

Walter Winterbottom, England's team manager, in his fourth World Cup.

Walter Winterbottom gives a team talk to England's players at the Bank of England ground, Roehampton, during pre-World Cup training.

Another East Londoner had just won a place in the team – Bobby Moore, capped for the first time in Peru *en route* to Chile. England had played extremely well, winning 4–0 on a ground where, three years earlier, they had lost 4–1, and the twenty-one-year-old Moore, tall, blond, quite imperturbable, had had a fine game at right-half. This imperturbability was evident even when he was a West Ham United youth player, running up a record number of youth caps for England. Haste seemed anathema to him; even in the tightest goal-line situations he would remain calm and relaxed.

Encouraged by Ron Greenwood, West Ham's manager, a disciple of Winterbottom, he had worked hard at his football, developing from a centre-half of great poise but unexceptional talents into a defensive wing-half who read the game superbly, covering and tackling faultlessly, using the long ball well. If he had weaknesses, they lay in strange, transient lapses in concentration and a vulnerability to small, quick-turning forwards who would play close up on him.

He well deserved his place, and would have an excellent World Cup, but the choice of the equally bold, equally large, straightforward Ron Flowers as the other wing-half meant that England lacked the ball-playing half-back they needed in a 4-2-4 formation. Bobby Robson, who had developed since 1958 into a thoughtful half-back, had dropped out in Lima through injury, and would otherwise have been a more sensible choice in the circumstances.

In goal was yet another Londoner, the cheerful, robust, fearless Ron Springett of Sheffield Wednesday. He was Fulham-born, resilient on the line, but vulnerable to shots from afar, as his colleagues knew. There was a worrying doubt about his vision.

At full-back there was a resilient pair in the calm, pipe-smoking Jim Armfield and the tough ebullient Ray Wilson, while at last there was a choice between two tall and powerful centre-halves, Tottenham's Maurice Norman and Sheffield Wednesday's Peter Swan. To Norman would go the preference, but each player had grim years ahead of him. Norman would retire prematurely after breaking a leg in a friendly match against a Hungarian team. Swan, seriously ill in Viña with dysentry, would serve a seven-year disqualification for helping to 'throw' a match at Ipswich, returning only in 1972 at the age of thirty-four.

For centre-forward there was the brave, blond Shropshire miner, Gerry Hitchens, who unlike Greaves had stayed happily that season in Milan, scoring freely for Inter. He arrived in Chile, to the admiration of his colleagues, dressed to kill. The 'new deal', the abolition of the maximum wage, had only just been negotiated in England, and the 'new footballer' with his *dolce vita* lay in the future. Indeed, the severe, short haircut of the British player would last beyond the 1966 World Cup, even if the long shorts and heavy boots had gone.

Hungary, Bulgaria and Argentina were the other teams in the Rancagua group, where England were favoured. Their own critics, however, feared they might again distil the familiar, bitter-sweet essence of mediocrity for which they were known in World Cups; and the opening game would bear out this pessimism.

Hungary, though they had just lost to Italy B, were in better plight than in 1958. They had beaten England two years before in Budapest, thanks to the prowess of Florian Albert, a fluent young centre-forward whose skills evoked the earlier Hidegkuti, and who combined beautifully with the lean Gorocs while Tichy was still there to fire his right-footed shells. Gyula Grosics alone survived from the great team of the 1950s. There was a tall, supple, blond, linking right-half in Erno Solymosi, a formidable double pillar in defence in Sipos and Meszoly, and an insidious right-winger in dark little Karoliy Sandor who played, like Kurt Hamrin, with his socks around his ankles.

The Argentinians had a new young manager in Juan Carlos Lorenzo, but were still playing with the traditional roving centre-half; this time the fair-haired Sacchi. He, with the strong, blond, attacking left-back, Silvio Marzolini, would give the team much of its propulsion. José Sanfilippo, their free-scoring inside-left, had tried to drop out after a period of poor form. Lorenzo had him medically and psychiatrically examined, got highly positive reports – and picked him.

The Bulgarians, built around the CDNA (Sofia) Army team, had beaten France in a play-off, yet seemed to have little to offer apart from the clever left wing of the experienced Ivan Kolev and the young Yakimov. Kolev, with his speed and ball skills, had now moved to the flank.

The Santiago group:
Italy, Chile, West Germany and Switzerland

Italy, playing in Santiago, had arrived in their customary state of chaos, warned by Herrera that it was always a bad thing to fall into the group which included the host country. At once flamboyant and dictatorial, hooded and extrovert, a coiner of slogans and of money, a ruthless manipulator and a superb preparer of players, Herrera had become the best paid, most controversial manager in the world, though the World Cup would elude him.

We have, of course, met Gioanin Ferrari before, in somewhat happier circumstances, as Italy's fine inside-left; with Meazza, the only man to play both in the 1934 and the 1938 World Cup winning teams. But with the Spal club's President, Paolo Mazza, on his back, and the usual tidal wave of intrigue to be confronted, there was not much he could do in Chile. At the end of it all, he wrote the Italian Federation an open letter disclaiming any responsibility.

By now, *catenaccio* had Italian football in its clammy grip, and bright young players who began with all the traditional joy in ball play and invention soon had it bred out of them when they reached the stony reality of Serie A, the First Division.

To qualify, Italy had to negotiate the low hurdle of Israel; yet at one point in the game in Tel Aviv they found themselves two down. They recovered to win 4–2, thanks partly to the accomplished left-footed finishing of the Veronese, Mario Corso of Inter. By the time the World Cup was due, however, Corso was dropped from the chosen twenty-two. It chanced that shortly before the party flew off he played a leading part in Inter's victory at San Siro over the Czech World Cup team. Afterwards, he made obscene gestures at Ferrari and Mazza, who were watching from the stand.

Ferrari, in fact, had taken Pozzo's old short cut of *oriundi*, provoking a ludicrous situation in consequence. José Altafini,

Eladio Rojas jumps for joy after scoring Chile's winning goal in the third place match against Yugoslavia.

lately Italy's chief goal-scorer, had in 1958's World Cup played centre-forward for Brazil. Humberto Maschio and the immensely talented little inside-left, Omar Sivori of the rolled-down socks, limpid control and deadly left foot, would have played for Argentina in the 1958 World Cup had Italian clubs not swooped on them in 1957. No policy could be more perfectly calculated to offend the South Americans in general, and the Argentinians, playing only ninety kilometres away in Rancagua, in particular.

As though this, and the presence of Italian club scouts hanging round the South American training camps, were not enough, two Italian journalists sent home articles about Chile which raised local hostility to a crescendo.

'Chile,' wrote Antonio Ghirelli, one of the most talented Italian football writers, bowing now to a fatal tendency to deal in sociology, 'is poor, small, proud. It has accepted the organisation of this edition of the Rimet Cup as Mussolini accepted that of sending his air force to bomb London. The capital has seven hundred bedrooms. The telephone doesn't work. A cable to Europe costs an eye out of your head. An air letter takes five days.'

Still more insulting to the Chileans was what a travelling correspondent called Corrado Pizzenelli – safely out of Chile before the trouble started – had to say. 'Malnutrition, prostitution, illiteracy, alcoholism, wretchedness. . . . Entire quarters of the city practise open-air prostitution. . . . In terms of underdevelopment, Chile must be placed on a level with many African and Asian countries . . . but while the inhabitants of those countries have not progressed, these have regressed.'

The Italians subsequently felt that the offence given by these articles was cunningly used and exacerbated by the Chileans to create a climate as hostile as possible to Italy's team before their match with Chile. Perhaps they were right. One had, at all events, to sympathise with the poor Italian (or putatively Italian) footballers, who would be obliged so painfully to bear the brunt of what had been written.

If there were *oriundi* in the team, there was also an authentic Italian star in Gianni Rivera, one of the most precocious and gifted footballers produced since Meazza. He was still only eighteen, yet already he had been capped against Belgium in their last international, won in Brussels. Already he had had two seasons as strategist of the Milan attack. He was a dark, grave, faun-like figure who, playing in the Olympic football team at the age of sixteen, had already been talking like a man of thirty. His technique was flawless; despite a fragile physique, he struck a ball beautifully, and his passing was wonderfully imaginative. The son of a railwayman from Alessandria, he had moved his family with him to Milan.

'The fact of being at home with one's father and mother and one's brother,' he said, sitting in the comfortable School of Aviation where Italy had their quarters, 'these are all little things that make the difference. When one lives all alone one goes all over the place with other people, because one has nothing else to do, but when one's living with one's family, one can refuse, and see it's not a good thing.'

West Germany were also in this group, bringing with them such doughty warriors as Uwe Seeler, Horst Szymaniak, Hans Schaefer and Karl-Heinz Schnellinger. They had qualified without hardship against Greece and Northern Ireland and, under the cunning leadership of Sepp Herberger in his last World Cup, had the tactical expertise, the physical hardness, to worry anyone. Despite the promise of the young Helmut Haller of Augsburg, however – Herberger had forbidden him to join Bologna till after Chile – there was no obvious heir to Fritz Walter; nor to the deadly Helmut Rahn.

Switzerland, the fourth team in the group, had accounted for Sweden in a play-off in Berlin, but were little fancied.

Of the Chileans themselves not a great deal was known, though they had lately thrashed and drawn with Hungary, and lost narrowly to Russia in Santiago. They were under the sophisticated managership of Fernando Riera, a debonair, good-looking man who had played football in France, they used a 4-2-4 formation, and were bound to be galvanised by an impassioned crowd.

Russian players Meshki and Dubinski, who broke a leg against Yugoslavia, in training.

Sepp Herberger, far left with ball, and Helmut Schoen, his eventual successor as German team manager, with the World Cup team in Frankfurt.

The Arica group: Uruguay, Russia, Yugoslavia, Colombia

Finally, in Group I, up in remote Arica, there were three giants and a probable pygmy. The giants were Uruguay, twice Cup winners; Russia, who had beaten them during their splendid November tour of South America; and Yugoslavia. The pygmy was Colombia, who had come down from high altitudes after unexpectedly putting out Peru. There were Yachine, Sekularac, Goncalves.

The opening games

In their opening game, Chile showed they would need to be reckoned with by beating Switzerland 3–1 in Santiago before a delighted 65,000 crowd. The *mis-en-scène* was glorious – bright sun, a soaring, snowy mountain. The President of Chile spoke, Sir Stanley Rous spoke, the President of the Chilean Federation spoke, and there was a minute's silence for poor Carlos Dittborn. After this came what seemed a brisk anticlimax when, in only seven minutes, a banal error by the Chilean defence allowed Wuthrich to score from over twenty-five yards. The Swiss *verrou* was working wonderfully.

Chile, with the tall, strong left-half Eladio Rojas and the energetic inside-right Toro giving them power in midfield, took half an hour to get into their stride. Their equaliser came at the most delicately telling moment – a minute before half-time, Leonel Sanchez, the rapid outside-left and son of a professional boxer – there would be reason to remember this – converting Landa's centre.

In the first ten minutes of the second half, Chile grasped their psychological advantage, overrunning the Swiss defence. Ramirez gave them the lead. Leonel Sanchez, tackling Grobety, beating man after man, then shooting home from the twenty-five yards, got the third.

Ken Aston, a large, blond referee from Ilford, headmaster of a primary school, had difficulty choosing a match ball. When he asked to see the five balls used for kicking-in, all were in a parlous, peeling state. He chose the least bad, and sent into Santiago for a Swedish ball which arrived ten minutes after half-time. He also took a Swiss player's name – 'Six stud marks on a man's thigh is good enough for me.' He and the other World Cup referees were meanwhile crammed three to a room in a second class hotel. Ghirelli was not wholly wrong about the organisation.

In the same group the following day, Italy and West Germany walked round and round one another like two cautious boxers, under a suitably leaden sky. There were no goals. Italy played, as expected, with the tough Torino half-back Ferrini as 'false' outside-right; a decision which, in those still relatively in-

Omar Sibori, Italy's Argentinian inside-left, has the ball snatched from his feet by Switzerland's Eisener.

152

nocent days, had roused much displeasure in their Press. Salvadore was sweeper; the inside forwards were Rivera, Altafini and Sivori. Germany, too, played *catenaccio*, with Schnellinger as sweeper. The two stoppers, Erhardt, a forbidding force in Sweden, and Willy Schulz, tackled implacably, and Seeler once struck the bar, but there was little variation of pace. Italy, matching greater power with greater skill, held their own, till the game degenerated into a kind of tank battle; a few of their movements were beautifully conceived and carried out. Their morale seemed to equal their skill, their possibilities seemed great; but for the Chilean match, they would make six silly changes, and their hopes would go out of the window.

In Rancagua, Argentina began by beating Bulgaria 1–0 through Facundo's early goal in a harsh, dull game, while Hungary beat England 2–1 the day after. The Argentinians, far from backward in physical contact, themselves cut an impressive figure when similarly treated. The gesture of hurt incomprehension, the slow, concertina-crumpling to the ground, the final, corpse-like prostration, would have touched a heart of stone.

England's prosaic attack found Hungary's packed defence an insoluble puzzle. It became all the more surprising that they had left behind a clever, perfectly-balanced forward like Johnny Byrne, purportedly because he had brawled in the players' tunnel after a League match with the 1958 World Cup right-back, Don Howe. 'It's England who lose, not Byrne,' remarked the Yugoslav coach Milovan Ciric. 'This is football; it's not a game for saints or women.'

England had no player to match the splendidly supple Albert and Solymosi, and it was a glorious individual goal by Albert which won the game, eighteen minutes from time. One of Tichy's long-range cannon balls had given Hungary the lead on the quarter-hour, and shown up Springett's costly weakness; Ron Flowers had equalised on the hour from a penalty given away by Meszoly's handling. So England went dispiritedly up the hill to Coya. 'You *want* us to lose,' Haynes reproached a journalist.

In Viña's little jewel of a seaside stadium, Brazil were given a surprisingly hard time by a brave Mexican team which lost four or five good chances to score. Brazil, aware that several of their team were bearing the burden of the years, had already pulled Zagalo deeper, in a 4-3-3 formation, and Zagalo it was, from the brilliant Pelé's cross, who headed the first goal.

Pelé, in splendid form, scored the other goal against Mexico – both came in the second half – after beating four defenders and then Carbajal, with a prodigious shot.

The Czechs then beat Spain 1–0 with a goal scored by their right-winger Stibranyi ten minutes from time; a brisk piece of opportunism when the injured Reija failed either to control a ball or to reach Santamaria (Uruguay's 1954 stopper) with his pass. That the Czechs were by then in a position to win was thanks to the way their defence, especially the impressive Schroiff, had withstood Spain's early pressure. Finally the ponderous Martinez had vented his frustration by kicking Schroiff in the stomach; which simply moved the stronger Czechs to punish their opponents with a series of mighty tackles. Schroiff continued, undaunted, to perform small miracles, and at last Spain exposed themselves to the counter-thrust which brought Stibranyi's goal. Czechoslovakia, with Masopust and the tall, lean, jog-trotting Kvasniak so skilful in midfield, had announced their candidature.

In far-off Arica, strange things were happening. Little Colombia, opening the ball, took the lead against Uruguay from a penalty and succumbed, 2–1, only a quarter of an hour from the finish. It took a characteristically clever run by little, dark Cubilla, the Uruguayan outside-right, and a thumping shot by Sasia to beat Sanchez, Colombia's fine goalkeeper, after half-time.

The next day a Russian team, including such heroes of 1958 as Yachine, Voronin, Ivanov, Netto and two lively wingers from Torpedo in Metreveli and Meshki, beat Yugoslavia 2–0 in a grim game. The Yugoslavs committed themselves furiously to the conflict, Mujic going so far as to break Dubinski's leg and to be sent home by his team in consequence. For all this, it was a fine, technically pleasing match; the only one in which the celebrated Yachine would justify his immense reputation. He made glorious saves from Galic and Sekularac, the wonderfully resourceful, little gypsy inside-right, who would trot through this World Cup with such coruscating effect. Swarthy and compact, subtle and unhurried, a player of great refinement and un-

Hungary v. England in Rancagua. Grosics, Hungary's goalkeeper, saves, challenged by Jerry Hitchens.

Arica. Coll of Colombia equalises straight from a corner against Russia, and Lev Yachine.

governable temper – mercifully controlled in Chile – 'Sekki' was the best inside-forward of the tournament.

Ponedelnik, Russia's muscular new centre-forward, was involved in both goals. After fifty-three minutes he struck a thundering free kick against the bar, and Ivanov beat Soskic, Yugoslavia's fine goalkeeper, to the rebound. Four minutes from the end Ponedelnik himself scored the second. He would later complain that his team's atmosphere was too cold, too impersonal; that at one crucial stage he and his room-mate had lain awake, side by side in their beds, far into the night, unable to speak a word to one another. It was plain that socialist realism had its limits and its nemesis.

England v. Argentina. Johnny Haynes of England shakes hands with the Argentinian captain, Navarro.

In the second round of matches Germany, in Santiago, beat Switzerland 2–1 in a tedious game which was spoiled when Szymaniak's brutal tackle broke a leg of the Swiss forward, Norbert Eschmann, after fourteen minutes. In the circumstances, the Swiss did well to hold the score to 2–1 and to have the last word, the last goal, themselves, when Schneiter scored fifteen minutes from the end.

The game was played in the deep shadow of what had gone on the day before in Chile's ghastly game against Italy; a game which produced two expulsions, a broken nose and a welter of violence. The ground, as we have seen, had been abundantly prepared by those two inflammatory articles, while the question of the *oriundi*, the recent accusations of drug-taking among Italian clubs, had made things worse. Omar Sivori, one of the discarded stars, later alleged that he had heard, in the depths of the night, a conspiratorial discussion between Paolo Mazza and two influential journalists, in which the team was picked. Other sources had it that there was never any question of picking Sivori for this match – 'He's too excitable, he speaks the same language as the Chileans, and would risk coming to blows with them.' If so, he would merely have been following the prevailing pattern.

For the Italian players, as their own correspondents wrote, were far too easily provoked by the Chileans, who were from the first busily spitting in their faces. The referee himself, tall Ken Aston, was accused by the Italians of being 'hostile and provocative'. He in turn, limping through the rest of the World Cup, *hors de combat* with a damaged Achilles tendon, insisted that the match was 'uncontrollable'. In the opinion of *L'Équipe*'s correspondent, 'The feebleness of the English referee Mr Aston, who never succeeded in hiding his lack of authority beneath an imperturbable front and who was too conscious of "the voice of the people", succeeded in transforming a lively match into a veritable street fight.' What is beyond dispute is that from this day Aston's career in refereeing went from strength to strength; to membership of FIFA's Referees' Committee, to the surveil-

he Battle of Santiago. Ken
ston, the English referee,
rders off David of Italy for
icking the now prostrate Leonel
anchez of Chile on the head.

lance of World Cup referees in 1966 and 1970.

Certainly he was ill-served by his linesmen who, when Leonel Sanchez, behind his back, broke Maschio's nose with a left hook that was televised around the world, elected to behave like the three wise monkeys. Thus Sanchez stayed on the field while Ferrini, for hacking down Landa in the seventh minute, and David, for a retaliatory kick at Sanchez's head, went off. Reduced to nine men, Italy still resisted till fifteen minutes from time, when Ramirez headed in Leonel Sanchez's free kick, Toro adding the second, in the last minute. It had been altogether a dreadful day for football.

The group concluded with a 2–0 win by a much more sophisticated, economical German team over Chile, and an easy but meaningless 3–0 victory by Italy against Switzerland. So Chile and Germany passed into the quarter-finals.

In Rancagua, England found form at last, beating Argentina by a clear 3–1; their first World Cup victory since 1954 outside the qualifying competition.

Much was achieved with the replacement of the disappointing Hitchens at centre-forward by Middlesbrough's Alan Peacock, a tall, straight-backed, guardsman-like figure even to the short haircut, who won many balls in the air despite ill usage from Navarro. A quiet young man, with the private and reflective smile of one enjoying a joke too good to be shared, he said philosophically, 'You expect it, don't you? I think my neck will be a bit stiff in the morning.' Though it was his first international, he showed great aplomb, provoking the first goal after seventeen minutes. When Charlton, in ebullient form, centred from the left, Peacock skilfully headed the ball on, Navarro desperately handled, and Flowers scored his second penalty of the series.

Argentina were clever but unincisive, best served by Sacchi and the adventurous Marzolini; but Moore and Flowers tackled briskly, Jimmy Armfield was impeccable, Bryan Douglas far more lively than he had been against Hungary. Charlton, with a crisp, low, right-footed shot, made it 2–0 before half-time. Douglas, midway through the second half, beautifully dummied his man, then struck a right foot shot which Roma could merely push out, Greaves then pushing it in. A late goal by little Sanfilippo was all Argentina could manage; in the dressing-room, sympathisers kissed their manager, Lorenzo, murmuring, '*Muy bien, Juan Carlos!*'

Then Hungary, in remarkable form, whipped Bulgaria 6–1, with a goal by Albert in the first minute and four goals by the twelfth. Albert and the greyhound Gorocs worked their fluent one-twos, their clever changes of pace, as easily as they had done in the 1960 Olympiad. Deprived of Iliev and Diev, Bulgaria could do little but let the wave wash over them. Hungary's was an iridescent performance, Solymosi, Albert and Gorocs bestriding the field as in the good old days of Bozsik, Hidegkuti and Puskas. Albert scored three; the result was 6–1.

In the final game, Lajos Baroti, the shrewd Hungarian coach, told his team not to exert themselves; a point was sufficient, and it was what they got, drawing 0–0 with Argentina. Albert and Sandor were rested. Gorocs, alas, tore a muscle in the eighteenth minute, while Meszoly, the blond stopper, played so majestically that the watching England players clapped him off the field.

England themselves, next day, gave a wretchedly mediocre performance against Bulgaria, drawing 0–0 in their turn, and lucky indeed to survive when Kolev beat Armfield on the line, to expose their goal with a cross nobody converted. England, second in the group, now had the daunting task of playing Brazil in Viña del Mar; while Hungary were much favoured to beat the Czechs in Rancagua.

Brazil had cataclysmically lost Pelé, victim of a torn thigh muscle, in their 0–0 draw with Czechoslovakia. After twenty-five minutes, taking a pass by Garrincha, he shot powerfully from twenty-five yards against the foot of the post; then hobbled off the field and out of the 1962 World Cup.

Brazil, with Pelé useless on the wing, drew all but Vavà and Garrincha back in defence; the Czechs gladly settled for a stalemate. No longer threatened by Brazil's explosive change of pace, they went their precise, skilful, somewhat monotonous way to a draw.

Brazil now pulled out of the hat the twenty-four-year-old Amarildo, Botafogo's inside-left; no Pelé, certainly, but a lithe, quick, enterprising player with a nose for a goal, a cheerful and emotional child of nature, brown-skinned, curly-haired, effervescent. Succeeding Pelé was clearly less of a burden than an adventure; and besides, Viña belonged to Brazil. A student band, dressed in paramilitary red jackets and blue trousers, roosted on the terraces, beating out endless encouraging samba rhythms during each game.

The final qualifying match, against Spain, proved a tough one. A goal by Peirò in the last minute had given Spain meagre victory against surprising Mexico, so well coached by the Argentinian, Scopelli. Carbajal, in his fourth World Cup, had kept an impeccable goal, and now Spain needed at least a draw, probably a win, to qualify. Herrera gambled by dropping his two famous forwards, del Sol and Suarez, his goalkeeper Carmelo, and his centre-half Santamaria. Now Puskas would lead an attack which had three Atletico Madrid players, and the flying Paco Gento at outside-left. This was the game, one had heard, in which Didì planned his revenge on di Stefano for the humiliations of Madrid; but di Stefano was still not playing. Greatest all-round forward of his generation, inexhaustibly versatile, he never took part in the finals of a World Cup.

The 'new' Spain played with immense commitment and no little flair. Indeed, the match was possibly the best of the whole tournament, and it took the sudden, soaring flight of Garrincha to save and win it for Brazil.

Herrera, high priest of *catenaccio* with Inter, now used it with Spain, Rodri playing sweeper, the other defenders marking man to man. For an hour these tactics, given force and bite by the team's intense commitment, had Brazil at full stretch, and in the thirty-fourth minute a short, swift dribble by Puskas, a clever pass, made a goal for the energetic Adelardo.

For thirty-eight minutes, Spain deservedly kept their lead, their drive and *brio* several times taking them close to another goal; once especially, through Peirò. Then Amarildo, rising splendidly to the occasion and the opportunity, converted Zagalo's centre to equalise. Again Spain almost scored, this time through Verges, but with four minutes left Garrincha got electrically away, crossed, and Amarildo darted in to head the winner. It was a very near thing; and a manifest injustice to Spain.

The last game of the group produced the strangest result, Mexico defeating Czechoslovakia 3–1 after giving away a first-minute goal. Later, rumours went about that the Czechs had de-

Brazil 2, Spain 1. Adelardo scores for Spain.

liberately let the game go, preferring rather to meet Hungary than England in the quarter-final. Yet they would have finished second even if they had beaten Mexico by 2–1 or 3–1; or had they drawn with them. It seems fairer to give Mexico credit for one of the best performances in their long but mediocre history in the World Cup.

Carbajal, celebrating his thirty-third birthday, had scarcely completed his ritual prayer when Masek beat him. Absorbing the shock, Mexico equalised in twelve minutes. Diaz, exploiting Reyes' cross, took the lead after a sinuous dribble by their outside-right del Aguila, and made it 3–1 with a last-minute penalty when Lala handled. Perhaps the Czechs, already qualified, were not at full pelt, but it remained a famous victory.

It meant that in the quarter-finals Czechoslovakia would play Hungary at Rancagua, while England came to Viña to meet Brazil. 'Don't tell me you're going to give us to beat Brazil!' Haynes bitterly apostrophised a journalist in England's dressing-room after the drab draw with Bulgaria.

In Arica, and Group I, strange things were happening. Russia, who had walloped the Uruguayans 5–0 in Moscow the previous month, now found that Uruguay in and Uruguay out of World Cups were two different teams; their 2–1 win was achieved only after eighty-nine minutes, and was extremely lucky. Reduced to ten men for an hour by an injury to Eliseo Alvarez, Uruguay pulled back their fine winger, Domingo Perez, and still had the best of the argument, equalising Mamikin's goal through Sasia after fifty-four minutes, and hitting the post three times. Their 4-2-4, with Nestor Gonçalves deploying his unhurried skills in midfield, would surely have prevailed at full strength.

Not that Russia had covered themselves with glory in their second game. Colombia, astonishingly, had held them to a 4–4 draw which *L'Équipe*'s annual described as 'one of the greatest surprises of modern football'. Russia, after all, were 3–0 up after eleven minutes, and if Acero reduced it to 3–1, that was still the score at half-time, while Ponedelnik brought it to 4–1, early in the second half.

It was then, after sixty-eight minutes, that something very strange happened. Lev Yachine, of all people, gave a goal away straight from a corner. Suddenly the options were open. The little black inside-forward, Klinger, began tearing holes in the strapping Russian defence, the whole team ran like furies, Rada scored a third goal, Klinger equalised. Though Yachine did make a couple of fine saves, *L'Équipe*'s annual solemnly, and prematurely, recorded that the match 'certainly marked an historic date, the end of the greatest modern goalkeeper, if not of all time: Lev Yachine.'

Yugoslavia, meanwhile, were winning their key match

against Uruguay 3–1, with Sekularac in such transcendent form, working such wonders of control and construction that the very Uruguayans bore him off on their shoulders at the end! His unhurried excellence, his faultless technique, his imaginative passing, his strength in the challenge, overwhelmingly gave Yugoslavia the edge after Uruguay had scored an early goal. His henchmen were the powerfully made, thrusting double spearhead, Galic and Jerkovic, scorers of the second and third goals. The first came through Josip Skoblar, a young left-winger later to make a great name in Marseilles, from the penalty spot, equalising Cabrera's goal.

Quarter-final: Brazil 3, England 1. Garrincha is too much for Ray Wilson.

Beating a now exhausted Colombia 5–0 in their third match, Jerkovic scoring three, Yugoslavia finished second in the group. Their quarter-final opponents, for the third consecutive World Cup, would be . . . West Germany.

The quarter-finals Brazil v. England

At Viña, to a background of swirling sea mist and the throbbing of the samba band Brazil – and Garrincha – accounted for England. Perhaps because he was no longer rivalled and obscured by Pelé, Garrincha continued in a vein of luminous virtuosity which would persist into the semi-final. Wilson did what he could with him; but it was inevitably little. To the panther swerve and acceleration, the deadly goal-line cross, which one had seen in Sweden, Garrincha had now added a thumping shot

Brazil v. England – a goal for Brazil.

in either foot and remarkable power in the air. The first Brazilian goal, after thirty-one minutes, came when he, at five foot seven, utterly outjumped Maurice Norman at six foot two, to head in a corner kick. That it was no fluke, no mere aberration by Norman, was shown when he did just the same against Chile.

A much worse error by Ron Flowers would have put Brazil 2–0 up, were it not for a marvellous save by Springett. Flowers, retrieving a ball on the right, bemusedly turned and pushed it straight across his own goal area. Amarildo was in like a ferret; only for Springett, still quicker, to dive and block at his feet. It was a save too easily forgotten afterwards when attempts were made to turn Springett into a scapegoat.

In fact, the English forwards gave another unhappy display; not least Jimmy Greaves, who had complained in Coya, 'There are some good teams here playing some bloody rubbish; they're all afraid to hold the ball in case they get killed.' Greaves may simply have been projecting, for he himself, especially in the second half, was curiously shy of physical contact. In the first, it was he who headed a free kick against the bar, giving Hitchens, replacing the indisposed Peacock, an easy equaliser.

Within five minutes of the second half, however, Garrincha decided the game. After fifty-four minutes, his fulminating, swerving free kick bounced off Springett's broad chest for Vavà to score as easily as Hitchens; then his diabolical swerving long shot utterly deceived the goalkeeper and curled in by the right-hand post. Afterwards, Brazilian radio reporters poured triumphantly into the dressing-room, solemnly addressing their microphones.

Brazil had been well worth their success, but they had not convinced everyone; among them Ferenc Puskas, who deplored the way football had gone, eight years after the World Cup had slipped from his grasp.

'Slow, very slow,' he remarked at Viña. 'The surprising thing to me is that they play so defensively. I don't like defensive football. I like the kind of game where one wins 5–4, 5–3, or even loses by the same score. Here, they're no longer playing football, it's war; very little play, very few goals, it's very tough. In 1954 there was more football. In 1954, they played.'

Eheu fugaces. There was much in what he said; but hadn't he, himself, been kicked out of the Cup in 1954?

Yugoslavia v. Germany

Yugoslavia flew down to Santiago to play Germany, staying at the Emperador Hotel on the busy, noisy, inconceivably shabby main thoroughfare, the Avenida Bernard O'Higgins. There, an endless procession of dingy, different-coloured buses, all of which looked ready for the junkyard, pressed nose to tail, festooned with patriotic slogans. Milovan Ciric, the Yugoslav manager, a large, bald, consistently amiable man, deplored his lack of wingers – though Kovacevic and Skoblar would do great things in France later on – and smilingly promised that his team would know how to cope with Germany's physical challenge.

'English methods,' he complained, 'are always so rigid. They must improvise more. Why must it always be wing-half to inside-left, inside-left to outside-right, and then a cross? If we had an outside-left like Charlton, we'd win the World Cup.'

Third time proved lucky; for at last Germany were conquered, at last their sheer, forbidding muscularity did not subdue Yugoslavia's greater finesse. The Germans played *catenaccio* again, the Yugoslavs 4-2-4. It was a spirited and splendid game, perhaps decided by its tactics. For the Germans, playing so tightly and cautiously, gave Radakovic, the little Yugoslav right-half, a scope and space that finally proved fatal.

Germany favoured the long pass, Yugoslav the short. In an absorbing half Germany initially forced the game, Seeler hitting a post, but then until the half-hour it was the Yugoslavs who dominated, making but not taking chances. The second half, though still exciting, was less distinguished, both teams appearing tired. Schnellinger, curiously anticipating Germany's 'total football' of a decade later, often left his post as sweeper to join in attacks, a dangerously effective strategem which several times almost brought a goal. As for the Yugoslavs, they now had Radakovic, who had collided with Seeler, playing with a bandaged head, and somewhat diminished in consequence. Germany, however, were getting far less than expected out of Szymaniak, who had crouched in midfield against Chile like an experienced giant spider but now had the daunting task of marking Sekularac; though he, too, pressed forward in the second half.

Extra time seemed certain, a German win the more likely, when at last, after eighty-six vibrant minutes, Galic pulled the ball back to Radakovic whose shot, from fifteen yards, flew under the bar to beat the able Fahrian.

The quarter-final at Arica: Chile on the attack against the Russians.

Chile v. Russia

In Arica, Chile astonished and uplifted their supporters by defeating Russia, with Yachine once more betraying strange deficiencies. He should have saved both Chilean goals, each a long shot. Leonel Sanchez got the first after ten minutes from a twenty-five-yard free kick, a searing cross shot from the left. Eladio Rojaz, the attacking half-back, scored the winner eighteen minutes later; two minutes after Chislenko had equalised from fully thirty-five yards. For all its formidable power, how so long a shot beat a goalkeeper as great as Yachine remains a mystery.

The Chileans, for the occasion, pulled Toro deeper, turning their 4-2-4 into a virtual 4-3-3, though at times Toro broke

The semi-final at Viña del Mar: Soskic, the Yugoslav goalkeeper, holds the ball, challenged by the Czechoslovakian Kadraba.

163

sharply and effectively from the back. It was not one of Chile's best days; if anything, the frenzied support of the 17,000-strong crowd, the knowledge that the whole country hung breathlessly on the result, inhibited more than it inspired them. Nevertheless, they were through.

Czechoslovakia v. Hungary

So, in the strangest fashion, were Czechoslovakia, outplayed at Rancagua by a Hungarian team which beat a tattoo on their goal-posts, but could not beat the incredible Schroiff; as brilliant that day as Yachine was fallible. Scherer, in the thirteenth minute, surprised Grosics with a cross shot in one of Czechoslovakia's pitifully rare breakaways. It was enough, however, to put his team in the semi-final, for on the one occasion when Hungary, and Tichy, seemed to have scored, Russia's Latychev, the veteran referee, gave it obscurely offside.

The semi-finals Brazil v. Chile

'*Con Pelé o sin Pelé, tomeremos Nescafé!*' boasted the slogans on the decrepit Santiago buses. With Pelé or without Pelé, we shall drink Nescafé! They would do, metaphorically speaking, nothing of the sort, though the city was in ferment. On the night of the victory at Arica, the streets had been choked with celebrating crowds, joyfully chanting slogans: '*Chee, chee, chee! Lay, lay, lay! Viva Chee-LAY!*' After the victorious third-place match it would all be repeated, the atmosphere one of surging, innocent delight, childlike celebration, while through the crowds, head down and unnoticed, prowled the old lion Vittorio Pozzo; in a shop doorway, grinning and eating monkey nuts, stood Puskas.

The Brazilians were so much superior to the Chileans that it was hardly a match. Garrincha, fiery and uncontrollable, seemed determined to win the game on his own. After only nine minutes, he pivoted on the ball in an inside-left position to beat Escutti with a killing twenty-yard left-foot shot. After thirty-two, he performed another of his trampoline jumps to head in a corner by Zagalo.

Chile, to their credit, were not supine. Ten minutes later Toro, right-footed, smashed a mighty free kick past Gilmar from the edge of the area to bring them back into the game; only for Vavà, a mere two minutes into the second half, to restore the margin, heading in Garrincha's dropping corner.

Once more the Chileans got up off the ground, inspired by the gifted Toro, the determined Rojas, the quick, slight, mobile right-back Eyzaguirre, fighting back into the game with a penalty by Leonel Sanchez for hands by Zozimo. But just as the match seemed alive again the indefatigable Zagalo moved up the

Garrincha, struck on the back of the head by a bottle, leaves the field after being sent off in Brazil's semi-final against Chile.

World Cup Final: the Brazilian team. Left to right, back row (players): D. Santos, Zito, Gilmar, N. Santos, Zozimo, Mauro; (kneeling) Garrincha, Didì, Vavà, Amarildo, Zagalo.

left wing, spun past his man with princely ease and delivered a short centre which Vavà headed in.

The closing minutes were displeasing. Garrincha, kicked by Rojas and tired of being kicked, kicked back and was sent off. As he made his way round the field towards the dressing-rooms, to a cacophony of whistling, a bottle struck him and cut open his head. Soon afterwards Landa, the Chilean centre-forward, followed him.

World Cup Final: the captains, Mauro of Brazil and Novak of Czechoslovakia, shake hands with the Russian officials.

Czechoslovakia v. Yugoslavia

In Viña del Mar, a mere, miserable 5,000 supporters stood under the pines, cypresses and willows to see Czechoslovakia beat the book again, this time defeating Yugoslavia. The Slavs, as Ciric had feared, were indeed weak on the wings, and could not breach the Czechs' packed defence in the centre. Tactically, Czechoslovakia were a credit to their manager, the silver-haired, silver-toothed, Austrian-born Vytlacil; surviving the first half, they they got the goals they needed in the second.

Kadraba gave them a fortuituous lead three minutes after half-time, but when Jerkovic equalised in the sixty-ninth minute, a Yugoslav win again seemed probable. Instead, Schroiff defied them as superbly as he had defied the Hungarians, Scherer scored ten minutes from time in a breakaway, and a silly handling offence by Markovic allowed the same tall player to make it 3–1 from a penalty. The Final would reunite Brazil and Czechoslovakia.

The Final Brazil v. Czechoslovakia

Needless to say, Brazil were favourites to beat the Czechs; but for that matter so had Hungary and Yugoslavia been in the quarter- and semi-finals. The Yugoslavs, in the third-place match, went through the irrelevant motions in Santiago and lost to a much more committed Chile with a last-minute goal by Eladio Rojas; the commanding Soskic would have saved it had the shot not been deflected. Sekularac, however, was splendid.

Perhaps Czechoslovakia *would* have brought off their greatest surprise of all had not the one crucial constant in their previous success been missing. Something snapped – Schroiff lost his form. Like a bomber pilot who has made one raid too many, an infantryman who cracks after too many campaigns, he would fall to pieces in the Final.

In the meantime, what of Garrincha? Would he be allowed to play? The World Cup Disciplinary Committee met to consider his case and Landa's. The Brazilian President, who had listened, it was said, to the radio commentary of the semi-final on earphones during Mass, sent a personal appeal. The world of football waited. The judgements were handed down. 'Seven and nine,' Sir Stanley Rous told a breathlessly expectant television commentator over the telephone. 'Seven was cautioned; nine was suspended.' Garrincha would play.

After this came a strange anticlimax, for though he played, Garrincha did very little. Ladislao Novak, the experienced Czech left-back, competing in his third World Cup, contained him well, it is true, but who could contain the 'real' Garrincha? At the very end, when the last goal had gone in and he swayed to and fro over the ball, the big, bald Popluhar confronted him, hands on hips, in weary exasperation.

The game began with a shock; the shock of a Czech goal which, with no Pelé, with Schroiff in form, might have worked wonders. After sixteen minutes a superb combination between Scherer and Masopust split Brazil's defence asunder. Scherer, deep on the right, held the ball and judged his diagonal pass as exquisitely as clever Masopust judged his run. Through the gap he went, calm and implacable, to strike the ball past Gilmar with his left foot. For the second successive World Cup Final, Brazil had conceded the first goal.

For the second time, too, they fought back, though it would take them till after half-time to get ahead. The equaliser took no time at all; and it was Amarildo's. Beating the sturdy Pluskal, he advanced on Schroiff almost along the left goal line. What would he do? Shoot for the near post or the far; or not shoot at all, pull the ball back? It was a fearful dilemma, and Schroiff's answer was wrong. Guarding the near post, he gave Amarildo enough room for an extraordinary shot, the ball flying in at the far corner, striking the side netting.

Brazilian fans celebrate after victory over Czechoslovakia in the Final.

Gilmar, Brazil's delighted goalkeeper, carried in triumph off the field.

A spectacular Czech clearance during the Final.

It was all very well for crafty Kvasniak to lope about in mid-field like an inspired stork, working his combinations with Haso-pust. The Brazilian centre held, things did not fall apart, and the 'ancient' Nilton Santos showed extraordinary powers of re-covery on the one or two occasions he was beaten.

Schroiff now saved well from Didì and Zagalo, but his charisma had gone. He was human, fallible.

In the second half the Czechs appeared to be holding their own, at their own *adagio* pace. Kadraba had a good shot, Jelinek another; Brazil seemed to have gone into their shell. Suddenly, after sixty-nine minutes, they struck, and again Amarildo was the decisive figure, a wonderfully effective replacement for Pelé. Boxed in on the left-hand goal line, he beat his man with a sud-den galvanic turn from left to right, centred across the exposed goal with his right foot – and there was Zito, to head into the empty net.

It was over and done with, and Schroiff might have been spared the small calvary of the third goal thirteen minutes from the end. Djalma Santos, reaching casually, massively backwards to a ball bouncing on his touchline, booted it with his left foot high, high up into the sun. It fell upon the dazzled Schroiff like unmerited retribution. He held up his hands to it, dropped it, and the impassive Vavà kicked it in.

Comes the hour, comes the man. In losing Pelé, Brazil had found Amarildo, and their elderly, distinguished team had kept the Cup.

Chile 1962

Group I

Uruguay 2, Colombia 1 (HT 0/1)
Russia 2, Yugoslavia 0 (HT 0/0)
Yugoslavia 3, Uruguay 1 (HT 2/1)
Russia 4, Colombia 4 (HT 3/1)
Russia 2, Uruguay 1 (HT 1/0)
Yugoslavia 5, Colombia 0 (HT 2/0)

	P	W	D	L	F	A	Pts
Russia	3	2	1	0	8	5	5
Yugoslavia	3	2	0	1	8	3	4
Uruguay	3	1	0	2	4	6	2
Colombia	3	0	1	2	5	11	1

Group II

Chile 3, Switzerland 1 (HT 1/1)
Germany 0, Italy 0 (HT 0/0)
Chile 2, Italy 0 (HT 0/0)
Germany 2, Switzerland 1 (HT 1/0)
Germany 2, Chile 0 (HT 1/0)
Italy 3, Switzerland 0 (HT 1/0)

	P	W	D	L	F	A	Pts
Germany	3	2	1	0	4	1	5
Chile	3	2	0	1	5	3	4
Italy	3	1	1	1	3	2	3
Switzerland	3	0	0	3	2	8	0

Group III

Brazil 2, Mexico 0 (HT 0/0)
Czechoslovakia 1, Spain 0 (HT 0/0)
Brazil 0, Czechoslovakia 0 (HT 0/0)
Spain 1, Mexico 0 (HT 0/0)
Brazil 2, Spain 1 (0/1)
Mexico 3, Czechoslovakia 1 (HT 2/1)

	P	W	D	L	F	A	Pts
Brazil	3	2	1	0	4	1	5
Czechoslovakia	3	1	1	1	2	3	3
Mexico	3	1	0	2	3	4	2
Spain	3	1	0	2	2	3	2

Group IV

Argentina 1, Bulgaria 0 (HT 1/0)
Hungary 2, England 1 (HT 1/0)
England 3, Argentina 1 (HT 2/0)
Hungary 6, Bulgaria 1 (HT 4/0)
Argentina 0, Hungary 0 (HT 0/0)
England 0, Bulgaria 0 (HT 0/0)

	P	W	D	L	F	A	Pts
Hungary	3	2	1	0	8	2	5
England	3	1	1	1	4	3	3
Argentina	3	1	1	1	2	3	3
Bulgaria	3	0	1	2	1	7	1

Quarter-finals

Santiago

Yugoslavia 1
Soskic; Durkovic, Jusufi; Radakovic, Markovic, Popovic; Kovacevic, Sekularac, Jerkovic, Galic, Skoblar.

SCORER
Radakovic for Yugoslavia
HT 0/0

West Germany 0
Fahrian; Novak, Schnellinger; Schulz, Erhardt, Giesemann; Haller, Syzmaniak, Seeler, Brulls, Schaefer.

Viña del Mar

Brazil 3
Gilmar; Santos, D., Mauro, Zozimo, Santos, N.; Zito, Didì, Garrincha, Vavà, Amarildo, Zagalo.

SCORERS
Garrincha (2), Vavà for Brazil
Hitchens for England
HT 1/1

England 1
Springett; Armfield, Wilson; Moore, Norman, Flowers; Douglas, Greaves, Hitchens, Haynes, Charlton.

Arico

Chile 2
Escutti; Eyzaguirre, Contreras, Sanchez, R., Navarro; Toro, Rojas; Ramirez, Landa, Tobar, Sanchez, L.

SCORERS
Sanchez, L., Rojas for Chile
Chislenko for Russia
HT 2/1

Russia 1
Yachine; Tchokelli, Ostrovski; Voronin, Maslenkin, Netto; Chislenko, Ivanov, Ponedelnik, Mamikin, Meshki.

Rancagua

Czechoslovakia 1
Schroiff; Lala, Novak; Pluskal, Popluhar, Masopust; Pospichal, Scherer, Kvasniak, Kadraba, Jelinek.

SCORER
Scherer for Czechoslovakia
HT 1/0

Hungary 0
Groscis; Matrai, Sarosi; Solymosi, Meszoly, Sipos; Sandor, Rakosi, Albert, Tichy, Fenyvesi.

Semi-finals

Santiago

Brazil 4
Gilmar; Santos, D.,
Mauro, Zozimo, Santos,
N.; Zito, Didì,
Garrincha, Vavà,
Amarildo, Zagalo.

Chile 2
Escutti; Eyzaguirre,
Contreras, Sanchez, R.,
Rodriguez; Toro, Rojas;
Ramirez, Landa, Tobar,
Sanchez, L.

SCORERS
Garrincha (2), Vavà (2) for Brazil
Toro, Sanchez, L. (penalty) for Chile
HT 2/1

Viña del Mar

Czechoslovakia 3
Schroiff; Lala, Novak;
Pluska¹, Popluhar,
Masopust; Pospichal,
Scherer, Kvasniak,
Kadraba, Jelinek.

Yugoslavia 1
Soskic; Durkovic, Jusufi;
Radakovic, Markovic,
Popovic; Sujakovic,
Sekularac, Jerkovic, Galic,
Skoblar.

SCORERS
Kadraba, Scherer (2) for Czechoslovakia
Jerkovic for Yugoslavia
HT 0/0

Third place match

Santiago

Chile 1
Godoy; Eyzaguirre, Cruz,
Sanchez, R., Rodriguez;
Toro, Rojas; Ramirez,
Campos, Tobar,
Sanchez, L.

Yugoslavia 0
Soskic; Durkovic,
Svinjarevic; Radakovic,
Markovic, Popovic;
Kovacevic, Sekularac,
Jerkovic, Galic, Skoblar.

SCORER
Rojas for Chile
HT 0/0

Final

Santiago

Brazil 3
Gilmar; Santos, D.,
Mauro, Zozimo, Santos,
N.; Zito, Didì,
Garrincha, Vavà,
Amarildo, Zagalo.

Czechoslovakia 1
Schroiff; Tichy, Novak;
Pluskal, Popluhar,
Masopust; Pospichal,
Scherer, Kvasniak,
Kadraba, Jelinek.

SCORERS
Amarildo, Zito, Vavà for Brazil
Masopust for Czechoslovakia
HT 1/1

ENGLAND 1966

Background to 1966

The 1966 World Cup was the first for thirty-two years to be won by the home side. To this extent England's achievement was an unusual one, and indeed their form in the exciting, pleasing semi-final and Final made up for much of the tedium which had gone before.

It was a passionate and controversial World Cup; controversy persisting long after the dramatic Final was lost and won, thanks to the shot by Geoff Hurst of England which struck the underside of the bar and came down – or did not come down – behind the line. It was a World Cup distinguished by the enigmatic presence, and final triumph, of Alf Ramsey, the collapse of the Brazilians, the astonishing prowess of the North Koreans, the turbulence of the Argentinians, the absolute superiority of the Europeans over the South Americans – who cried conspiracy and threatened mass withdrawal, in consequence. It was a World Cup in which, for the second consecutive occasion, the fabled Pelé was laid low by injury, though this time in displeasing circumstances; in which Hurst scored the first hat-trick in a World Cup Final, and extra time was needed for the first time since 1934.

It is probable but scarcely demonstrable that England would not have won without Ramsey; a great deal more probable that it would not have won even with Ramsey anywhere but in England.

Whatever else may be said about the tournament's quality, the merits of England's win, there is no doubt that the Final was a glorious climax, the best there had been since 1954, and a great deal better than the one-sided Brazilian exhibition of 1970. Again, though England may not at any time have matched the technique and artistry of the Brazilian teams which won the two previous competitions, though they may have struggled all the way to the semi-final putting effort above creativity, hard work above joy in playing, the team had its undoubted stars. The commanding Bobby Moore, captain and left-half, was properly voted best player of the tournament, and this was followed by the immensely popular Bobby Charlton's election as European Footballer of the Year. Then there was Gordon Banks, whose splendid displays excelled even those of the veteran Lev Yachine – playing in his last World Cup – not to mention Geoff Hurst and the indefatigable Alan Ball, the two true heroes of the World Cup Final.

Nor must one forget the goblin figure of Nobby Stiles who, tiny and tearful, socks around his ankles, shirt dangling over his shorts, front teeth safely in the dressing-room, assured Ramsey after the Final, 'It was you Alf, you did it! We'd have been nothing without you!' Stiles, indeed, would not. More sombre were the words of a *New Statesman* critic, brought up on the *Wunder-*

'World Cup Willie' – the 1966 poster.

team, who wrote, the day before the match: 'Next week I shall describe how England won the World Cup – and what we can do about it.'

Alf Ramsey

Nobby Stiles autographs a football.

We have met Ramsey, in this World Cup saga, before; as England's right-back in Brazil, when the United States so saucily and painfully twisted the lion's tail. As though this were not trauma enough, he had also played in the team which was beaten 6–3 at Wembley by Hungary in November 1953.

Born to a poor family in Dagenham, the London 'overspill' town, in 1920, his early ambition was to become a successful grocer. As a footballer, he was a curiously late developer. Southampton discovered him during his Army service when he was an inside-forward, but eventually converted him to full-back where his strength, vision of play and somewhat deliberative approach put him more at his ease. By December 1948, he was good enough to play for England against Switzerland, but only as a second choice. In the summer of 1949 his career took a crucial turn when Arthur Rowe signed him for Tottenham Hotspur in a deal involving the Welsh international left-winger Ernie Jones, and which, overall, valued Ramsey at the surprisingly low figure of £21,000. It must have been the best bargain Tottenham ever made.

World Cup Final: Bobby Moore, Gordon Banks beside him, carries the Cup off the field.

A toast by Bobby Charlton at the World Cup victory banquet.

For Ramsey fitted instantly into the new, push-and-run, quick, wall-passing tactics devised by Rowe. Though he was not the captain of the team, his nickname at Spurs, 'The General', shows clearly enough who was in command. His moral influence over the side was immense. He may have lacked pace, but his positional sense was admirable, his tackling strong, and above all he made consistently fine use of the ball. It was long before the days of the overlapping full-back, but Ramsey was what one might call a constructive full-back, whose thoughtful, scientific play set the tone for the whole ebullient team. He was also a dab hand at penalty kicks, with one of which he would temporarily save England's unbeaten home record, in October 1953 against FIFA at Wembley. When Hungary destroyed it a few weeks later, Ramsey again, to some degree, had the last word; or at least the last goal – from the penalty spot.

Quiet, intense, passionately dedicated to the game, he learned much from his manager, the Londoner and former Spurs captain Arthur Rowe, who warmed to him from the first and has never ceased to admire him. They could scarcely, in character, have been more different; Rowe so much the Londoner, quick, fluent, funny and caustic, yet beneath all this as passionate and vulnerable as the cautious, taciturn Ramsey. They in fact complemented one another superbly, helping Tottenham to win

Second and First Division Championships in consecutive seasons. In the meantime, Ramsey settled down in the England team. He was twenty-nine when he came to Tottenham, but his best playing years were undoubtedly those which lay ahead of him.

His approach to the game, his unfailingly thoughtful play, made it probable he would succeed as a manager, and so he did, taking Ipswich Town, a small East Anglian club which had entered the Football League only in 1937, from the Third Division to the Championship of the First, an extraordinary feat, achieved with a team of obscure and rehabilitated players. His relationship with the Ipswich Chairman, John Cobbold, member of a family as wealthy and patrician as Ramsey's was plebeian, was fruitful and harmonious. When Ramsey frequently resigned in his first difficult days at Portman Road, days complicated by the fact that the previous veteran manager, Scott Duncan, remained as Secretary, the ebullient Cobbold as frequently pacified him.

Ramsey's tactics at Ipswich, involving a deep-lying left-winger in the fragile veteran Leadbetter, and two strong, thrustful centre-forwards, were interesting and shrewd.

The England team badge.

When, after the 1962 World Cup, it was decided to appoint a full-time team manager with no other interests – Walter Winterbottom, disappointed in his ambitions for the Football Association secretaryship, had resigned – Ramsey was not the first choice. Indeed, he was probably no better than the third; Jimmy Adamson, the dedicated Burnley player who had coached the 1962 team, being first. He turned the job down.

Ramsey, who must have known he had got all he was ever likely to get out of his Ipswich side, poised on the verge of rapid disintegration, accepted the job, but on the specific understanding that he and he alone picked the team, that the Selection Committee which had for so many years theoretically held sway over the team manager would disappear. Vittorio Pozzo once remarked that a selection committee implied compromise, 'and no great team was ever built on that'. As we have seen, there were times when the selectors could drive a team manager to distraction, other times when he could hide usefully behind them while having his own way. Ramsey never pretended to have much time for selectors and their ilk. Indeed, he told a member of what now became, grandiosely, the Senior International Committee, on a tour of the Americas, that as far as he was concerned, he would rather have extra players; their one useful function was that they saved his going to cocktail parties.

Ramsey built his success and his managerial reputation on the fact of being a player's man, and if this image, over the ensuing years, would not always stay refulgent, there is no doubt that it was his strength during the years which led to his success in 1966. Winterbottom, by contrast, had been, for all his virtues and his charm – a quality which scarcely distinguished Ramsey – an 'Establishment' man. He had been Sir Stanley Rous' choice, Sir Stanley's *protégé*, a theorist and an idealist whose chief concern, by his own admission, was the development of coaching. The players, who gave him a hard time when he first took over, came to like and accept him, but for all his own career in professional football, he did not move on their level, live in their world, talk in their terms. Ramsey did. Indeed, he seemed uncomfortable in any other world, afflicted by a feeling of social and cultural inadequacy reflected in a suspicion of the unfamiliar, a deep mistrust of the Press, a lurking xenophobia. In all this – and it was marginal to his undoubted gifts of leadership and inspiration – Ramsey was largely the victim of his times. He was born and brought up in an era when the ideal of the English gentleman, the public school accent, the patrician stance, were all still relevant. Soon, after the war and the alleged bloodless social revolution, a Cockney accent would be something to flaunt rather than conceal, a working-class background would no longer be a barrier but a springboard to success in politics, cinema, the theatre or that new El Dorado, photography.

However tense and taut he might be with the world at large, Ramsey with his players was generally relaxed, friendly, avuncular, even humorous, cheerfully joining in their training games, never losing his authority but never wielding it in the paternalist manner of a Vittorio Pozzo.

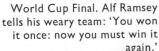

World Cup Final. Alf Ramsey tells his weary team: 'You won it once: now you must win it again.'

The contenders England

Ramsey's first international fixture, against France, was held in Paris in the Nations Cup early in 1963, and was a disaster; England were thrashed 5–2, though goalkeeping errors made the defeat look worse than it should have been. Having taken stock, Ramsey then quickly rebuilt the side, and by the European tour of the summer of 1963 it was a very good one; well balanced, incisive, well 'motivated'. Ramsey had also made it his business to do something which Winterbottom had not done over his sixteen years; he appointed a team doctor. It seems quite unthinkable that after so many years of foreign tours, and World Cups, the Football Association should go abroad with a posse of officials and selectors, yet not bother to take a doctor. Perhaps a better word would be 'symptomatic'; symptomatic of a state of mind in which the Establishment and its needs and comforts came first, the players a very distant second. As we have seen, it was only when Peter Swan, given dangerously mistaken treatment, almost died in Viña del Mar during the 1962 World Cup, that the FA woke up to the need for a regular medical adviser.

England v. Uruguay. The Queen shakes hands with the England right-back, George Cohen, before the opening World Cup game.

They were especially fortunate in the man they chose, a gifted Harley Street consultant called Dr Alan Bass, Arsenal's team doctor, a native of Leeds, who carried his knowledge lightly, got on splendidly with the enigmatic Ramsey and his trainer, Harold Shepherdson, and just as well with all the players. Bass, indeed, was a perfect bridge between Establishment and team. A large, unaffected, vigorous young man, with huge physical and intellectual energy and a passion for research, he would be equally successful in running the medical services for the 1966 World Cup, keeping a keen and successful eye on the problem of 'doping'.

On that 1963 tour, Ramsey's relations with the Press were for once as good as they were with the players. He conceived and patiently explained successful tactics, in which wingers were of the essence; vital in their role of getting round the back of a packed defence and pulling the ball back into the goalmouth.

Gradually, as we shall see, he abandoned this tactical conception in favour of a 4-3-3 system, modulating at times into a 4-4-2, which eschewed orthodox wingers, putting its emphasis on hard work and hard running.

That his strategic grasp was less than impeccable was shown the following summer, when he took England to play in an international tournament organised by Brazil. The opening match, against Brazil themselves at the Maracanà Stadium in Rio, was disastrous. Ramsey had unwisely chosen the Blackpool goalkeeper, Tony Waiters, to make his international debut instead of Banks. Still more unwisely, he allowed Pelé to run wild and free, with devastating results. England lost 5–1; nor did they win either of their two subsequent games in the competition, against

Argentina and Portugal. Before the Brazilian match, moreover, Ramsey had a taste of the gamesmanship he was likely to meet in major international football. The Brazilians, having fixed the kick-off time, blithely arrived over an hour late, while the English players sat and fretted in their dressing-room. Shades of Pozzo's foresight before the 1938 World Cup Final. Ramsey would see that nothing like this happened again.

The 1964 tour was also significant for his collision with Bobby Moore. The tour, ill-planned, began with a meaningless game against the United States in New York, followed by the long haul down to Rio and inadequate time to prepare. In New York, certain English players broke curfew, but more serious was the stand made by several, Moore among them, against a training session organised on the tour by Ramsey. The 'revolution' quickly petered out, but had its strange, though not uncharacteristic, sequel in Ramsey's refusal to confirm Moore as England's captain till the very eve of the subsequent match against Northern Ireland in Belfast the following October.

Ramsey has a long memory, and it was some while before he and Moore achieved a reconciliation. Indeed, before the 1966 World Cup there seemed a real possibility that Moore would be replaced by the infinitely less commanding, but considerably more aggressive, Norman Hunter of Leeds United. It was perhaps not entirely fortuitous that during the pre-World Cup tour Moore's closest companion should be another East Londoner, another player never truly *persona grata* with Ramsey, Tottenham's Jimmy Greaves.

Players like Greaves, whose immense natural talent allowed them to do in a flash what other players could not achieve with endless effort, clearly worried Ramsey. Greaves, a goal-scoring prodigy in his teens, a nervous, humorous, iconoclastic Cockney who had begun brilliantly with Chelsea, stayed briefly and reluctantly with Milan, then return to London and the Spurs, manifestly worried him. 'All right, Alf!' Greaves exclaimed, climbing out of the coach as the England team arrived in the gloomily industrial city of Katowice, last port of call on its pre-World Cup tour, 'You've proved your point. Now let's go home!'

Despite his critics, Ramsey was not at bottom without his own particular humour, but Greaves' irreverence was not something he could easily accept or understand. Indeed, his first real fracas with the Press had come a year before, on tour in Gothenburg, when he omitted Greaves from the team, said there were no injured players, then was incensed when newspapers reported that Greaves had been dropped. It was, however, equally characteristic of the man that he should in due course cool down and have the generosity to apologise.

Greaves, on the summer tour, looked fit and sharp again after long months fighting the effects of jaundice. He scored four splendid, self-deprecated goals in Norway and his stomach, in the words of one writer, looked 'as flat as a spade'. He did much less well in Denmark, where on a dreadful pitch England won crudely, 2–0, but then so did Geoff Hurst, the West Ham striker.

Since Ramsey's accession, and since the 1962 World Cup, the team had been greatly modified. Gordon Banks, making his debut in May 1963 at home to Brazil, and letting in, to Ramsey's displeasure, a wildly swerving free kick by Pepe, had confirmed himself as the best goalkeeper since Bert Williams; perhaps since Frank Swift.

A Sheffield man who played for Leicester City, he combined physical strength and courage with astounding agility. His high cheekbones, his narrow eyes, gave his face an almost Red Indian, rather than a Yorkshire, look. He was modest, quiet and diligent. Ramsey, he said, on the day before the World Cup Final, had convinced him that 'my mind's got not to wander'. Nor did it.

To partner the still excellent Ray Wilson at full-back Ramsey had chosen George Cohen, an immensely amiable Londoner who had played all his professional football with Fulham, a strong, fast, endlessly determined player with a penchant for overlapping and a bottomless good humour.

At right-half there was . . . Nobby Stiles, the players' player, *bête noire* of the purists, a tiny, toothless, urban, gesticulating figure, perenially in the bad books of referees and opponents, forever urging on, castigating, his own defenders, a player with no obvious physical or technical gifts, a poor passer of the ball, but a formidable marker and an extraordinary competitor. By the end of this World Cup he would be the player whom most of the footballing world loved to hate, yet his was the satisfaction of nullifying Eusebio, the tournament's leading scorer and, till then, most dangerous forward.

The attack was clearly more of a problem than the defence. Bobby Charlton had been transformed, by Ramsey and by Manchester United, from a flowing, accelerating left-winger with a terrific shot in either foot into the general of the team, the role that he preferred. 'You're active all the time, you're in the game,' he declared. He exercised this role, however, in a very different manner from Johnny Haynes. A naturally more gifted player in terms of technique – though Haynes' ball control was often undervalued – he had none of Haynes' vision of play, eye for an opening, great strategic sense. His long, powerful cross-field passes were usually cause for a delighted roar at Wembley, but often they were merely lateral and spectacular, making no real impact. Yet his sinuous ability to beat a man with a lovely swerve could set problems to a defence which then found itself obliged to commit another defender, while his glorious shooting when he did come forward was a harbinger of goals. 'They're easier missed than scored.' As it would turn out, the fear he instilled in opposing teams could win a strategical battle before ever a ball was kicked, for in the Final, Helmut Schoen would fearfully and mistakenly commit the gifted Beckenbauer to shadowing him.

His brother Jack, of Leeds United, had become the regular centre-half. A veteran by now, his spectacular improvement had much to do with the new spirit at Leeds inculcated by its manager, Don Revie. Charlton, a tall, tough, laconic man from a miner's family, with a miner's robust attitudes, could scarcely have been more of a contrast to his gentler brother, whom he so admired. As children, it appeared, they had never been close. There was none of Bobby's Prince Myshkin-like quality about Jack who, immeasurably less gifted, relied on strength, experience and intelligence.

When Charlton and Stiles once had a blazing argument in a training game, Ramsey simply let them get on with it before intervening and setting things to rights. He had said from the moment he took office, with quite untypical bravado, 'We shall win the World Cup'; nor did he waver from his prediction, till he had shown that it was more than bravado.

England's players embrace after their semi-final victory over Portugal: Bobby Moore and Nobby Stiles in the foreground, and Bobby Charlton and Gordon Banks behind them.

He had had much more time and chance than Walter Winter-bottom to get his men together and drill them into a team. Not only did they have the customary pre-World Cup tour, but they also spent hard weeks at the physical recreation centre at Lilleshall – 'Stalag Lilleshall', they nicknamed it. By the time the tournament came they were immensely fit, though it was high summer, and their morale was exceptional.

Geoff Hurst had been something of a marginal choice for the party. When a journalist in Oslo expressed surprise that the brilliant young Chelsea forward Peter Osgood had not been chosen, Hurst replied, with uncharacteristic bitterness, 'Instead of me, I suppose'. Like Bobby Moore, he owed much to the coaching and percipience of West Ham's manager, Ron Greenwood. He was superbly built, tall, with immensely muscular thighs, a fine jumper, shot and header, but he had originally been no more than a moderate wing-half, and Greenwood had countermanded a decision to sell him to a Second Division team. The son of an Oldham Athletic half-back, Hurst had moved early to Essex, for whom he had played cricket. He was marvellously philosophical about the harsh treatment he often got from opponents, superbly unselfish and intelligent in his movement 'off' the ball, especially to the left wing.

Martin Peters was a third West Ham player in the party, a quiet, almost withdrawn, Londoner whom Greenwood had described as 'ten years ahead of his time', technically exceptional, a right-half by preference and position, who had just 'made' the England team in time the previous May. Ramsey had chosen him against Yugoslavia at Wembley and he had done well; many had felt his choice long overdue. Now he would blossom in a new role as a midfield player exploiting his flair for the unexpected, Panglossian appearance in the penalty area.

The little, red-haired, twenty-one-year-old Alan Ball, Blackpool's inside-forward, was quintessentially the kind of player Alf Ramsey wanted. He had first capped him on his twentieth birthday the previous year against Yugoslavia in Belgrade. The son of a former professional inside-forward, whom physically he closely resembled and who had been the Svengali of his career, Ball was a passionate enthusiast. Some felt he was neither fish nor fowl, that he lacked the subtlety of a great midfield player, the power and acceleration of a great goal-scorer; but in the Final none would play better or contribute more than he.

Roger Hunt, the Liverpool inside-forward, was another Ramsey player *par excellence*, fair-haired, sturdily built, as quiet as Martin Peters but much less talented, a doer of good by stealth, but essentially a workhorse. Once, given a lift to Hampden by mocking Scottish supporters, Ramsey was told that Hunt was 'a poor player'. After the brief, ritual pause, Ramsey smiled and replied, 'Roger Hunt? Roger scores twenty goals a season,

World Cup referees visiting the lions of Longleat as guests of the Marquess of Bath.

every season. Yes, Roger Hunt's a poor player.'

England were drawn in Group I, which would play all its matches but one at Wembley; Uruguay and France were scheduled to play at the White City, a gesture towards the owners, who had allowed it to be used as World Cup headquarters. The fourth team in the group was Mexico, and England's passage to the quarter-finals seemed pretty secure. It was unfortunate that a Football Association booklet on the competition should give the impression that should England win the group they would play the quarter-final at Wembley but the semi-final at Everton. In fact, no such decision had been taken, as FIFA's own rules made clear. Nor, as some supposed, had it been decided that the winners of Group I would, if they cleared the quarter-finals, automatically play the semi-finals at Wembley. Instead, it was left to the World Cup committee to choose the respective venues, and it was not without considerable discussion and disagreement that it did so.

Indeed, given the nature of the discussion, it is especially ironical that certain European and South American journalists, pursuing what one might perhaps call the Conspiracy Theory of football, should darkly have blamed Sir Stanley Rous for loading the dice in favour of England.

Nothing could have been farther from the truth. What in fact happened was that a strong group urged that England play their semi-final at Wembley, on purely – or pragmatically – economic grounds. This group argued that if England played at Wembley, it would be in front of a 90,000 crowd, whereas if Russia and West Germany played there, probably the crowd would be no bigger than 50,000. At Liverpool, the crowd would probably be a 'capacity' one, whoever played there. Rous argued strongly against this, but was finally persuaded to accept the majority's view.

In Liverpool itself, there was much disappointment and resentment that England should not be there – as was expected. Before the Russia-Germany game, there was a small demonstration by fans with placards, who were briskly thrown out by the police.

There were fears, a few months before the competition, that the celebrated Rimet Cup itself might have followed the fate of the first FA cup, stolen while on exhibition in a Birmingham shop window.

The considerably more valuable Rimet Cup was in its turn stolen, while on display in a showcase at an exhibition in Westminster. To give the story a suitably English twist and conclusion, it was rediscovered in a rubbish heap, in the remote suburbs, by a mongrel dog called Pickles, which was being taken for a walk by its owner.

The World Cup 'proudly presented by Stanley Gibbons', but mysteriously stolen by persons then unknown from the National Stamp Exhibition in Westminster.

Brazil

Brazil were in the Liverpool-Manchester Group III, though all their matches would be on Everton's ground. Once again the 'draw' had been a somewhat premeditated affair, the admirable Dr Hilton Gosling having long since picked out the pleasant Lymm for his team's headquarters. Vicente Feola was back again as team manager. In the event the selection would display a reverence for the past bordering on gerontiphilia, but in prospect Brazil seemed well equipped to defend their title and even to win it a third consecutive time. Alf Ramsey had taken advantage of England's Scandinavian tour to fly to Gothenburg to watch them win 3–2 against Sweden; a match in which they had seemed at no better than half pace, but in which the traditional weaknesses in their central defence had been apparent. Amazingly, they had not only stayed faithful to most of the old guard of 1962, they had even recalled Bellini and Orlando, their two centre-backs of 1958.

Of Garrincha, who had played only the second half in Gothenburg – the ground where he tormented Russia – and had virtually sunk from sight after one fine run, Dr Gosling said, 'He has recovered (from injuries in a motor accident) but not completely. The problem with Garrincha is this; he can't play as often as he used to play, his recovery is quite slow now.' It was a point Brazil's selectors would wantonly ignore.

An ageing Djalma Santos and a fading Zito were also among the elect, while a third survivor of 1958, the thirty-four-year-old Dino, who had gone home from Italy to São Paulo promising to retire, was now in such splendid form with Corinthians that he seemed likely to win a place. In fact he did not even get into the final party. Lima, a powerful but straightforward half-back, did, while the gifted but inconsistent Gerson, a member of the 1960 Olympic team, was the designated successor to Didì. In Gothenburg he scored a beautiful, Didì-type 'falling leaf' goal with his left foot from a free kick, but was inconsistent. Two goals were smartly scored by a nineteen-year-old striker from Belo Horizonte called Tostao.

Brazilian players relax at Lymm. Pelé is fifth from the left in the back row.

But when all was said and done there was always Pelé, the sublime *deus ex machina*, throbbing with power and energy, capable of resolving and transforming any game in a flash. He, too, had had his problems with injuries, but at twenty-five he was at the peak of his career.

'Sooner or later,' warned Rudolf Vytlacil, who had managed the Czech team against Brazil in the 1962 Final and would now be in charge of Bulgaria in their group, 'their nerves will crack.' Nobody, however, believed it.

Vytlacil had done well with Bulgaria, surprisingly knocking out the Belgians in a play-off, and for the last month of the season his chosen men had been called brusquely into training camp, denied to their clubs in the last throes of the Championship. His star was a tall, strong centre-forward with a fine left foot and great acceleration called Gundi Asparoukhov. Alas, an ankle injury would reduce Asparoukhov to anonymity, while worse still would befall him in 1971, when he died in a motor accident.

Hungary

Florian Albert, Hungary's centre-forward.

Portugal and Hungary were in the same strong group. The Hungarian team manager had promised that his side would abandon 4-2-4 and play with Matray as a sweeper, because otherwise 'we'd have no chance against Brazil and Portugal'. The Hungarians had won their qualifying group well, without losing a match. They still had the immaculate, Hidegkuti-like Florian Albert for centre-forward, and could afford the indulgence of playing Ferenc Bene, a huge success in the 1964 Olympic tournament, small and clever and fleet, on the right wing. As we shall see, however, their tactics were rather more than mere *catenaccio*.

Portugal

Ferenc Bene, the Hungarian forward.

Portugal had staggered through the last phases of *their* group, losing in Romania, but in Eusebio they had one of the game's few authentic stars, a very great striking inside-forward with a staggering right foot, flowing control, wonderful acceleration. Born in Lourenço Marques, Mozambique, he had at the age of nineteen established himself in the Benfica team in 1961 in a world club championship match in Montevideo, having previously electrified Paris in a friendly tournament. His face had a pristine innocence and beauty in respose, his movements were graceful yet enormously powerful. If Europe had found a rival to Pelé in spectacle and efficiency, then this was unquestionably he.

There were several other stars from a Benfica team which had played superbly in the European Cup over the past five years, winning it twice and twice losing narrowly in the Final. Eusebio himself, after his thunderous shooting had resolved the 1962 Final against Real Madrid in Amsterdam, had been symbolically presented by Ferenc Puskas – scorer of three that night – with his jersey. José Augusto, formerly the team's fast and clever outside-right, would now play in midfield as a subtly creative inside-left, little Simoes would appear with great effect both on the left flank and on the right, while the immensely tall Torres would be a menace in the air.

Alas, two superb defenders had dropped out; and this would finally prove decisive. Costa Pereira, a tall, calm goalkeeper, and Germano, a mighty, resilient centre-half, had been the very props of the Benfica defence and there was no replacing them.

The groups

In England's group, Uruguay, who would be met in the curtain-raiser, were clearly the toughest nut to crack. They were managed by the elderly, dedicated, courteous Ondino Viera, a man rich in experience of South American football. They brought such stars of the 1962 team as the dazzling inside-forward Pedro Rocha in midfield, and Ladislao Mazurkiewiecz in goal, but to Viera's chagrin he could get hold of none of the Uruguayans playing in Argentina – Silveira, Pavoni, Matosas, Sasia, Cubilla.

At their motel in Harlow, the young team played exuberantly with a model electric racing track like happy children, untroubled by the disappointing results of their European tour. Viera studied the England team and wondered aloud why they might 'leave out a great *puntero* like Connelly. They must have a defensive idea if they do, not an attacking one; tremendously defensive.'

In the Birmingham-Sheffield group there were Argentina, Spain, Switzerland and West Germany. Luis Suarez, the Internazionale (Milan) inside-forward, the first £200,000 transfer of all and a World Cup player of 1962, had given England to win. His own country had qualified most laboriously with a play-off in Paris against little Eire, won only 1–0 by a goal from Ufarte, the Atletico Madrid right-winger, who had played almost all his football in Brazil with Flamengo of Rio.

Argentina, who had progressively hardened their hearts since 1958 and had won Brazil's International Tournament of 1964, which included England and Portugal, with ruthless defensive methods, had had a palace revolution, Juan Carlos Lorenzo, their 1962 manager, replacing Zubeldia. They had unexpectedly recalled Luis Artime, centre-forward, and Ermindo Onega, inside-left, two players who had till quite recently been playing in the River Plate reserves, for all their celebrated understanding. Artime, known as *El Hermoso*, 'The Handsome', would go on scoring goals all over South America for the next six years. As the perambulating half-back in a team hanging somewhere between *catenaccio* and *metodo* there was the tall, strong, unhurried Antonio Rattin; a proper successor to Luisito Monti in more senses than one.

The Swiss had been fortunate to edge ahead of Northern Ireland, baulked by a frustrating draw in Albania, while the West Germans had come in at the expense of Sweden. The return of the ever-resilient Uwe Seeler, amazingly recovered from an operation to fit an artificial Achilles tendon, had enabled them to win the vital match in Stockholm. Seeler, announced a pessimistic German journalist in London, had lost his *détente*, and what was Seeler without his *détente*? In the event, it would be shown that he still had it – England, four years later, must have wished in Leon that he had not. Indeed, he remained the moral impulse of his team. 'Uwe, Uwe, Uwe!' cried the German fans, waving their efflorescence of flags and banners, and Seeler never stinted his efforts.

In midfield there was abundant young talent: Helmut Haller, now with Bologna in Italy, Wolfgang Overath and his splendid left foot, and a tall, dark, immensely elegant young attacking right-half called Franz Beckenbauer from Bayern Munich, who was said to be better than either.

The Italians, who played in the north-eastern Group IV with Russia, Chile and . . . North Korea, came with a bevy of impressive recent victories behind them. In charge of them was the tiny, spectacled Edmondo Fabbri, who had vacillated between the kind of large-souled, attacking tactics which thrashed Poland 6–1 in Rome and the wretched *catenaccio*-ridden negativity which brought about a 1–0 defeat in Scotland. The return, in Naples, was won against a much depleted Scottish side, several of whose stars were kept at home by their English clubs for reasons more or less convincing. Jock Stein, the forceful and able Celtic manager who had been in charge, resigned in disgust.

When the draw was announced, after Italy's 3–0 win over Scotland, qualification for the quarter-finals seemed inevitable; even if, by a malign concatenation, Chile had to be met again. Then things began to go wrong. There was a disappointing 0–0 draw with France, in which Inter's turbulent midfield player Mario Corso not only played badly but previously insulted the assistant manager, Ferruccio Valcareggi, who elected not to hear the worst of his epithets. Poor Mora, meanwhile, after scoring a fine goal against the Scots and confirming himself as one of Italy's few natural wingers, had broken his leg.

Inter were angry enough when Corso was dropped from the team leaving Gianni Rivera unchallenged in midfield. They were incensed when Fabbri also left out their captain and sweeper, the superbly combative and resilient Armando Picchi, whose presence would be so badly missed. One Sunday morning, during the World Cup, I found myself taking part with Picchi in an enthusiastic kick-about game in Battersea Park beneath the looming towers of the power station, and Picchi, in his underpants, played as if it were the World Cup Final itself, shouting at his Italian friends, scoring the winning goal. How pitiful that he should die from cancer in 1971. Fabbri also surprised the critics by omitting Giuliano Sarti, his most experienced goalkeeper, and the heavy-scoring Luigi Riva of Cagliari.

The Russians had made their customary pre-World Cup tour of South America. They still had the incomparable Lev Yachine, not to mention a fine winger in Chislenko and a forceful midfield half-back in Voinov. The charge against them, however, was the old one of lack of flair.

Chile no longer had their midfield pair of Toro and Rojas,

both of whom had gone abroad, and failed, while North Korea – what could be expected of *them*? They had had to beat only Australia to qualify, since the rest of the Afro-Asian block had walked out in a huff because they were allowed only one representative. The two necessary games had taken place on neutral territory, at Pnom-Penh in Cambodia. Australia, who seemed to have enough experience to win comfortably, were thrashed 6–1, then beaten 3–1, by a team of little men who moved sweetly and finished splendidly. Sir Stanley Rous, who was present, warned everyone prepared to listen that this was not a team to be taken lightly; Jean Vincent, France's left-winger in 1958, now coaching in Laos, said that the North Koreans were better than that famous French team. But scepticism remained.

Little, after all, was known about the North Koreans, and when their delegation arrived in the north east, speaking next to no English and parrying questions with a smile, little more was learned. The players, it appeared, were all commissioned in the Army, living an almost monastic life, dedicated to football, in a barracks at Pyong Yang, under an exigent coach. Their contacts with football beyond their own remote confines were small, and beyond the range of Communist countries sympathetic to Russia – rather than China – nil. A couple of games in eastern Europe on the way to the World Cup was simply not enough. Had they

Brazil v. Bulgaria: Pelé, the victim of harsh treatment.

deserted their sombre, rather than splendid, isolation as soon as they had beaten Australia, who knows how much more they might have done; though they would, it is true, have lost their aura of inscrutability, the charisma of the unknown.

The opening matches The first round

The opening match of the tournament, held at Wembley, was a dreadful one; the most arid of goalless draws between England and Uruguay. The Uruguayan tactics had been predictable from the beginning; *catenaccio* defence and minimal ambitions. In the circumstances, Ramsey's own tactics and team selection were curiously obtuse. Connelly *did* play instead of Peters, but far from guaranteeing the attacking game Viera had expected it simply meant that England, with only one winger, Bobby Charlton out of form and neither Hunt nor Greaves making much impression on Uruguay's solid, contemptuously resourceful defence, had little chance of a goal.

Portugal v. Hungary: treatment for Eusebio.

On tour, Jimmy Greaves had said, 'I think every player senses in the England team that we all could be on the edge of virtual immortality as far as the football's concerned. I think it's something you don't want to speak about. It's something you want to put behind you and hope to God you do the right thing at the right time. You've got to be honest. We're in with such a good chance, it's unbelievable.'

Many, as we have seen, agreed with him, not least Edmondo Fabbri who had prophesied, 'England will win, because they are strong', but after this sterile game, their prospects seemed infinitely poorer.

Brazil's beginning, at Everton, was better; they beat Bulgaria 2–0, thanks to two fulminating goals from free kicks, one in the first half by a splendid Pelé, one in the second by Garrincha. Pelé had been ruthlessly shadowed, often mercilessly dealt with, by Zhechev, with little protection from Jim Finney, the English referee. He still looked as wonderfully versatile as ever, but a French journalist, looking sombrely down from the Press box, observed, 'Pelé won't finish the World Cup. It's amazing he hasn't gone mad.' Bulgaria's Yakimov, meanwhile, matched the Brazilians in virtuosity.

At Old Trafford their rivals, Portugal and Hungary, played, and an injury to Szentmihalyi, Hungary's goalkeeper, only a few seconds after the kick-off, tipped the balance. José Augusto's first goal soon followed, Szentmihalyi missing a corner, and all Hungary's clever, furious attacks came to naught. Playing with a novel formation, three midfield men breaking splendidly to support Bene and Farkas up front, they twice hit the bar. At last Bene equalised, after sixty-one minutes, but six minutes later, with Szentmihalyi again at fault, Augusto made it 2–1. Torres got the third goal from an 'impossible' angle with almost the last kick, giving Portugal a 3–1 win which ridiculed the actual play.

In Sheffield the Swiss collapsed 5–0 before the West Germans, Beckenbauer gliding through for a couple of fluent goals. At the last moment Switzerland had dropped two of their best players, Leimgruber and Kobi Kuhn, for breaking curfew. They had, it was said, found themselves far from training camp, and taken a lift from a couple of girls. The punishment seemed rather severe, both for team and players.

At Villa Park, Argentina, who had lost 3–0 in Italy on the way to England, beat Spain 2–1 in a disappointing game, twice cruelly hacking down Suarez, early on. Artime, sharply exploiting Onega's clever suggestions, scored both goals for Argentina, while Pirri, in his first international, replied with a curious, looping header for Spain. Argentina had the blond Silvio Marzolini again as one of their two overlapping full-backs, Roberto Perfumo as a composed and elegant sweeper.

At Middlesborough the North Koreans, who would be taken to the hearts of the Ayresome Park crowd, referred to lovingly as 'us', for all their exotic remoteness, began badly. Russia, physically much too powerful, brushed their over-cautious team aside, 3–0, Malafeev and Banichevski, the big strikers, getting the goals. There still seemed no reason to believe that the Koreans could do anything.

Italy, at Sunderland, laboriously beat Chile 2–0 with an early goal and a late goal. Something strange had happened to them since their string of 'friendly' victories; the cynical would whisper afterwards of the effects of strict drug control. The players seemed tense, reflecting the tension of little Fabbri, which seemed unassuaged by the fact that the Italian Federation had extended his contract to 1970. After the match, perhaps foolishly, he violently upbraided his team for their poor display, forgetting the maxim of Pozzo: 'Italians like to feel you are on their side.'

The French, meanwhile, ensconced at Welwyn Garden City, began badly with a draw against Mexico, whose goal was scored by the alert Enrique Borja. The bone of contention was Lucien Muller, an experienced midfield player now with Barcelona, who had been brought from Spain but would not play a match. At their motel, Press conferences were a diversion in themselves. Tracksuited and affable, Henri Guérin, the team manager, and Jasseron, his tall, moustached, Tati-esque assistant, would stand behind a table. When they attempted to speak, one of the senior French journalists, as likely as not, would interrupt them to deliver a measured and eloquent oration. After one such, following the match against England, Jasseron said pleadingly, hands outspread, 'For me, Bosquier played well. We're all agreed?'

'No, no!' cried the journalists. 'Not for me, not for me!'

Succumbing 2–1 to Uruguay at White City, the French thus lost all chance of qualifying; they could hardly hope to beat England.

Hungary v. Brazil

The second round of matches brought a glorious game between Hungary and Brazil at Everton, worthy of standing with the best the World Cup has ever produced. It was exciting, dramatic, full of fine goals and delightful football, played at extraordinary speed. It also represented the first defeat of Brazil in a World Cup since 1954.

Pelé, let it be said at once, could not play, his place being taken by young Tostao. Gerson replaced Denilson, essentially a half-back, in midfield, while the veterans Djalma, Santos and Garrincha were most unwisely committed to their second match in a few days. The Hungarians made several changes, including Gelei for Szentmihalyi in goal.

It was Albert, however, who dominated the field, left to wander at will by the Brazilians, orchestrating Hungary's flowing attacks, now running beautifully with the ball, now passing cleverly, always willing and able to beat his man, consummately versatile. At the end of the remarkable match, when he stood by the tunnel in the rain taking a pull from a bottle of water, the Everton crowd were chanting, 'Al-*bert*, Al-*bert*!' paying a great performance the tribute it deserved. 'Football that day,' wrote a French critic, 'found an expression of its truth which touched on absolute art.'

After only three minutes, little Bene was wriggling in from the right, infiltrating Brazil's ponderous defence, and striking his shot from the narrowest of angles past Gilmar. From that moment, Hungary had the bit between their teeth. Their defence was excellent, the prematurely grey Matrai sweeping diligently behind the muscular Sipos and Meszoly, with Sipos always ready to go forward. The attack, marvellously fast and fluid, struck now from this angle, now from that, as midfield players and even defenders dashed into the open spaces left by the clever two front runners.

rance's goalkeeper, Arbour, houts to his defence in the match gainst Uruguay, the only one to e played at the White City.

France v. Uruguay: Mazurkiewicz, Uruguay's goalkeeper, saves.

Brazil were reprieved when, after fifteen minutes, Lima's free kick rebounded to Tostao, who whipped it smartly home, but the half-time score of 1–1 was illusory. Hungary finally regained a lead they would not lose with an exhilarating goal by Farkas. Albert's clever run and pass exposed the Brazilian defence again, sending Bene flying down the right. Bene pulled back a fast, low cross which Farkas met with a ferocious right-footed volley on the near post, a goal which left the crowd first breathless, then exultant. Ten minutes later a penalty by Meszoli, conceded by an overplayed Brazilian defence, fouling Bene, knocked the last nail in the Brazilian coffin.

Portugal v. Brazil and Italy v. Russia

Pelé came back for the final throw against Portugal, but he was obviously not fit, and the match was lost and won long before a brutal, inexplicable double foul by Morais put him out of the game. In the panic after the match with Hungary, Brazil made seven changes, ejecting the veterans Gilmar, Bellini, Djalma, Santos and Garrincha, yet restoring the veteran Orlando for his first World Cup match since 1958. Manga, a tall, agile goalkeeper nicknamed 'Frankenstein' for his bizarre appearance, replaced Gilmar, and crossed himself anxiously as he emerged from the tunnel; all nerves, despite his excellence on a tour of Europe the previous year.

After fourteen minutes he had given away a goal, feebly punching out Eusebio's centre for Simoes, who had begun the move, to head in. After twenty-five minutes, another goal: Coluna, Portugal's splendid black captain and left-half, a beautiful striker of the ball, sent over a free kick which Torres nodded back from the far post. Eusebio headed in again.

The game was in Portugal's pockets, and there was no excuse, not even that of cynical necessity, for Morais to chop down Pelé. Later, Pelé would say that it was only when he saw the incident on film that he realised how bad it was. He would swear, then, never to play in a World Cup again. The indulgent, flaccid Eng-

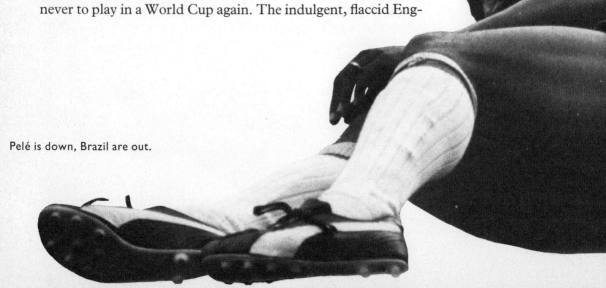

Pelé is down, Brazil are out.

elé carried off the field by
r Gosling and Mario Americo
uring the match against Portugal.

lish referee, George McCabe, allowed Morais to stay on the field, so that now Portugal were virtually playing against ten men. Silva, Brazil's new centre-forward, had also been hurt, while even at full strength they had been quite unable to curb a rampant Eusebio, whose speed and flexibility were a dreadful torment to their defenders.

The second half was curiously barren of goals until, after sixty-four minutes, Rildo, the young, attacking left-back, gave Brazil false hope with an enterprising run and goal. Five minutes from time, Eusebio appropriately ended such illusions when, after a right-wing corner, he thrashed the ball back into goal.

Brazil were out, and with both Hungary and Portugal defeating Bulgaria, these two passed into the quarter-finals.

England's group went on its weary way. Calderon, Mexico's goalkeeper, knelt in prayer beneath his crossbar before the kick-off of another tiresome game, against England, ruined by a Mexican team which kept nine or even ten men in defence. At last, with the crowd chanting, 'We want goals!' – it was a crowd immeasurably more vocal than in Winterbottom's reign – Bobby Charlton obliged them. Seven minutes from half-time, from well outside the area and at a sharp angle, he struck a memorable right-footed cross shot past Calderon. In the second half, his excellent pass sent Greaves through, for Hunt to put in the rebound, but though Peters had been added to the midfield and Terry Paine tried at outside-right, the team was still creaking. Stiles, whatever his inspirational function, gave nothing in creativity, and seemed in these games, when goals had to be scored, no more than a testimony to Ramsey's penchant for counter-attacking football and at least one 'hard man'.

A crisis was reached in the subsequent game against France, again won 2–0, laboriously, against a French team which played most of the match with the injured Herbin at centre-forward. The English players complained afterwards that opponents spat at them. Be that as it may, Stiles' foul on Jacky Simon late in the game seemed a gross one. Two officials of the Football Association insisted that Ramsey withdraw him from the team. Ramsey, loyal to his players and his somewhat contentious ideology, said that if Stiles went, so would he. Stiles, inevitably, remained.

This, however, was the only match after which Ramsey reproached his team. Once back at the Hendon Hall Hotel, their headquarters, he castigated them for sins of presumption, though exempting the hardworking Roger Hunt, who had scored both goals. To the onlooker, England's performance had seemed, if anything, rather better than in the previous two games. The match was significant for an injury to Greaves which allowed him to be gently discarded, and Ramsey's last attempt to play with an orthodox winger, Ian Callaghan of Liverpool. It must also have convinced him of the value of the absent Ball.

If Calderon had prayed, Carbajal, after Mexico's 0–0 draw with Uruguay, kissed both goalposts. It was the thirty-seven-year-old 'keeper's final match, in his fifth World Cup; and a most satisfactory one for his country. This time it was the Uruguayans, cynical and negative, masters of the 'tactical' foul, who shut up shop, knowing that a draw would take them into the quarter-final.

More cynical and provocative still were their Argentinian neighbours, in a deplorable, goalless match against West Germany at Villa Park. This time the Germans could not frolic as they did against the Swiss, Beckenbauer being much too concerned with countering the clever, inventive Onega. Albrecht, who had outrageously rugby-tackled Haller, was sent off after sixty-five minutes for another bad foul, on Weber, but still the Germans played it close to the chest; though Perfumo, acrobatic and resilient, cleared from beneath his own bar.

These two now proceeded to qualify, Argentina beating the Swiss 2–0 with goals by Artime and Onega, Germany defeating Spain 2–1 at Birmingham in a very tight match. A powerful shot from an astonishing angle by the hefty Emmerich, their left-winger, gave them the lead, but Fuste equalised, and Seeler won the match only six minutes from time.

Meanwhile the travails of Italy continued – and multiplied. Fabbri, in an evident state of alarm, put out a curiously unbalanced, hitherto untried, team against Russia at Sunderland, dropping Gianni Rivera and both wingers, choosing Giacomo Bulgarelli of Bologna, despite a knee injury.

With the vastly tall Giacinto Facchetti of Inter, essentially an overlapping full-back, helpless against clever Chislenko, Russia's outside-right, the Italians never found a rhythm, never made adequate chances for their chief bombardier, the slender but incisive Sandrino Mazzola, son of Valentino. A goal by Chislenko in the second half settled the match. Some critics remarked on the officiousness of the referee, a tiny, bald, dark West German called Herr Kreitlein, of whom more would be heard.

North Korea astonish Italy at Middlesbrough. Li Chan Myung at grips with the Italian attack.

Italy v. North Korea and Russia v. Chile

So to the ultimate Italian trauma: Middlesbrough, and the match with North Korea. Finding confidence, the little Koreans had come out of their shells against Chile and, to the delight of the friendly Middlesbrough crowd, gained a draw which could have been something better. Speed, in Fabbri's view and that of others, was the North Koreans' only real weapon; it was generally agreed that quick, flexible men were required to counteract it. Fabbri, however, surprisingly chose for his defence two slow players in Janich and Guarneri. Worse still, he called up again the manifestly unfit Bulgarelli, who was out of the game in half an hour after attempting to foul an opponent and definitively injuring his knee.

The Koreans played with splendid spirit and refreshing sportsmanship: the kind of 'professional' foul to which the World Cup exposed them clearly filled these straightforward little men with pained surprise. After forty-two minutes their inside-left, Pak Doo Ik, tackled Rivera – who was back in the team – advanced, and beat Albertosi with a searing cross shot. There were no more goals.

The effect in Italy and on the team was cataclysmic, a gigantic *mea culpa*, in which few were spared. When the team sneaked into Genoa Airport at dead of night they found outraged supporters waiting to bombard them with insults and tomatoes. For many months the mocking cry of 'Ko-re-a!' would echo over Italian stadiums when Fabbri or any of his World Cup men ap-

North Korea v. Italy: the Koreans are too many for Italy's Facchetti.

peared. He himself, in a volley of accusation and counter-accusation, would lose his job.

Russia, beating Chile 2–1 at Sunderland with a couple of goals by a new left-winger, Porkujan, maintained a one hundred per cent record, and passed into the quarter-finals, against Hungary, on the same ground.

Quarter-final at Wembley England v. Argentina. Kreitlein the German referee, rushed into the midst of a fracas

The quarter-finals England v. Argentina

In this round, run again on a knock-out pattern, the most brilliant and exciting match was unquestionably that between Portugal and North Korea at Everton, while it would be hard to decide which was the more turbulent – Wembley's England v. Argentina, or Sheffield's West Germany v. Uruguay.

The Wembley match, or fiasco, would reverberate for years to come, would polarise European and South American football, evoking almost paranoic reactions from the River Plate. The Brazilians were already away, arriving by train at Euston with the faces of condemned men, muttering, not without justice, of the inadequacies of English referees. Now Argentinian cynicism and provocation met the authoritarianism of Herr Kreitlein; and all was chaos.

The sad thing about it all – and about so many similar performances by Argentinian teams during that period – was that had they approached the occasion as a football match, Argentina might have won. Even playing with ten men for most of the match they succeeded in making England look ponderous and unintelligent. Had they fully exploited the great gifts of a team which by now was playing far better than when it started, goals might have come. The all-round competence of the unhurried Rattin, the daring combinations of Artime and Onega, the brilliance of the acrobatic Roma, the incisiveness of Oscar Mas; all these were thrown away in a stupid commitment to destruction, obstruction, the wasting of time, the apparent seeking of a draw which would finally give Argentina an even chance of winning the toss.

Scarcely had the game begun than the Argentinians embarked on a maddening series of deliberate fouls so that England – who had left out Greaves and brought in Hurst for his first game – found every attack choked at birth. Herr Kreitlein rushed hither and thither, an exacerbating rather than a calming influence, inscribing names in his notebook with the zeal of a schoolboy collecting engine numbers. Where Herr Kreitlein's tiny form perambulated, there generally followed the much larger form of Rattin, looming above him like a tree in the cork forest he was supposed to own, arguing, protesting, provoking. When he was booked, ironically, it was for a trivial foul on Bobby

Charlton, but his whole attitude was one incompatible with the proper running of the game.

At the same time his large, loping figure was at the centre of Argentina's elaborate web of short passes, of the occasional attacks which once caused Banks, unsighted, to dive vigorously to a sudden shot by Mas.

Nine minutes from half-time, however, objecting to the 'booking' of a colleague, Rattin was sent off; and refused to go. The incident itself may, in isolation, have been unexceptional, but cumulatively things had gone too far. Herr Kreitlein, bald head gleaming in the sunlight, had had enough. He said the day after that though he understood no Spanish, the look on Rattin's face was enough.

For ten long minutes there were arguments, petitions, appeals. Albrecht at one point seemed to beckon his whole team off. The tall, de Gaulle-ish figure of Ken Aston, victim of Santiago and now chief of the World Cup referees, appeared by the touchline to intercede. And at last, slowly and with huge reluctance, Rattin went, making the long, long circuit of the pitch, accompanied by his trainer, exchanging insults with the crowd, pausing now and then to watch as the game went on, like some reluctant phantom.

England v. Argentina: police save Herr Kreitlein from the Argentinian reserves at the final whistle.

The ten Argentinians held out astonishingly well, harshly exposing England's bankruptcy in midfield, where there was no one with Onega's subtlety. Hurst, playing his first competitive match since Copenhagen, found the going quite exhausting at first, but his was the first really dangerous English shot of the match, a reward for his power and perseverance. Four minutes after the interval, Wilson, receiving from Moore, dropped a centre over the defence. Hurst seemed almost surprised when it bobbled beneath his feet on the far post, but he recovered in time to strike an immensely strong shot. Roma, with a jackknife dive of fabulous agility, got a hand to it, and turned it round the post.

Argentina, when they did break, were dangerously effective, with Artime and Mas so quick on the turn, the full-backs so keen to overlap, Onega so inventive. Thirteen minutes from the end, however, Wilson found Peters, whose high cross curled in from the left was met by Hurst, this time at the near post, with a prodigious jump, a header glanced beautifully into the right-hand corner. Mas, having cuffed a small boy who ran on to felicitate Hurst, was nearly through to score from the kick-off, but England were in the semi-final.

After this, mayhem; Argentinian players rushing to attack Herr Kreitlein – without success – urinating in the dressing-room corridor, spitting at a linesman, banging on the England team's door. Ramsey, who had tried to prevent George Cohen exchanging shirts with an Argentinian, was interviewed soon afterwards and pronounced the fateful words, 'Our best football will come against the team which comes out to play football, and not to act as animals!'

It was paraffin on the bonfire, insult added to injury; especially to those who could have no idea of what had gone on in the tunnel. In the next three years, Argentinian club teams competing for the alleged Intercontinental Championship would do far worse things than Rattin and his crew, against Celtic, Milan, Manchester United, Feyenoord; but the words would persist – almost in letters of fire.

Quarter-final: Uruguay v. West Germany. Tilkowski, West Germany's goalkeeper, in full flight challenged by Silva, who was later sent off.

Uruguay v. West Germany

Meanwhile, at Hillsborough, Sheffield, two Uruguayans were sent off and West Germany won, 4–0. Neither side was blameless; much went on which escaped notice at the time. Uruguay, beginning well, should have scored early on, but instead fell behind, Haller flukily diverting a shot by Held past Mazurkiewicz. The flashpoint came when Uruguay believed Schnellinger to have handled on the line. When Emmerich painfully kicked Troche, the Uruguayan captain, Troche kicked him back in the stomach, and was sent off, slapping Seeler's face on the way for good measure.

To those who accused the Germans in general, and Haller in particular, of 'acting', it might be pointed out that when Haller at one point collapsed and writhed, it was because a Uruguayan had seized his testicles, and that night he was oozing blood.

Troche had gone five minutes after half-time. Five minutes later, Jim Finney, the English referee, expelled Silva, the Uruguayan inside-forward, for chopping down Haller.

Uruguay v. West Germany. Police persuade Silva to leave the field after being expelled.

The nine surviving Uruguayans resisted with the determination for which their football is famous, but it could not last. With Beckenbauer able now to go fluently forward as he had not done since the Swiss match, the writing was on the wall; even if it was twenty minutes from time before Beckenbauer brought off a one-two with Seeler, casually dribbled round Mazurkiewiecz, and scored. Seeler and Haller added two more.

In the quarter-final Bene scores for Hungary against Russia, beating Yachine; but it wasn't enough.

Russia v. Hungary and Portugal v. North Korea

Hungary, after their excellence against Brazil, now blew up, losing, as they so often have done, to the Russians' greater physical power. Albert was consigned to the obsessive care of Voronin, who forsook, for the occasion, his usual constructive game to take part in the man-to-man marking. Sabo – ironically himself Hungarian by origin – outshone Albert as a general, splendidly abetted by Chislenko, who had begun the World Cup so well, and would finish so depressingly. He it was who exploited yet another in the series of Hungarian goalkeeping errors which had followed the going of Grosics, Gelei dropping an easy ball after only six minutes.

Porkujan, two minutes after the interval, made it 2–0, at a corner Gelei did not catch, little Bene replied, and hope revived; only for the energetic Rakosi, ten minutes from time, to miss the equaliser. A marvellous save by Yachine from Sipos' thumping free kick; and the Russian steamroller rolled on.

At Everton, the beginning of Portugal v. North Korea was sensational; a goal in a minute, followed by a second and a third; and all for North Korea. Their opening was extraordinary, a thunderclap of dazzling, attacking football, Pak Seung Jin driving home after a cutting right-wing move.

Russia v. Hungary: Gelei, the Hungarian goalkeeper, watches Matrai tackling Russia's Banischevski.

Portugal had some twenty minutes to ride the punch, but could not do so, Li Dong-Woon scoring a second, Yang Sung Kook, the outside-left, a third. The Portuguese team, conquerors of Brazil, seemed now quite *bouleversés*. It would take genius to revive them; and Eusebio provided it, running, shooting and fighting with indomitable flair, long legs threshing past the little Korean defenders.

After twenty-eight minutes Simoes put him through for his first goal. Three minutes from half-time a Korean brought Torres tumbling like a forest giant. Eusebio belted in the penalty, then urgently picked up the ball and galloped back to the centre-spot, to be intercepted and upbraided by an obscurely outraged Korean; a man from Pyong Yang arguing with a man from Mozambique on a football field in Liverpool!

Eusebio would, in the event, have the best of the argument. Fifteen minutes from half-time, he sprinted through again to equalise, then, after another of his exhilarating left-wing runs, in which he negotiated tackles with electric ease, he was hacked down – and scored another penalty. At a corner kick Augusto got the fifth, and the Koreans, too generous and ingenuous to sit on their lead, were out. Alas, they would sink back into their strange isolation, leaving us with memories of their courage, their talent, their generosity. On Teesside, they would be recalled as long as such folk heroes as Camsell, Mannion and Hardwick.

Eusebio congratulated after equalising for Portugal in the quarter-final against North Korea.

The semi-finals Germany v. Russia; England v. Portugal
The semi-finals pitted West Germany against Russia at Everton; England against Portugal at Wembley. The first match, played a day earlier, was a wretched parody of football; the second, if it fell short of the glories of Hungary v. Brazil, a tribute to the game.

The Germans and the Russians produced a sour, ill-tempered, impoverished match, refereed without illumination by the handsome, obtrusive Sicilian, Concetto Lo Bello. Sabo, stupidly trying to foul Beckenbauer and laming himself in the process, set the tone, and it was only the majestic goal-keeping, the immaculate sportsmanship, of Yachine that gave the game any distinction. It was especially ironic that afterwards he should be blamed by Morozow, the team manager, for conceding a goal, when he had kept Russia afloat for so long.

A minute from half-time Russia found themselves in still worse plight. A powerful tackle by Schnellinger robbed Chislenko, and hurt him in the process. The left-back ran on to send a perfect crossfield ball to the blond Haller, who ran on to it and scored. Russia then ill-advisedly brought the hobbling Chislenko straight back on to the field. He at once lost the ball to Held and, in his pain and frustration, kicked him. Lo Bello instantly sent him off; and then there were nine.

The semi-final at Wembley: England have won against Portugal.

These nine the Germans treated with extraordinary respect and caution. They scored only once more, with a remarkable left-footed shot, curling from outside the box around the Russian wall and in at the far post, by Beckenbauer. But with Voronin and Khusainov fighting bravely and skilfully the Russians actually managed a goal of their own. A couple of minutes from the end Tilkowski, always vulnerable in the air, dropped a left-wing cross under pressure, and Porkujan put the ball in. It was a meagre victory.

England won much more handsomely, though the score was the same. At the end the great crowd stayed behind, singing joyfully: 'We'll win the Cup, we'll win the Cup, Ee-ay-addey-oh, we'll win the Cup!'

Ramsey proved, *grosso modo*, to be right; Portugal did *not* 'act as animals', and England did play much their best football so far. Ramsey was subsequently ordered by FIFA to apologise for his remarks, which he did. It was a pity, in the circumstances, that the Argentinians never apologised for their behaviour.

Having so comprehensively kicked Pelé, the Portuguese behaved against England like angels of light. Indeed, when Bobby Charlton, the hero of an agreeable evening, scored his second goal, they chivalrously shook him by the hand as he returned for the kick-off.

It was a game which England should have won with ease, but nearly allowed to slip away from them, a game in which Eusebio, the tournament's leading scorer, was simply blotted from sight by the tenacious Stiles, who also found time to exhort, upbraid and castigate his own defence.

Bobby Charlton had much his best game of the World Cup, perhaps the best he ever played for England, his distribution for once being quite the equal of his fine running and shooting. When, after half an hour, Ray Wilson cleverly sent through Hunt, and Pereira could only block the shot, Charlton coolly drove it back into the net. At half-time, with Ball running like a Zatopek – or a Zagalo ('That's what it's all about') – the score

usebio leaves the field in tears fter Portugal's defeat in the emi-final.

An uncomfortable moment for Uwe Seeler, West Germany's centre-forward, in the semi-final against Russia.

1–0 remained, and England had missed a dangerous number of chances.

For a quarter of an hour after the break, Portugal's gifted forwards pressed, only to find a defence in which the tall, blond Moore and Jackie Charlton, the faultless Banks, the galvanic Stiles, defied them, too compact to be breached.

So England regained ascendancy, and eleven minutes from the end they at last scored again. Hurst forcefully shook off Carlos' challenge, went to the right-hand goal line, pulled the ball back, and Bobby Charlton's right foot struck a fulminating goal.

Portugal again revived, driven on by the muscular, tireless Coluna. In another three minutes Simoes had curled the ball over from the right, Torres rose to it above the defence and headed over Banks, Jackie Charlton punched it out, Eusebio scored still another penalty.

Now Portugal assailed the English goal, and only Stiles' fine covering tackle thwarted Simoes, after which Stiles turned on his defence with a wealth of outraged gesture. Bobby Charlton let fly a left-footed shot which Pereira smothered but again could not hold, and Banks had to tip over a raking, right-footed shot by Coluna. Then it was time; England had reached the Final.

The semi-final: Germany v. Russia. Held, No. 10, tries for goal.

Bert Trautmann, former Manchester City goalkeeper, and Dr Gerhardt of the West German FA, with chimney sweep mascot and a forecast.

The Final England v. Germany

They had reached the Final without Greaves, and the question now was whether he would return. To Greaves himself, it was one of absolute importance; this was the match on which he had set his heart. Hurst, who had replaced him, was obviously playing far too well to be dropped; if anyone went it would plainly be Roger Hunt, diligent but mediocre, a selfless and intelligent runner, a more than adequate finisher, but never a forward of true international class.

The Germans had two problems: goalkeeper and outside-left. They were not satisfied with Tilkowski's performances, above all when it came to dealing with high crosses, and he had injured his shoulder against Russia. Helmut Schoen, their team manager, would have liked to replace him with the fair-haired Bayern Munich goalkeeper Sepp Maier; but Maier was himself injured.

Then there was the question of Lothar Emmerich, the Bundesliga's most prolific scorer, a tall, strong player with a ferocious left foot who had got that important goal against the Swiss, but was not renowned for his audacity. The temptation was to drop him; the fear was that should Germany then lose, fury would break about Schoen's head. He chose Emmerich.

Ramsey, following a strangulated Press conference on the Bank of England grounds at Roehampton at which, after agonised reflection, he reaffirmed that England would win the World Cup, chose Hunt.

So, after a meaningless third-place match in which Portugal, with yet another penalty by Eusebio, beat Russia 2–1, the lines of battle were drawn.

History spoke firmly in England's favour. After sixty-five years they had yet to lose to Germany, whom they had been beating regularly since a team of amateurs overplayed them 12–0 at Tottenham in 1901. The Germans, now ensconced at Welwyn Garden City, were all too cognisant of the fact. To beard the lion in his den was no joking matter. Perhaps if the match had been played elsewhere, Schoen would have been more enterprising than to sacrifice Beckenbauer to the ungrateful task of 'policing' Bobby Charlton. The Germans would in fact again play a flexible version of *catenaccio*, with the robust Willy Schulz as sweeper, Weber at centre-back, Haller and Overath in midfield, Seeler, Emmerich and the rapid Held up front.

Ramsey had hoped to exploit the relative slowness of Schnellinger by getting Ball to draw him into the middle. In fact this slowness would be much more fully and logically exploited out on the wing, where Ball would show an unsuspected talent for beating his man, then leaving him standing.

England, however, made a bad beginning. After only thirteen inconclusive minutes Ray Wilson, most uncharacteristically, headed Held's left-wing cross straight to the feet of Haller on the far post. Haller crisply controlled the ball and drove it low and wide across Banks into the left-hand corner. The flags and banners waved in triumph.

It took England, morale as high as ever, only six minutes to equalise. Tilkowski had already looked unhappy on crosses, had already needed treatment after a collision in the air with Hurst. Handsome and anxious, he fretted on his goal-line; alas, certainly no Turek.

Now, when Overath fouled Bobby Moore, the English captain took the German defence unawares with a quick, long, accurate free kick from the left. Hurst, timing his run immaculately, ran in from the right to glide the ball with his head past Tilkowski, who exchanged recriminations with his colleagues.

The match was open again – in both senses of the word, for though Beckenbauer's fluent excursions into midfield to link up with Overath were inevitably limited, the Germans were certainly not committed to mere defence. With Held running forcefully on the left, Seeler finding space on the right, Haller lurking slightly behind the strikers, they were flexible and dangerous, a different team from the grim company that beat the Russians.

Tilkowski's weakness showed again when he could only palm

World Cup Final: the exchange of pennants between Uwe Seeler and Bobby Moore.

out Hurst's gentle header, and Ball whipped it across an empty, tempting goal. Germany soon struck back, twice. Held, strongly tackled on the goal line by Jackie Charlton, took the corner himself. It was weakly headed out, Overath drove it back again, Banks blocked, Emmerich, still nearer, shot again, and again Banks saved. His mind was indeed not wandering.

Three minutes from half-time Hunt's preference to Greaves was put severely in question. When Wilson brought off yet another of his overlaps and well-judged crosses, Hurst outjumped the German defence and glided the ball to Hunt on the left-hand post. Greaves would surely have put the chance away, but Hunt's left foot was his 'swinger'. Tilkowski raised his arms like a man in prayer, and his prayer was answered as the ball struck him and bounced loose. There was time for a shot by Seeler, a tip-over by Banks, then a pleasing, inconclusive half was at an end.

The second half began with a heavy shower, and two intricate, fine pieces of control on the right by Ball who, in the first half, had been tirelessly pulling Schnellinger across the whole face of the forward-line. Then came a period of stalemate, phoney war, in which no chances were made. Each defence had the measure of its opposing attack, and if Bobby Charlton still ran gracefully, there was a gaping space on England's left wing unless Wilson filled it.

Only twelve and a half minutes remained when England broke the deadlock. Ball thumped into Tilkowski, bundling him over the goal-line for a left-wing corner which he then took. The ball ran loose to Hurst, who shot, Weber lunged in to block and the ball rose tantalisingly into the air as though on a jet of water in a shooting gallery. It was Peters who shot – and scored.

The end of the World Cup Final. Bakhramov, the Russian linesman who awarded Hurst's decisive goal, takes leave of Uwe Seeler and the West Germans. Haller, right, seems inconsolable.

World Cup Final. Weber of West Germany is challenged in the air by Martin Peters.

Weber lunges to equalise for West Germany in the World Cup Final.

After the hugging, the congratulations, Stiles and Wilson turned to the touchline, eyebrows questioningly raised, fingers upstretched, as if they had some premonition of what was in store.

With four minutes left England spurned a handsome chance to finish the job. With Germany now desperately committed to seeking the equaliser they broke away, a superb through pass by Ball cutting the defence to shreds and putting Hunt quite clear. On his right he had not only Bobby Charlton but Geoff Hurst, while in front of Tilkowski there was only Schulz; a *three* to one situation which should automatically have produced a goal. But for the second time in the match Hunt blundered, making his pass to Charlton too soon, before Schulz was fully drawn; too shallow and too square. This haste communicated itself to Charlton, who sliced wildly at the ball and hit it wide.

Martin Peters, No. 16, the scorer, and Roger Hunt, No. 21, run back in triumph after England's second goal in the Final.

For this England paid heavily. There was less than a minute left when Held and Jackie Charlton jumped for a header. Many thought Held had backed into Charlton. Herr Dienst, the Swiss referee, was of the view that Charlton had fouled Held. He gave a free kick on the left, just outside the penalty area, which at last allowed the hesitant Emmerich to justify his choice. His strong, left-footed shot hit Schnellinger in the back, was sent across the goal-mouth by Held, and there was driven home past the lunging Wilson and the plunging Banks by another defender, Weber. There would now be extra time.

Exhausted by the drama, the tension of it all, as much as by the running, the players sprawled about the grass. Ramsey, in his bright blue tracksuit, marched on to the field and told the England team that they had won the World Cup once; now they must win it again. 'Look at them!' he said, indicating the weary Germans. 'They're finished!'

Alan Ball was anything but finished. Within ninety seconds he was tearing down the right wing yet again, a miracle of perpetual motion, far too much for heavy Schnellinger, letting go a shot which Tilkowski turned over the bar.

England had the wind in their sails. Jackie Charlton came up and passed to his brother, whose blistering left-footed shot Tilkowski – a new goalkeeper, now – turned full stretch on to the post. After a hundred minutes, however, a long, excellent pass to the right wing by Stiles found Ball again. Ball would later write that he thought, 'Oh, no! I can't get that one! I'm finished!' He had already, he said, 'died twice', but once more he found the energy to leave Schnellinger standing, then centre on the run.

This time, Geoff Hurst met the ball on the near post with a furious right-footed shot. Tilkowski had no chance with it; it tore past him, hit the underside of the bar and bounced down. Roger Hunt stood with arms joyfully raised, not troubling to apply the *coup de grâce* which, in retrospect, would have avoided so

A sad Uwe Seeler leaves the field after West Germany's defeat in the Final.

The gold medal which was presented to each member of the winning World Cup team.

much controversy. Clearly he was sure the ball had crossed the line.

Herr Dienst was not. Besieged by protesting German players, he marched to the right-hand touchline to consult his Russian linesman, Bakhramov. He, a tall, silver-haired, distinguished figure, reminiscent of a chess-player or a violinist rather than a referee, quickly ended the poignant hiatus, jerking his flag with the utmost emphasis towards the centre spot. For the English crowd, the England players, it was a moment of ecstatic catharsis. The goal stood; the World Cup was clearly theirs.

Once more the Germans threw their men into unbridled attack; once more their defence broke down in consequence. It was in the last seconds that Moore's long pass, capping an immaculate performance, sent Hurst through, and this time there would be no erring. As joyful small boys dashed on to the pitch, anticipating the goal, the final whistle, he carried on alone, blew out his cheeks, and beat Tilkowski with a terrible left-footer. He was the first man to score three in a World Cup Final; and the Cup itself had at last come to the country where football began.

Bobby Moore kisses the World Cup.

England 1966

Group I

England 0, Uruguay 0 (HT 0/0)
France 1, Mexico 1 (HT 0/0)
Uruguay 2, France 1 (HT 2/1)
England 2, Mexico 0 (HT 1/0)
Uruguay 0, Mexico 0 (HT 0/0)
England 2, France 0 (HT 1/0)

	P	W	D	L	F	A	Pts
England	3	2	1	0	4	0	5
Uruguay	3	1	2	0	2	1	4
Mexico	3	0	2	1	1	3	2
France	3	0	1	2	2	5	1

Group II

West Germany 5, Switzerland 0 (HT 3/0)
Argentina 2, Spain 1 (HT 0/0)
Spain 2, Switzerland 1 (HT 0/1)
Argentina 0, West Germany 0 (HT 0/0)
Argentina 2, Switzerland 0 (HT 0/0)
West Germany 2, Spain 1 (HT 1/1)

	P	W	D	L	F	A	Pts
West Germany	3	2	1	0	7	1	5
Argentina	3	2	1	0	4	1	5
Spain	3	1	0	2	4	5	2
Switzerland	3	0	0	3	1	9	0

Group III

Brazil 2, Bulgaria 0 (HT 1/0)
Portugal 3, Hungary 1 (HT 1/0)
Hungary 3, Brazil 1 (HT 1/1)
Portugal 3, Bulgaria 0 (HT 2/0)
Portugal 3, Brazil 1 (HT 2/0)
Hungary 3, Bulgaria 1 (HT 2/1)

	P	W	D	L	F	A	Pts
Portugal	3	3	0	0	9	2	6
Hungary	3	2	0	1	7	5	4
Brazil	3	1	0	2	4	6	2
Bulgaria	3	0	0	3	1	8	0

Group IV

Russia 3, North Korea 0 (HT 2/0)
Italy 2, Chile 0 (HT 1/0)
Chile 1, North Korea 1 (HT 1/0)
Russia 1, Italy 0 (HT 0/0)
North Korea 1, Italy 0 (HT 1/0)
Russia 2, Chile 1 (HT 1/1)

	P	W	D	L	F	A	Pts
Russia	3	3	0	0	6	1	6
North Korea	3	1	1	1	2	4	3
Italy	3	1	0	2	2	2	2
Chile	3	0	1	2	2	5	1

Quarter-finals

Wembley

England 1	**Argentina 0**
Banks; Cohen, Wilson; Stiles, Charlton, J., Moore; Ball, Hurst, Charlton, R., Hunt, Peters.	Roma; Ferreiro, Perfumo, Albrecht, Marzolini; Gonzalez, Rattin, Onega; Solari, Artime, Mas.

SCORER
Hurst for England
HT 0/0

Sheffield

West Germany 4	**Uruguay 0**
Tilkowski; Hottges, Weber, Schulz, Schnellinger; Beckenbauer, Haller, Overath; Seeler, Held, Emmerich.	Mazurkiewicz; Troche, Ubinas, Gonçalves, Manicera, Caetano; Salva, Rocha; Silva, Cortes, Perez.

SCORERS
Held, Beckenbauer, Seeler, Haller for West Germany
HT 1/0

Everton

Portugal 5	**North Korea 3**
José Pereira; Morais, Baptista, Vicente, Hilario; Graça, Coluna; José Augusto, Eusebio, Torres, Simoes.	Li Chan Myung; Rim Yung Sum, Shin Yung Kyoo, Ha Jung Won, O Yoon Kyung; Pak Seung Jin, Jon Seung Hwi; Han Bong Jin, Pak Doo Ik, Li Dong Woon, Yang Sung Kook.

SCORERS
Eusebio (4) (2 penalties), José Augusto for Portugal
Pak Seung Jin, Yang Sung Kook, Li Dong Woon for North Korea
HT 2/3

Sunderland

Russia 2	**Hungary 1**
Yachine; Ponomarev, Chesternijev, Voronin, Danilov; Sabo, Khusainov; Chislenko, Banichevski, Malafeev, Porkujan.	Gelei; Matrai, Kaposzta, Meszoly, Sipos, Szepesi; Nagy, Albert, Rakosi; Bene, Farkas.

SCORERS
Chislenko, Porkujan for Russia
Bene for Hungary
HT 1/0

Semi-finals
Everton

West Germany 2
Tilkowski; Hottges,
Weber, Schulz,
Schnellinger;
Beckenbauer, Haller,
Overath; Seeler, Held,
Emmerich.

Russia 1
Yachine; Ponomarev,
Chesternijev, Voronin,
Danilov; Sabo,
Khusainov; Chislenko,
Banichevski, Malafeev,
Porkujan.

SCORERS
Haller, Beckenbauer for Germany
Porkujan for Russia
HT 1/0

Wembley

England 2
Banks; Cohen, Wilson;
Stiles, Charlton, J.,
Moore; Ball, Hurst,
Charlton, R., Hunt, Peters.

Portugal 1
José Pereira; Festa,
Baptista, José Carlos,
Hilario; Graça, Coluna,
José Augusto; Eusebio,
Torres, Simoes.

SCORERS
Charlton, R. (2) for England
Eusebio (penalty) for Portugal
HT 1/0

Third place match
Wembley

Portugal 2
José Pereira; Festa,
Baptista, José Carlos,
Hilario; Graça, Coluna,
José Augusto; Eusebio,
Torres, Simoes.

Russia 1
Yachine; Ponomarev,
Khurtsilava, Korneev,
Danilov; Voronin,
Sichinava; Metreveli,
Malafeev, Banichevski,
Serebrianikov.

SCORERS
Eusebio (penalty), Torres for Portugal
Malafeev for Russia
HT 1/1

Final
Wembley

England 4
(after extra time)
Banks; Cohen, Wilson;
Stiles, Charlton, J., Moore;
Ball, Hurst, Hunt,
Charlton, R., Peters.

West Germany 2

Tilkowski; Hottges,
Schulz, Weber,
Schnellinger; Haller,
Beckenbauer, Overath;
Seeler, Held, Emmerich.

SCORERS
Hurst (3), Peters for England
Haller, Weber for Germany
HT 1/1

MEXICO 1970

The challenge of Mexico

The 1970 World Cup, played, inexplicably and inexcusably, in Mexico, was gloriously won by Brazil. For all the appalling problems of heat and altitude, all the preceding threat of violent, negative play, they triumphed with a panache, elegance and enterprise which raised new hope for attacking football. It was especially suitable that in the Final they should thrash an Italian team which stood for all that was most cautious and destructive in the contemporary game.

The decision to make it Mexico, rather than Argentina, had been taken by FIFA at their Congress in Tokyo during the 1964 Olympic Games, thus following the dubious example of the Olympic Committee which had decided to hold the Games in Mexico City in 1968. What may euphemistically be described as lobbying by the interested parties was particularly fierce. Several delegations, including that of the Football Association, whose Secretary had personal experience of conditions in Mexico City, opposed the choice of Mexico. What possibly swayed the final choice was the inconsistency of Argentina's support for the World Cup, and their tenuous economic situation.

The displeasing machinations in Tokyo – one delegate admitted that his fare had been paid by an aspirant World Cup host – the whisperings in hotel corners and corridors, prompted Sir Stanley Rous to cry 'Enough!' Mexico, as it was, prevailed by fifty-six votes to thirty-two, with seven abstentions, but he, and others, wanted no more of such gerrymandering.

'Subsequently,' said his motion on the order paper, 'the Executive Committee intends to ask Congress to authorise them to allocate future World Cup competitions and Congresses on the lines . . . set out below.

'If accepted, this will enable national associations concerned to make adequate preparations without encountering strong competition which regrettably is occurring in connection with the present campaign.

'The present uncertainty causes national associations much expense to canvass for votes; puts strain on friendships of some who do not like to discriminate between the applicants, particularly when both claimants have much in common, involves them in much worry and expense and prevents them from concentrating their efforts on more fruitful activities. The Committee feel that many of the delegates who exercise their right to vote do so without having seen the facilities which are offered by the various applicants and are therefore forced to base their choice on not wholly relevant issues.'

The intense heat of the Mexican summer – rising to well over ninety degrees – and the breathing difficulties experienced at heights of over seven thousand feet, in Puebla, Toluca, Mexico City and the rest, were problems enough. To make matters

Juanito, Mexico's 1970 World Cup mascot.

214

worse, the World Cup Committee entered a lamentable agreement with international television to begin their Sunday matches – including the Final – at twelve noon. In almost every one of the chosen venues noon is an hour at which it is inadvisable even to walk about. To attempt to play football, and World Cup football at that, was both ludicrous and potentially dangerous. It was particularly difficult for teams from northern Europe; the holders, England, would find themselves melting in the torrid ninety-eight degrees of Guadalajara, when up against Brazil, and finally succumbing in the still stickier heat of Leon.

In retrospect, the decision to play in Mexico, and to play frequently at noon, looks as shameful as it did in prospect. True – to quote one of those humane father figures who make the Olympics what they are – nobody died. True, it is hard to prove that permanent harm was done to any player. But the cynicism and callousness of condemning footballers to play in such circumstances may not so easily be forgiven. The World Cup of 1970 ultimately succeeded in spite of the abominable conditions, and one hopes, though without any great confidence, that the lesson has been learned.

Acclimatisation

One inevitable effect, just as in the case of the 1968 Olympiad, was a huge increase in the cost of preparation. Though medical opinions varied sharply on the best means of acclimatisation and the optimum period of adaptation, there was no doubt that such a period was essential. The Olympic soccer tournament of 1968 had provided valuable and, on the whole, quite encouraging data, while several European teams, among them England, Italy and Russia, had come to play in Mexico. In general, they had found very great difficulties on these short visits, difficulties which seemed at their very worst not immediately after arrival – though they were bad enough – but after a week or so. The

The rebuilt Guadalajara Stadium where England and Brazil played their group matches.

Olympic tournament, however, in which Mexico's team of young League players was well beaten by France and Japan, showed that teams from sea level could settle down quite happily after three weeks or so. The Final, after all, had been between Hungary and Bulgaria.

The Brazilian team badge.

The contenders Brazil

Brazil's preparation, heavily and generously underwritten by the President of their Sports Confederation, João Havelange, was a protracted one, extending over some three months. Their prospects, however, were seriously compromised by a sudden change of horses in mid-stream when, in March 1970, João Saldanha, the team manager, was replaced by Zagalo. It was a situation heavy with irony, for Zagalo, Brazil's left-winger in the victories of 1958 and 1962, had been a protégé of Saldanha's when he was managing Botafogo.

Saldanha's own personality and career were nothing if not spectacular. A tiny, slender, polyglot man of great charm and fluency, now some fifty years old, he was born in Rio Grande do Sul, the son of a wealthy landowner. Football was his passion; he even went to the 1938 World Cup in France under his own steam, and there obtained the signed autograph of his idol, Vittorio Pozzo. In Rio, he became a journalist famous for his trenchancy, and a devoted fan of the Botafogo club. Indeed, in 1957, when Botafogo were at an extremely low ebb, they heeded his insistence that he alone could save them and made him manager. Saldanha promptly won them their first Championship since 1948, took them to second place the following year; and returned to journalism.

His was one of the few dissentient voices when the World Cup was retained by Brazil in 1962. The team, he said, was old and vulnerable. After the rout of 1966 his criticism became, predictably, more violent still, until Brazil resorted to the stratagem of Botafogo; they invited him to become manager. On February 6, 1969, he took over, and promptly detonated his first petard. He announced an A and a B selection which, he promised, would not only carry Brazil through their qualifying group a year later, but, saving injury and disciplinary lapses, would also represent them in Mexico. It is interesting to note that every one of the Brazilian team which eventually beat Italy in the 1970 Final was among the twenty-two footballers Saldanha chose; seven in the A selection, four in the B.

With his intelligence, enthusiasm and vigour, he gave the national side new direction and allure. It did not look terribly impressive when it scraped through 2–1 in the Maracanà against England in June 1969, with late goals by Tostao and Jairzinho, but the following August, with Tostao scoring abundantly, it swept through its qualifying group against Colombia, Paraguay and Venezuela, uniting the vast country behind it.

Saldanha, intellectual and revolutionary, dialectician and, we were to understand, master of unarmed combat, departed for Europe trailing clouds of glory, saw seven international games, locked horns with the dour Alf Ramsey in a television interview; and returned to Brazil a changed man. Something had happened; something at once radical and puzzling. Now Saldanha's policies, always unexpected and spectacular, became frenetic and bizarre. In November 1969, without an international match being played for four months, he suddenly dropped four defenders, including both goalkeepers, and called up five new men.

There was instant outrage and protest, compounded the following February, when Toninho and Scala were, on medical grounds, sent back from training camp to their clubs by Dr Toledo, the Brazilians' medical adviser, only to be pronounced perfectly fit by their own infuriated clubs. On March 4, Brazil played at Porto Alegre, and lost to Argentina, who had already been eliminated from the World Cup by Peru. Four days later, Saldanha committed the ultimate and unforgivable crime: he contemplated dropping Pelé, with whom he had for some time been embroiled in a struggle for power. The heavens opened, Saldanha disappeared, Zagalo took over.

Thorough, calm, reputedly and invariably 'lucky' in all that he did, Zagalo made certain small but vital changes. The most important of them was using Rivelino, a powerfully built inside-left with a magnificent left foot, the equal of the celebrated Gerson's, as a nominal left-winger. This, at one blow, solved the problem of incorporating both these splendid talents in the team and also relieved Rivelino of the necessity to play flat out for ninety minutes. His previous appearances had been distinguished but insufficient, falling away after one dazzling half.

Zagalo's famous luck was confirmed by the recovery of Tostao from a severe eye injury. Suffered in training, when a ball hit him, all unaware, and detached the retina, it had necessitated two operations in Houston, Texas. Since his brief appearance in the 1966 World Cup, Tostao had developed into a player of glorious technical skill, great subtlety and considerable courage. Certainly the lack and loss of him had clipped the wings of Saldanha's Brazil; but now he was back.

Brazil's team manager and former World Cup winger, Mario Lobo Zagalo.

Back, too, though less significantly, came the little Fluminense goalkeeper, Felix, first called up and then jettisoned by João Saldanha. Felix would play every game in Mexico, but his performances, his vulnerability to the high cross, would, *mutatis mutandis*, recall the old, cruel Harry Truman joke; that indeed, 'anybody' could be President; 'any' goalkeeper could win a World Cup medal. A far cry, this, from the immaculate, imperturbable Gilmar.

Brazil were assigned to the same qualifying group as England, Guadalajara, together with Romania and Czechoslovakia. They arrived there with an evident, shrewd policy of 'beads for the natives'. Clearly they knew their Mexicans. Distributing flags, smiles and pennants, full of protestations of good will, admiration and affection for the local populace, they had done a thorough job of seduction by the time they took off for their training redoubt at Guanajuato. On their return, they ran their training camp, outside Guadalajara at the Suites de Caribe, like a fortress, even obliging journalists to obtain and produce a separate identity card from that required and issued by the World Cup Committee. It did not matter. Good will had been shown and reciprocated. It would cost England dear.

For England displayed no such calculated graces. This was the more unfortunate as they had something to live down. Sir Alf Ramsey's allusion in 1966 to 'animals', after the quarter-final against Argentina may, as we have seen, been pardonable, but it had done nothing to improve relations between England and Latin America, nothing to demolish the image of substitute *gringos* – the hated North Americans – with which the Mexicans, especially, seemed determined to endow them.

England's team manager,
Sir Alf Ramsey.

England

It was clear at the time, and is still clearer now, that the confrontation between Ramsey and the Mexicans, ultimately so disastrous for his team, should have been mediated. Indeed, it was quite clear on England's exploratory tour in 1969. It was Sir Alf's hope and ambition, frequently and fervently expressed, that England in 1969 would make friends, and create the climate they required for success in 1970. In these circumstances, his own performance was sometimes a little surprising.

After the goalless draw between Mexico and England in the Azteca Stadium in May 1969, he gave a short Press conference outside the dressing-rooms, and was asked if he had anything to say to the Mexican Press. 'Yes,' he replied. 'There was a band playing outside our hotel till five o'clock this morning. We were promised a motor cycle escort to the stadium. It never arrived. When our players went out to inspect the pitch, they were abused and jeered by the crowd. I would have thought the Mexican public would have been delighted to welcome England. Then, when the game began, they could cheer their own team as much as they liked. But' – a happy, hasty, afterthought – 'we are delighted to be in Mexico, and the Mexican people are a wonderful people.'

In Guadalajara a few days later, after an England XI had thrashed a Mexican XI 4–0, there were further solecisms. When the game was over, the Governor of the state of Jalisco made a presentation to Ramsey, and was then escorted into what were then, before the building of the World Cup stadium, the underground dressing-rooms. After them scuttled a flock of Mexican journalists, who re-emerged almost instantly, chivvied by an irate Sir Alf, very much like the money-changers being driven from the temple. '*You've* got no right in here!' Nor had they, but the point, perhaps, was unwisely taken. 'What can you expect,' cried a Guadalajara newspaper the following morning, 'from one who referred to the Argentinians as animals?'

Whatever Ramsey's many solid qualities, diplomacy was scarcely one of them, and in the difficult circumstances it was of the essence. Instead, apparent xenophobia was compounded by his well-known aversion to the Press; one which had by now been widely reciprocated. It was no use explaining to Mexican journalists that they were being treated no more brusquely, no more indifferently, than their English counterparts. The Mexican capacity for self-hatred, wounded feelings, is large; the seed fell upon ground already dangerously fertile.

Some sort of buffer, some kind of public relations man, might, in the circumstances, have been thought mandatory. But the best the Football Association could do was to send, man after elderly man, their Senior International Committee, who used to be called selectors before Ramsey had their powers taken away and reduced them to tourists, or to the state of the French aristocracy after Louis XIV had comfortably immured them in Versailles. Their function in Mexico was exquisitely obscure; their motto might almost have been: They Also Serve, Who Only Eat and Drink.

England, indeed, had clearly become the team the Mexicans loved to hate: 'a team of thieves and drunks', as one local newspaper amiably put it. There had been Ramsey's indifference to the Press, Bobby Moore's absurd persecution in Colombia, and the arrival of Jeff Astle, most nervous of air travellers, at Mexico City airport in a state of some disarray.

Moore's astonishing, impregnable calm, that icy self-possession which had made him such a force in the England de-

Les Cocker, the assistant trainer, exhorting England's Bonetti, Jackie Charlton and Sadler in pre-World Cup training in Mexico City.

fence, had never been so impressively manifest as it was in his Colombian tribulations. While the England team were staying at the Tequendama hotel in Bogotá – a sombre city of criminals and cripples, and no friend to England in 1950 – he and Bobby Charlton visited the Green Fire jewellery shop inside the hotel. While they were afterwards sitting just outside it, they were approached, and asked to explain the alleged disappearance of a bracelet. Both were naturally astonished, unaware of the well-established Colombian pastime of thus accusing visiting celebrities. Indeed, when the news of Bobby Moore's subsequent arrest and detention broke upon the world, a rash of similar cases was exposed, their victims ranging from singers to bullfighters.

England, despite the eight thousand-foot altitude, won easily against Colombia in Bogotá – as did their second eleven, on the same night – then travelled for two similar matches in Quito, Ecuador (nine thousand feet), both of which they also won, Moore behaving throughout with his customary poised detachment. On arriving once more in Bogotá, on the way back to Mexico City, he was arrested by the Colombian police and put under house arrest in the care of the President of the Millonarios Football Club.

Accusations were made against him by the proprietor of the jewellery shop, the shopgirl, and a mysterious 'witness', whose background would turn out to be, at the least, equivocal, and who would ultimately disappear. Following diplomatic intervention, Moore was 'bailed' to play in the World Cup, played superbly, and was persecuted for a few months more with threats of further charges before the case died a belated, murky death. Plainly it was a fabrication from the start (its perpetrators were charged for conspiracy in 1972), but this cannot detract from the extraordinary qualities of resilience shown by Moore, whose 1970 performances outstripped even those of 1966.

England's hopes of keeping the World Cup seemed quite substantial, for all the oppressive conditions. Though Cohen and Wilson, the full-backs, Nobby Stiles, Hunt and Jackie Charlton had dropped out of the 1966 side (Stiles and Charlton remaining in the 1970 party) morale was excellent. New stars had been discovered. A most useful aid, slow sodium, had been adopted. Of the old brigade, Bobby Moore, Gordon Banks and Geoff Hurst seemed better than ever. Terry Cooper, a small, strong, immensely mobile left-back who had begun with Leeds as a left-winger, was the perfect man for an overlap, full of pace, control and enterprise. Alan Mullery, a cheerful Londoner, had efficiently succeeded Stiles. He was a solid, all-round player who, though scarcely an artist, was technically better endowed than his predecessor, even if he lacked Stiles' galvanising qualities. Both he and Manchester City's lean inside-right, Colin Bell, had excelled on the 1969 Latin American tour.

Bobby Charlton and camera in Mexico.

Francis Lee, the blond, stockily-built Manchester City striker, had come into the team at outside-right in 1968 and shown a heartening response to the great occasion. An explosive runner with a strong shot, especially happy when operating on the left flank, he was a most useful ally for the muscular, self-sacrificing Hurst, whose positional play now equalled his admirable finishing.

Perhaps the team had no great flair; it had gone out to Yugoslavia in the violent semi-final of the 1968 European Championship, had continued to exalt effort over talent. Nevertheless, it was respected and feared.

Some World Cup countries perhaps took caution too far – England among them. The English players arrived in Mexico early in May, the best part of a month before their first game. The West Germans, who would ultimately beat them, arrived weeks later.

The 1970 World Cup poster.

Germany

West Germany, playing in the group at Leon – a small, hot, rather squalid city north-west of Guadalajara – were moderately fancied. They could again call on the gracefully inventive Franz Beckenbauer and Wolfgang Overath in midfield, not to mention the resilient Uwe Seeler, playing his fourth World Cup. Moreover, there was a new and formidable threat in the person of Gerd Muller, the young Bayern Munich centre-forward. Short, dark-haired, with heavy, powerful thighs, Muller was a finisher *par excellence*, deadly in the box, a splendid volleyer.

How, though, could he be reconciled with that other fine centre-forward, the veteran Seeler? Helmut Schoen, though violently and vociferously criticised by his lieutenant of 1966, little Dettmar Cramer, resolved the question masterfully. First, Pozzo-like, he set Seeler and Muller to share a hotel room. Secondly, he decided to play Seeler in midfield; an inspired choice.

West Germany had strong rivals in Peru, whose ebullient, inventive, highly adventurous team had put out dour Argentina. Skilfully managed by Didì, the old Brazilian general of 1958 and 1962, the Peruvians scorned negative methods – even in their last, decisive qualifying game in Buenos Aires, when they had daringly used two wingers in a 4-2-4 formation, forced a draw, and come through. Though star players had been suspended for violence perpetrated in that eliminating series, there was talent to burn: the black, effervescent, twenty-year-old Teofilo Cubillas at inside-forward; the powerful, adventurous Chumpitaz, with his mighty right foot; the experienced black striker, Gallardo.

Italy

The Italians, drawn in the high altitude Puebla-Toluca group with Israel, Uruguay and Sweden, were placing almost messianic hopes in Luigi Riva. Long before they flew off to Mexico, it was clear to any visitor that the country was burdening the Cagliari forward with a responsibility and a mission he could scarcely hope to discharge.

I remember, that May, attending a 'debate' held in Milan, attended by famous former players, managers and journalists. When one of them resonantly proclaimed that there was one great difference between 1966 and 1970 – Riva! – the hall burst into ecstatic applause.

Gianni Rivera of Italy with sombrero. He was the centre of turbulent controversy

Of Riva's great, goal-scoring talent, of his control, acceleration, his mighty left foot, his courage, there was no doubt. Yet his very fame and presence were enough to confirm Italy in their dreadfully sterile addiction to *catenaccio* tactics; enough to lull them into a belief that if ten men stayed in defence and Riva was upfield, it was sufficient to guarantee goals. On top of this, and the North Korean complex which exacerbated it, there was the contretemps of Rivera and Mazzola, which threatened to split the team asunder before ever a ball was kicked.

We are familiar by now with both players. Gianni Rivera, as poised, elegant and economical as ever, captain and orchestrator of Milan, was now a ripe twenty-six, playing in his third World Cup, chosen as European Footballer of the Year. Sandrino Mazzola, who had made his name as a scoring centre-forward or striker, had in 1968, when Rivera was injured, used the Nations Cup final against Yugoslavia, in Rome, to affirm himself as a superb midfield player. Finals, indeed, seemed to bring out the best in him, for he played heroically well in Mexico City.

Meanwhile, it came to Rivera's ears at second hand, in the Hotel de la Ville in Mexico City where Italy were staying, that he was to be dropped. Mazzola would play in the opening game, against Sweden. Rivera, incensed, publicly excoriated the Italian team's officials Ferruccio Valcareggi, the amiable and un-ambitious manager, and Walter Mandelli, the *éminence grise*, chief of the Federal Technical Centre in Florence. They reacted with equal wrath, threatening that if Rivera did not apologise he would be sent home. The confrontation was resolved by the hasty and pacifying arrival of Artemio Franchi, President of the FIGC, the Italian FA, Franco Carraro, the young President, and Nereo Rocco, the manager, of Milan. Mandelli objected to the way Rivera had been treated, called his troops together, and encouraged them with a forceful and well judged speech. Rivera did not withdraw, but he did make his peace with Mandelli and Valcareggi, observing that if, in future, he were dropped, he hoped his first knowledge of it would not come from a journalist. The problem was only partly solved.

Italy's players in training. Sandrino Mazzola is in the middle of the front row.

If the Italians were haunted by nightmares of North Korea, at least the North Koreans were not there to trouble them in person. After their mysterious and remarkable presence in England, they had characteristically withdrawn from the 1970 World Cup, refusing to play qualifying games against Israel. The Israelis, in consequence, were able to win in an immensely far-flung group, including South Korea and the ultimate runners-up, Australia. Their team had already played, and played well, in Mexico in the 1968 Olympics, and had an excellent inside-left in Mordecai Spiegler, an Israeli of Russian birth.

This time, there was both an African and an Asian entrant, for the Afro-Asians had had their way, the groups had been separated and a displeasingly anomalous situation thus created. De-zoning alone could at once content the Afro-Asians and see to it that Europe had a proper representation. As it was, Morocco and Israel qualified, while such teams as Scotland, Yugoslavia and Spain did not.

Italy in training. The middle three players are Rivera, Facchetti and Mazzola.

Belgium

Group 1, in Mexico City, had the Mexicans themselves, the mathematical and solid Russians, El Salvador – whose elimination of Honduras had provoked a short and bloody war – and Belgium, greatly favoured. Discovering a fine midfield player in Odilon Polleunis, reaffirming the talents of Paul Van Himst, 'motivated' by a forceful coach in Raymond Goethals, they had surprisingly put out both Yugoslavia and Spain, though they had flagged towards the close.

Alas, they would disappoint everybody with their wretched performances in Mexico. At the bottom of them was dissension, and the cause of this dissension – as in the case of the flaccid Czech team – was football boots. The sordid machinations of the 1968 Olympics, when two German sports boot manufacturers competed to suborn the leading runners, had their parallel in 1970. In the Belgian team, it was said, there were three mutually antagonistic groups: two were shod, and rewarded, by rival manufacturers, the third was ignored, unsubsidised, and resentful.

The opening games

The tournament opened with a ploddingly dull midday game between Mexico and Russia at the immense, vertiginous Azteca Stadium. No goals were scored, little drama was distilled. Mexico did not choose their admirable striker, Enrique Borja, who had been enmeshed in the coils of their tangled football politics, transferred from Universidad to America and mysteriously kept on sidelines. Russia, with their big captain, Albert Chesternijev, sweeping up in his diligent, crouching bird dog's manner, obviously suffered from the great heat, and showed scant initiative. The most passionate moment was evoked by the appearance of the Union Jack in the parade before the game; it was fervently and ferociously whistled.

If the Mexico-Russia game was notable for anything, it was for the fussy, officious refereeing of West Germany's Herr Tschenscher. Strong in what to many of us seemed the equivocal experience of the Olympic tournament, the FIFA Referees' Committee had once more put its trust in the flourishing of coloured cards, and in Draconian instructions to its officials. In the event, coloured cards meant as little as they did in 1968, when the Final was ruined by the authoritarian refereeing of Diego de Leo. There were good referees and bad referees, permissive referees and officious referees. Herr Tschenscher, all too keenly conscious of the occasion, 'booked' a succession of largely inoffensive Russians, dealt much more leniently with the Mexicans, and was partly responsible for the tedium of the occasion, which was to a certain extent redeemed by a fine save in each half by the Russian goalkeeper, Kavazashvili. Mexico certainly felt the unlucky loss of their midfield player, Onofre, who had broken a leg in training only a few days previously.

England v. Romania: Keith Newton prostrate after being fouled by Mocanu.

That Herr Tschenscher's interpretation of the new refereeing dispensations was largely personal was shown the following Tuesday, when England opened their series against Romania in Guadalajara. Mocanu, the Romanian left-back, committed at least three brutal, crippling fouls, swinging knee-high kicks which lamed two English players, yet was so indulgently treated by M. Loraux, the Belgian referee, that he did not even have his name taken.

England, winning with a goal smartly and powerfully taken by Geoff Hurst's left foot in the second half, certainly deserved their victory. The star of the afternoon was unquestionably Terry Cooper, who exploited Romania's defensive tactics to overlap, on both flanks, with high spirit and effectiveness.

Alan Ball, the hero of the 1966 World Cup Final, who would not, for all his dedication, make the same impact under Mexico's conditions, said afterwards, 'I've never seen a team as terrified in my life as we were, with the fear of having a bad result against Romania. I've never been so frightened as when we went out. I always write home to my wife and my parents on the afternoon of a game for England, it's a superstition. I wrote to my Dad: "I'm really looking forward to it, but I'm frightened to death!" Normally I'm not that kind of lad, but I was really keyed up the other day. But when we got it over, relief came into the camp in general. We'd got the hardest over, and now we think we can beat these.'

Brazil v. Czechoslovakia: Pelé appears to be enjoying himself.

'These' were the Brazilians, who had themselves begun more impressively with their 4–1 victory over the Czechs, featuring the prodigies of Pelé, Jairzinho, Gerson and Rivelino. As so often in the past, the Brazilian defence had not looked remotely equal to the attack, yet it had not mattered. Perhaps it would have done had the Czechs been less prodigal with their chances. 'They played basketball football,' said Ball scornfully. 'As soon as the Brazilians got the ball, they all ran back, seven of them. The midfield was wide open.'

Petras, the stalwart, blond Czech centre-forward, swept easily past Brito to give his side the lead, and might in that opening period have had at least one other goal. One of Rivelino's swerving, fulminating, celebrated free kicks brought an immediate equaliser, and just after half-time Pelé, who had almost beaten Viktor with an astonishing, sublimely impertinent fifty-yard lob, got the second. He immaculately caught a long, high pass from Gerson's superb left foot on his chest, before volleying in.

The tall Kvasniak, a star of the 1962 World Cup Final, who had come on as a slow substitute, missed a palpable chance to equalise, after a corner, and the error was punished at once, Jairzinho breaking away to score from what might have been an offside position. There could be no doubts, however, about his and Brazil's last goal. Running with marvellous control and power, shaking off three defenders and an attempted foul, he cut in to drive the ball home with his strong right foot.

If Pelé had been in transcendent form, then so, in midfield, had Gerson, the great orchestrator of the team, at last displaying the gifts and the repertoire associated with him. His precision was equalled by his imagination, his power by his economy. Off the field, he looked the picture of the anti-athlete: thick-thighed, unshaven, cupping in his hand one of his reputed forty cigarettes a day as though it would be his last.

Tostao also made a large contribution, especially with his ability to hold the ball or lay it off with his back to the goal. The operations on his eye had clearly diminished his value in the air, and perhaps his willingness to take chances; though as England would find out, he could still be a robust combatant.

Though they played with two men largely on the flanks, Brazil's formation could not really be classified as 4-2-4, both Rivelino and Pelé being always prepared to work in midfield.

The defence, meanwhile, looked extremely porous both in goal, where Felix's preferred policy with high crosses seemed to be to watch and hope, and in the middle, where Brito looked slow and Piazza, converted from a linking half-back, uncertain. Later, little João Saldanha, who lived, like the England players, in the Guadalajara Hilton Hotel, with its swimming pool and its proliferating hordes of English tourists, would blame not the defenders but the midfield men, reluctant to drop back to help them. In the event, as we shall see, the question was sublimely and hearteningly academic. Brazil prevailed because they had a fine *creative* midfield and a wonderfully gifted forward line.

Didì, their black master spirit, and strategist of two World Cups, meanwhile took his gifted Peruvians into action. The omens and the beginning could scarcely have been more depressing. A minute's silence was observed in Leon for the appalling Peruvian earthquake. No doubt the psychological reaction had something to do with the fact that the Peruvians quickly went two goals down to Bulgaria, who cleverly exploited a couple of free kicks. But then, bringing on substitutes, in Campos to tighten the defence and the coloured Hugo Sotil to enliven the attack, Peru hit back. The elusive dribbling of Cubillas, the powerful breaks from the back four of Hector Chumpitaz, the running of Sotil and Gallardo, turned the tide. Gallardo, once an unsuccessful Milan player, later with Cagliari, answered Bonev's goal quickly with a cross shot. In the second half, Chumpitaz's mighty right foot scored from a free kick for Peru, by way of revenge, and Cubillas ran on to the impressive Mifflin's pass to get the winner.

The following day, on the same ground, the untrumpeted Moroccans gave West Germany an appalling fright. Who would have expected these minnows to come out and attack furiously for the opening twenty minutes? Not the puzzled Germans, whose *catenaccio*, Schulz, sweeping up again, was overcome when Hottges headed weakly back to his blond goalkeeper, Sepp Maier, and the ball fell as a gift before Houmane, who scored.

For the first but by no means the last time in this tournament, Grabowski came on as substitute, with telling effect. This was, indeed, the first World Cup in which substitutes had been al-

Germany v. Morocco.
...n to the ball is Gerd
...r (white shirt), West
...any's centre-forward and
...ournament's leading scorer.

lowed – two for each side, at any juncture of the game, the formality and fiction of being able to replace only an injured man having been abandoned. Ironically, as we shall see, the Germans would later be hoist with their own petard. Meanwhile, Helmut Schoen made his first good use of Grabowski, a fair haired right-winger of pace, initiative and subtle control, who replaced Helmut Haller and created the winning goal.

Not until eleven minutes after half-time did the anxious Germans equalise, and Schoen must have been particularly pleased that it should come from the co-operation of Seeler and Muller, the old warhorse driving home Muller's pass. Twelve minutes from the end, Grabowski got away on one of his characteristic runs, Loehr, the other winger, headed against the bar and Muller, forever in the imminent, deadly breach, scored the first of his ten World Cup goals.

The second game in Group 1 saw Belgium's talented team make a good enough start, easily defeating, 3–0, an El Salvador side which clearly had no real business to be there; indeed, would not have been, had Mexico's status as hosts not exempted them even from their customary facile passage to the finals. Wilfried Van Moer, the sturdy and dynamic little Standard Liège midfield player, scored two of the goals, Raul Lambert, the powerful Bruges striker, the other. With Van Himst and another fine opportunist in Devrindt also in the attack, goals seemed potentially abundant. In fact, this was the merest flash in the pan.

The Puebla-Toluca Group II produced a couple of deadly dull games. Uruguay made very heavy weather of winning 2–0 against a determined Israeli team. Worst of all, their splendid midfield inside-forward, the lithe, dark Pedro Rocha, hurt himself so badly after twelve minutes that he would take no further part in the competition. Playing in his third World Cup, a fitting successor, in his different style, to Schiaffino, Rocha might have enabled Uruguay to do rather better than take fourth place. He could even have troubled Brazil and their suspect defence.

The Italians, in all their three opening games, played in a lather of foreboding, as if defeat would result in execution. In the first match, against Sweden at Toluca, they scored through Domenghini after eleven minutes, with a shot that might have been saved, then sat on their lead. The Swedes could have done with Roger Magnusson, their fast, strong outside-right, whom the Olympique Marseille club had refused to release without prohibitory payment. The still more gifted centre-forward, Ove Kindvall, who had recently been the hero of Feyenoord of Rotterdam's European Cup Final victory over Celtic, could not score one goal in the tournament.

Riva was equally sterile at this stage, and Domenghini's was the only goal Italy would get in their group matches.

The remaining games, against Uruguay and Israel, were

both of them grim and goalless. Not unexpectedly, the exaltation of Riva had inhibited the functioning of the team; for what
star footballer, used to earning his 40 million lire a year, takes
kindly to being reduced to a kind of water carrier?

Certainly not the centre-forward, Roberto Boninsegna, who
had left Riva and Cagliari, returning to his original club, Inter,
largely for that reason. Combative, well sprung, with a splendid
left foot, Boninsegna was something of an ironic choice for the
series, owing his place only to the fact that Pietro Anastasi, at
666 million lire the most expensive player in Italy, should have
to drop out and undergo an operation. Anastasi had already
suffered from being forced out on to the left flank – and a right-
footed player, at that – through Riva's wish to play in the middle.
The group psychology – or pathology – of the whole thing was
sombrely intriguing, but it did nothing to further Italy's chances.
As for Rivera, he made only one appearance in the Group II
games, substituting for Domenghini against Israel. It was not
till the quarter-finals that Valcareggi produced his inspired
compromise: itself destined to rebound on him in the Final.

Uruguay were lucky to join them in the quarter-finals, for
they lost 1–0 to the Swedes in the final game, Grahn heading the
only goal. Previously, they had been held to a draw by the determined Israelis, who had surpassed themselves in their results
and their competent displays.

The group had its displeasing and gratuitous scandal.

On the very morning of the match between Uruguay and
Sweden, Sir Stanley Rous, who happened to be in Puebla, replaced the Brazilian referee, De Moraes, in consequence of
rumours which were current in the city. The Uruguayans later
protested angrily, naturally piqued at what seemed to them an
implication that they had tried to corrupt the referee. In fact
there was never any such evidence; yet at the same time it is
difficult to see how Sir Stanley, in the interests of the competition, could have done other than he did, even if his action may
have seemed arbitrary.

'When the referee appointments were made,' he later explained, 'the President of the Referees' Committee and I were
told of a plot to discredit Mr De Moraes by suggesting that if a
sum of money was paid to him by the officials of one of the teams,
he would favour that team. We did not believe the allegations. . . .

'On the eve of the match, however, when the Swedish team
arrived in Puebla, the rumour was widespread, and after dis-
cussing the matter with the Swedish delegate, I decided to interview Mr De Moraes. This interview could only take place at
9 a.m. on the day of the match. Mr De Moraes denied that he had
made approaches to either team, but agreed that it would be better if he did not referee in Puebla as any decision he might give,
especially if strict, would be used by his accusers in support of

the accusations.' To the recriminations of Señor Fernandez, the head of the Uruguayan delegation, Sir Stanley replied that he was 'surprised at his attitude about something which was done for the benefit of his team'.

Sir Stanley further pointed out that it was impossible for him to make contact with members of the Referees' Appointments Committee, as they were on duty in different parts of Mexico. Investigations, meanwhile, were still in train 'to discover the origin of the malicious rumours'.

These investigations never quite bore fruit, though there were strong reasons for believing that the rumours were initiated by a jealous Brazilian colleague of De Moraes. Certainly the World Cup committee were satisfied that a Brazilian accredited journalist had been at the bottom of them. The rumour was first communicated to the authorities by a Swedish business-man, Mr Bjore Lantz, who gave an unspecified Brazilian Press man as his informant. There was never reason to believe that De Moraes was anything but an innocent party.

Meeting of champions Brazil v. England

The meeting of England, the holders, with Brazil, the former holders, was without doubt the *pièce de résistance* of the qualifying rounds. The conditions would certainly favour Brazil, but news that Gerson, with an injured thigh, would probably miss the game, threw it open.

On the previous afternoon, Romania beat the disappointing Czechs 2–1, though Petras, with a fine, glancing header, got his customary early goal. Petras ran powerfully and dangerously on either flank, but the Romanians came back into the game, equalised through Neagu after half-time, and won through a penalty by the blond, talented Florea Dumitrache, a centre-forward whose individualism was deplored by his manager. The cult of personality was indeed out of favour, for another of Romania's best forwards, Dobrin, had been excluded for disciplinary reasons, while the giant, comedian goalkeeper, Raducanu, missed this match on similar grounds. It was whispered that he had pushed someone into the swimming pool at the Romanians' hotel in a whimsical moment.

As in 1958, England had elected to stay at an hotel in the middle of town, and now it would cost them still dearer. The previous year, on their arrival from Mexico City on their tour, to them the Guadalajara Hilton, with its swimming pool, its sham-colonial style, had seemed a quiet haven. What no one had been percipient enough to realise was that it would be flooded with supporters, and within easy access of the malevolent.

Day by day, as the rows of half-naked bodies formed around the swimming pool, the England players in their blue tracksuits

England v. Brazil: Gordon Banks precedes Pelé to a high cross.

229

looked like wistful trusties out on parole, denied the benefits of sun and still water. Considerably worse was to befall them on the eve of the Brazilian match.

From quite early in the evening, the advance guard of the besieging army began to arrive; on foot, in cars, on motor cycles, shouting, honking and chanting. The chant was largely for '*BRA-sil, BRA-sil!*' though its intention was fundamentally hostile to England. Round and round the hotel drove the cars and motor cycles, honking obscenely and provocatively, while the crowd in front of the hotel steadily grew.

There was to be no remission. As the night wore on, so the noise increased – now an obvious, malign attempt to disturb the English players' slumbers. It succeeded. Several English players had to change their rooms in the middle of the night; all appeals to the police were futile. Famous for the ruthlessness with which they dispersed a crowd, on this occasion the police were clearly prepared to do no more than guard the actual doors of the hotel. When the crowd attempted to storm them, they were turned back without trouble, suggesting that the whole demonstration could as easily have been ended, had the spirit been willing. As it was, many of the English team were forced to add the effects of a broken night to the already formidable hazards of the next day's game.

Ramsey made only one change for the match. Mullery would again look after Pelé; Brian Labone, the strong Everton defender, would play stopper. At right-back, however, Keith Newton, who had been one of those kicked by Mocanu, was replaced by Tommy Wright of Everton. 'He can beat you,' Ramsey warned Wright of Paulo Cesar, who played on Brazil's left wing; and he did. He was picked to replace Gerson, to advance from deep positions and give help in midfield to Rivelino and the young right-half Clodoaldo, a player who would not come fully into his own till later on.

'It's when they get to the eighteen-yard box,' said Bobby Charlton of the Brazilians, 'if you *let* them get to the eighteen-yard box.' He himself had shown greater fire and efficiency against Romania than he had for a long time – the unquestioned prince of midfield, where only a year before he had been threatened by the excellence of Colin Bell. Though Bell would substitute him in both this match and against the West Germans, he would never show the form he had shown the previous year, when he played so hearteningly well, with such stamina and versatility.

Character, perhaps, had much to do with it, for Bell, a fellow north-easterner, showed something of the same shy temperament as the young Charlton. There was no question of his talent, there seemed to be no doubt of his temperament and his flair for great occasions, but in Mexico he, like his club-mate Francis Lee, would disappoint.

England v. Brazil. Francis Lee, No. 7, has his name taken for a foul on the Brazilian goalkeeper, Felix.

Many have seen the England versus Brazil game as the 'real' Final, England as the 'real' runners-up, and there is no doubt that they gave Brazil a far more courageous and substantial fight than craven Italy. Yet the absence of Gerson cannot be discounted, while if England missed a couple of fine chances, then only Gordon Banks could have made the miraculous save from Pelé's header that came in the tenth minute of the game.

The groundwork was done by Jairzinho, confirming fears that Cooper would not be able to hold him, nor be able to attack as he had done against largely wingless Romania. Brushing past the left-back with all the strength and acceleration of his predecessors, Garrincha and Julinho, Jairzinho dashed to the line and centred perfectly. Pelé headed the ball down hard, on the bounce, inside the left-hand post, and was already shouting, 'Goal!' when Banks, with incredible, gymnastic agility, somehow launched himself across his goal from the opposite post, to flail the ball, one-handed, over the bar. 'He got up like a salmon

Pelé enjoins silence in Mexico City.

231

out of fresh water,' Pelé observed afterwards, adding modestly, 'it's a pity it came to no avail.'

With the dry, blazing heat reaching ninety-eight degrees, it was extraordinary, even with their slow sodium tablets, that England resisted as they did. No English player lost less than ten pounds in weight, and their doctor pointed out that an American Army manual forbade even training to be done when the thermometer exceeded eighty-five degrees. The World Cup Committee had prostituted their tournament and sacrificed its players to the demands of European television.

England threw away a couple of good opportunities in each half. In the first, Geoff Hurst, clear through the Brazilian defence, made the elementary mistake of presuming himself in an offside position, hesitating, and at length shooting hastily and feebly. Francis Lee, when a right-wing cross by Tommy Wright put the goal at his mercy, contrived to head straight at Felix.

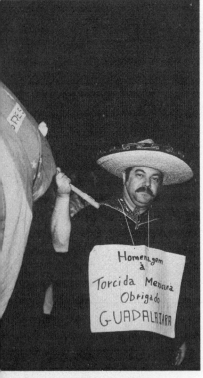

Brazilian thanks for Mexican support in Guadalajara.

The goalkeeper again betrayed his fallibility with high centres, but England's long inimicality to orthodox wingers meant that he was not often under pressure. It was only late in the game that Ramsey at last sent on the tall Jeff Astle, whose greatest strength was in the air, while Charlton gave way to Bell. Astle, though he would miss horribly, at once set the Brazilians problems; but by this time England were a goal down.

It came after fourteen minutes of the second half, and Tostao was its motivating force. His splendid dribbling on the left took him past three English defenders; though he certainly pushed off Bobby Moore, who played throughout with superb aplomb. Finally, he passed to Pelé in the goalmouth, and Pelé, without ado, laid the ball off beautifully to his right, for Jairzinho to dart in and score.

A cross headed down by Astle gave Alan Ball a chance which he squandered; Astle himself contrived to shoot over the bar when a panicky defender headed the ball straight to his feet, and another shot by Ball clipped the bar. Brazil, however, held out. It had been a magnificent, enthralling display of football, admirably refereed by the obscure Israeli referee, Abraham Klein; an inspired appointment. In the English defence, Alan Mullery had played Pelé as cleanly and resourcefully as he had a year before in Rio. Next morning, Ball sat disconsolate by the swimming pool: 'How could Jeff miss that chance?'

Towards the Finals

In Group I, the Russians suddenly cut loose against a surprisingly feeble Belgium, thrashing them 4–1. Two of the goals went to the Dynamo Kiev striker, Bychevetz, and the Russian midfield functioned sweetly with another Kiev player, the elegant Muntijan, in incisive form.

Mexico then disposed of El Salvador 4–0, though they owed their first goal to an abominable refereeing error; one which presaged the decision which would win them their match against Belgium. El Salvador in fact began well, Rodriguez, in the ninth minute, hitting the post, then Calderon with successive shots. A couple of minutes from half-time, however, Hussain Kandil, the Egyptian referee, gave El Salvador a free kick. It was promptly taken by Perez of Mexico, who pushed it to Padilla. The latter centred, Valdivia scored, and Kandil gave a goal. In vain did the El Salvador players argue, weep and lie on the ground; the goal, disgracefully, stood. Mexico went on to score three more against a demoralised side. A supporter who questioned the merits of the victory was shot dead by his patriotic neighbour; a reminder that during the Olympic football tournament two Mexicans who said that their country would not win the title had been stabbed to death by another patriot, left only with the posthumous consolation of being right.

So to Belgium, a crowd of 112,000 in the immense Azteca, and another gravely dubious goal. This time it was the only one of the game; a penalty, given after fifteen minutes. Jeck cleared the ball, Valdivia, rushing onward after the event, fell over his leg. Señor Coerezza, of Argentina, gave a penalty kick. Despite two minutes of Belgian protests, Pena took it and scored, and Mexico narrowly survived the remainder of the game. 'The penalty,' said Goethals, Belgium's manager, 'was the worst I have ever seen, nor have I ever experienced such a hostile, biased crowd.' So Mexico attained the quarter-finals for the first time in their long World Cup career.

Russia beat El Salvador 2–0 in the ante-penultimate game.

In Leon, Peru, with a couple of goals from the exciting Cubillas, disposed of Morocco 3–0, while the West Germans thrashed a flaccid Bulgaria 5–2, Gerd Muller scoring three, one from the penalty spot. The blond Karl-Heinz Schnellinger, playing, like Seeler, in his fourth World Cup, took over from Willie Schulz as sweeper.

It was plain that Brazil would win Group III, probable that England would accompany them. The Brazilians put out a diminished team against Romania, lacking both Rivelino and Gerson, pushing Piazza into midfield, and winning only by 3–2. Pelé got a couple of crisp goals, Jairzinho the other when Paulo Cesar – again emphasising what Brazil could do and wingless England could not – went to the by-line and pulled the ball back. The Romanians, after a poor start, played brightly, Dumitrache once more casting doubt on Brazil's central defence with his first half goal, Dembrowski heading a second near the end. Felix again looked vulnerable, but Brazil were hardly extended.

England, next day, looked quite abysmal. Drafting in a bevy of reserves, they struggled pitifully to find rhythm against the

Brazil celebrate a goal against Romania.

Czech team who, as Keith Newton ruefully observed, never stopped running, and ridiculed their previous form. Allan Clarke, far from a success, scored the only goal of the match early in the second half, from a penalty so dubious that even the French referee, M. Machin, gave a mysterious explanation. When Kuna tackled Bell he appeared to fall on the ball and handle it, yet Machin said afterwards he had given the penalty for tripping. With Jackie Charlton sadly at sea in defence, Astle easily mastered in the air and ineffectual on the ground (the Czech defence was not Brazil's), the English display was embarrassing. Indeed, the enterprising Czech right-back, Dobias, almost equalised with a shot which deceived Banks but hit the bar. As against that, Ball hit the bar, for England.

The quarter-finals Italy v. Mexico

The quarter-finals drew West Germany against England in Leon, Brazil against Peru in Guadalajara, Italy against Mexico on the heights of Toluca, Uruguay against Russia in Mexico City, where the rejoicing at the home team's success had reached frightening proportions. Santiago, eight years before, was almost docile by comparison, as the mobs gave vent to their fearful joy.

It would not last long. Freed at last from the Korean complex, Italy and Riva came out of their shell; their extravagantly talented players, for once allowed to express themselves, swept the weak Mexican team aside.

Though Riva scored two goals, it was Gianni Rivera's day. Valcareggi's compromise was to play Mazzola for the first half, Rivera in the second, and it was with Rivera's arrival that Italy took charge of the game. At half-time, the score was 1–1, Gonzalez giving the Mexicans a false dawn with a goal in twelve minutes, which was equalised when Domenghini's shot was deflected home. In the second period, Rivera ruled the field.

Exchanging passes with the clever little Picchio De Sisti, Rivera crossed to Riva, who burst past two defenders, then beat Calderon from a sharp angle. Next his shot, then Domenghini's, were blocked, but Rivera drove the second rebound home. Finally, Rivera's immaculate pass sent Riva through for the fourth. There would be no more rowdy rejoicings in Mexico City.

Uruguay v. Russia

The Azteca Stadium confirmed its recent reputation for dubious goals when Uruguay defeated Russia 1–0 in the last seconds of extra time. As little, dark Cubilla, the serpentine Uruguayan right-winger, pulled the ball back, it seemed quite clearly to have crossed the goal-line. But neither the referee nor his linesman thought so, and when Esparrago scored the goal stood. So the

Russian team, purportedly fed up that promises to pay them a large bonus had not been kept, went out of the Cup. Their attack had again lacked flair and punch, but disappointment may have had something to do with that.

As for the Uruguayans, their achievement in reaching the semi-finals without Rocha had to be saluted. Apart from the experienced Cubilla, who had not long since returned from playing in Buenos Aires for River Plate, their stars were in defence; Ancheta, the big, dark, young centre-half, splendid on the ground and in the air, and of course the famous Mazurkiewiecz, keeping a superb goal in his third World Cup.

Brazil v. Peru

In Guadalajara, Brazil, still the darlings of the crowd, accounted for Peru in a spectacular and effervescent game, a game in which both sides delighted in attack and scorned caution. That Peru's defence was very far from the equal of their shining attack had been plain in their concluding group game with West Germany. Again, the persisting importance of wingers was shown as the Germans, despite their *catenaccio* formation, used Libuda – then Grabowski – and Loehr wide on the flanks, to pour out a cornucopia of centres. Gerd Muller, seldom troubling to move out of the middle, as his future opponent Brian Labone remarked, made superb use of them, scoring three times; once with a magnificent header. Indeed, despite his lack of height, or perhaps because of its lulling effect on opposing defences, he was sur-

Gianni Rivera prostrate after scoring Italy's third goal against Mexico in Toluca.

England v. Czechoslovakia: an apprehensive Viktor, the Czech goalkeeper, seizes the ball from Allan Clarke.

prisingly dangerous in the air. Curiously enough, he also missed a very good chance, when the score was still 0–0, and the subtle Beckenbauer lobbed a free kick above the wall to find him unguarded. Peru scored just before half-time, and had the better of the second half, when the height and heat seemed to have sapped the Germans and given the Peruvians the advantage their native conditions implied. But there were no more goals, and a dull 1–1 draw between Bulgaria and Morocco completed the group.

Now, against Brazil, Peru played with dash and spirit but ultimately with little hope. Brazil had Gerson back again; and Rivelino, with his thumping left foot and his bandit's moustache. Both left feet, indeed, thumped to excellent purpose, with Rivelino often working alongside Gerson in midfield. Peru brought back their black winger, Baylon, of whom so much had initially been expected, but though Brazil had to use the young Marco Antonio in place of the injured Everaldo, Baylon got little change out of him. On Brazil's right wing, the muscular Jairzinho was ill, and even though he scored Brazil's fourth from Tostao's insidious pass, was not the force he had been in the group matches.

An embrace between Sir Alf Ramsey and Helmut Schoen, the team managers, after England's elimination by West Germany.

Brazil went ahead after eleven minutes with a goal which emphasised their quick thinking and equally swift reflexes. When Campos, trying to breast the ball down, slipped, Tostao instantly found Rivelino, whose deadly left foot struck again. The ball beat Rubinos, to go in off the post. Hard on the heels of that Tostao, now moving with all his old provocative sleight of foot, feinted right to unbalance an opponent, then beat Rubinos with his left.

Peru, inevitably depressed, were allowed to come back into the game on the half-hour, with the complicity of Felix, who totally misjudged Gallardo's long spinning cross from the left.

It didn't matter. Just after the interval, Pelé's long shot was deflected home by Tostao. Again Peru reacted, Sotil, who had replaced Baylon as he did in their first match, having a shot which Brito could not clear, Subillas driving in from twenty yards. Then came Brazil's fourth, from Jairzinho.

West Germany v. England

At Leon, it may with hindsight be said that England lost the match at the moment when Gordon Banks drank a bottle of beer. 'The world's best goalkeeper!' his colleagues had jokingly been calling him throughout the tour, but it was no more than the truth. On the Saturday, however, he was taken ill, and on the Sunday morning, on the large green lawn of the English team's hotel in Leon, he was to be seen hobbling, white and manifestly sick, on the arm of the England team doctor, Neil Phillips. There was plainly no hope of his playing and so it might be said, a little callously, that his place went to Peter Bonetti and the match to West Germany.

That it was by no means so simple as this is shown by the controversy which has surrounded the game ever since; not the kind of controversy evoked by Hurst's goal in the two teams' previous World Cup meeting, but by the question of tactics, the question of Ramsey, the question of Bonetti's fallibility. Was it an oversimplification, too easy an escape for Ramsey, to say that if Banks had played England would have won – or had his mistaken tactics, his ill-handled substitutions, been fundamentally responsible?

What is quite beyond doubt or argument is that England, forty minutes from the end, were leading 2–0, and that they finally lost, in extra time, 3–2.

The match, in prospect, had several fascinating attributes. In the first place, it included the teams which had contested the 1966 Final. In the second, West Germany had at long last broken their protracted run of defeats against England; a run which had begun in 1901 with the visit of the first German team to play in England. Admittedly, the crucial victory had more extrinsic than intrinsic significance, for West Germany's 1–0 win against England in Hanover in May 1968 was a trivial one. The England team was below strength, the standard low, the occasion tedious. Nevertheless, after sixty-seven years, a win was a win.

The West Germans, however, looked strong favourites. After their dull beginning against Morocco they had swept aside Bulgarians and Peruvians in a flurry of goals, Wolfgang Overath, with his splendid, long, 'quarter-back's' left-footed passes, combining with Seeler and the matchless Beckenbauer in midfield, to make the bullets for the formidable Muller to fire. The wingers, all three of them, had been fast and dangerous, ideas had been many. By contrast, England had scored only a couple of goals, and though admittedly below full strength had looked dreadful against the Czechs. Their 4-4-2 plan, described by the Manchester City manager and former England left-half, Joe Mercer, as 'cruelty to centre-forwards', had been neither effective nor entertaining. Later, the handsome, multilingual Romanian World Cup captain, Mircea Lucescu, an anglophile and an admirer of British football, would complain that England had come to Mexico with the too narrow ambition of keeping the World Cup rather than of playing good football.

Among England's senior players there had been a rumble or two; some would have preferred a more active policy against the Brazilians. But Ramsey, putting Lee back into the team alongside Hurst, was unshakeably committed to 4-4-2, and it was only to be hoped that the full-backs' overlap would compensate for the lack of wingers, that Martin Peters would at last rediscover his 1966 form in midfield and around the goal area, and that

Quarter-final in Leon: Bobby Charlton painfully tackled by West Germany's Hottges. Alan Ball is on the right.

The victorious Brazilian team. Players left to right, back row: Carlos Alberto, Brito, Felix, Piazza, Clodoaldo, Everaldo; front row: Jairzinho, Gerson, Tostao, Pelé, Rivelino.

Bobby Charlton would do something special in his record-making 106th appearance.

Bonetti, Banks' replacement, was no tyro. A vastly agile, slim, spectacular keeper, he had made his debut just before the 1966 World Cup, and in his sporadic games for England had always shown a fine response to the occasion. But he had never played in so important a match before, and he had not taken part in a competitive game for a month.

Yet for an hour England played quite splendidly, showing strength, pace and invention, together with a finishing power quite absent in their previous games. Bobby Moore was as majestically dominant as he had been in Guadalajara; Geoff Hurst, his West Ham club-mate, gloriously combative and intelligent. Terry Cooper not only played Libuda almost literally out of the game, but overlapped exuberantly; as did Keith Newton. Bobby Charlton did many admirable things, Lee and Peters had their best game of the series, Mullery perhaps the best of his life. The two goals came, but they were not enough.

England v. West Germany: Sir Alf Ramsey controversially takes off Bobby Charlton.

The first was scored after half an hour; a goal transcendently Mullery's from start to finish, in conception and execution. First giving and taking passes with Lee, he hit a splendid crossfield ball out to Newton on the right. As the full-back made ground, Mullery raced diagonally towards the far post, getting there, meteoric and unexpected, exactly with Newton's centre, which he drove past Maier.

Five minutes after the interval Geoff Hurst, tirelessly unselfish, set Newton off again. Once more the run finished with an excellent cross, and this time it was Martin Peters, in his best 1966 manner, who popped up, to score.

It was just after this that Schoen took off Libuda and put on Grabowski; and the game changed. In a nutshell, Grabowski was fresh and full of running, Cooper exhausted by the killing heat and unaccustomed altitude. From being one of England's most effective players, he now degenerated into one of their most vulnerable; and was not substituted. It was the second German substitution, for Willi Schulz had come on instead of Hottges at half-time to take over the marking of Hurst, who had been rather too much for Fichtel.

Grabowski's pace and enterprise gave the Germans new heart, and it is significant, given the subsequent theory that all went awry when Charlton departed, thus allowing Beckenbauer to come forward, that Beckenbauer scored his vital goal *before* Charlton was replaced. It came when he advanced, picked up a rebound, and sent a low, right-footed, unexceptional shot towards the left-hand corner. Bonetti went down too late, the ball ran under his dive, and the score was 2–1.

England v. West Germany at Leon. A dramatic moment in the West German goalmouth as Labone, left, and Lee challenge Beckenbauer and the West German goalkeeper, Maier.

Now Bell came on for Charlton, who had been showing certain signs of wear; though hardly as obviously as Cooper. On, too, subsequently and quite inexplicably, came the hard-tack-ling, quintessentially destructive Norman Hunter of Leeds in place of Peters. Thus, almost at a stroke, the English midfield had been radically altered. Moreover, the obvious inference that Hunter had been brought on to stiffen the defence was proved wrong when he began to run wild and free; even, at one moment, taking a corner.

England were far from recumbent. Ball unleashed Bell, to whose low, near-post centre Hurst – who had had far too few of them – stooped in his most effective manner. The ball flew across the goal, beating Maier, but passed just outside the far post.

So Germany, with an extraordinary headed goal by Uwe Seeler, were able to equalise. Throughout the match, Seeler had been pressing and challenging with characteristic gusto, often winning balls in the air which seemed unattainable.

It was thus that he scored West Germany's equaliser. A weary Labone cleared out of the goalmouth straight to Schnel-linger, who lobbed back again. The English defence had not moved up quickly enough to put Seeler offside, and the stocky little forward, leaping mightily with his back to goal, managed to send the ball in a remarkable, tantalising parabola over the head of Bonetti, who was off his line and in limbo.

Thus there was extra time, and the initiative was now pal-pably Germany's. England's last chance went when Lee wrig-gled past Schnellinger on the right-hand goal-line, delivered one of the few perfect, pulled-back crosses which England produced in the series, and Hurst drove it in. The goal was disallowed for no evident reason; neither English player could have been off-side, and Lee had certainly not fouled Schnellinger. So Muller, with a thundering volley, knocked the last nail into England's coffin. Inevitably, the goal derived from Grabowski's mastery of Cooper. Beating him again, he crossed, Loehr headed the ball back from the left, and once more Bonetti was out of the picture.

It was a splendid recovery by West Germany, a harsh blow to England, whose exhausted players sprawled in the sunshine on the lawn of their hotel like the casualties of a war. The burden placed on their overlapping full-backs in such cruel conditions had finally worn them out; and yet it had been such a close thing.

No one had fought harder, more selflessly, than the gallant Hurst, who was in a sorry state during the drive back through the arid country to Guadalajara; a tired hero indeed. The slow sodium pills which the English team had used with such good effect were not enough, when 120 minutes had to be played in such conditions. Hurst, the personification of his team's plight, slept for much of the time, stopped in a squalid village, grateful for soft drinks and a badly-needed salt pill. He had played, like Moore, still better than in the World Cup Final, yet his subsequent career would suggest that Mexico had taken more out of him than could be put back. In a very real sense, he was a victim of the World Cup committee's arcane decision to play there.

The semi-finals Brazil v. Uruguay

The semi-finals pitted those old foes, Uruguay and Brazil, against each other at Guadalajara, and Italy against West Germany in Mexico City. The Uruguayans were highly displeased to be playing on what was by now Brazil's home from home ground. They maintained, not without some logic, that the game should take place in Mexico City, arrived late in Guadalajara, and snubbed the Governor's reception.

Nonetheless, with poor Felix's complicity they took the lead. Little, dark Cubilla advanced with the ball along the right-hand goal-line, to be confronted by Piazza. He shot from the 'impossible' angle and the ball, against all probability, bounced past Felix into the goal.

Uruguay held their lead till late in the first half, when Clodoaldo ran in on the blind side to score a fine equaliser. The sturdy, twenty-year-old right-half had now come into his own, after looking, in the early games, understandably overawed by the glittering company, content to be basically a defender who, when he got the ball, pushed it to his elders and betters. Now, however, he was expressing the full range of his exceptional talent; a self-expression which would bear strange – and bitter – fruit in the Final.

Pelé, Clodoaldo's idol and mentor at Santos, was again in glorious form and, as in the opening match, came close to scoring a spectacular goal. Having observed Mazurkiewicz's habit of kicking the ball out, short, to his defenders, he once whirled to intercept one of these clearances, volleyed superbly, and brought from the goalkeeper an equally superb save.

The first half was marred by a great deal of violent play by the Uruguayans; Zagalo, indeed, had feared the consequences of Uruguay scoring first, then tried to shut up shop. Though Jairzinho had too much speed and power for Mujica, Ancheta and the veteran Matosas covered well, the Uruguayan defence survived the free-kicks they ruthlessly and recklessly gave away, and it was only in injury time that Clodoaldo raced on to Tostao's fine pass to make it 1–1.

Brazil, in the second half, took hold of the game, and Uruguay's resistance became still more cynical and physical. Repeating their quarter-final ploy, they substituted Maneiro with Esparrago. This time, however, the quick sequel was a goal to Brazil. Tostao, that inspired artificer, was again behind it, serving Jairzinho under full, imposing sail. Mujica had neither the

The semi-final between Brazil
and Uruguay: Pelé and Rivelino
go for goal.

pace nor the force to hold the winger, who raced in to drive the ball past Mazurkiewiecz. Uruguay, to their credit, retaliated, and Felix now came into his own when he saved from Cubilla. Then Pelé cunningly drew the defence before rolling the ball aside to let Rivelino do proper and spectacular execution. By way of a last, bravura flourish, Pelé, fiendishly inventive, confronted Mazurkiewiecz on a through ball, ran to one side, *away* from the ball, drawing the keeper after him, then shot fractionally wide of the unguarded goal.

Semi-final: Poletti in despair after presenting West Germany's second goal to Muller, No. 13. The plaintive goalkeeper is Albertosi.

Italy v. West Germany

In Mexico City, meanwhile, a thrilling, fluctuating but scarcely classic match was taking place between Italy and West Germany. There had been a tendency to enshrine it as a great game, a masterpiece of attacking football, thrust and counter thrust. To many of those, like myself, who were there, a better summing up was that of the Italian journalist who described the frenetic, goal-filled period of extra time caustically as 'basketball!'

This time, Germany's fortune would rebound on them; and so would Schoen's penchant for substitution.

Playing for the first time in the Azteca, and doubtless weary after their quarter-final, Germany were slow into their stride; it was Italy, through the persistent Boninsegna, who scored the only goal of the first half. Boring his way through in the eighth minute, he twice had lucky rebounds from the German defence, and finally drove the ball past Maier, left-footed, from the edge of the box.

At half-time, Italy duly took off Mazzola to bring on Rivera, but the switch was less relevant than the fact that they fell back cautiously and characteristically to defend their lead. This allowed the Germans, who had generally been making little progress, to occupy the midfield and surge forward. It is always unwise to allow space to such players as Beckenbauer and Overath, and the initiative passed to Germany; indeed, their supremacy steadily turned into a bombardment. Seeler, when the sweeper Cera allowed a ball to run past him, Grabowski, who for once played a full match, and Overath all missed very good chances. Libuda succeeded Lohr early in the second half, and twenty minutes later Schoen gambled doubly by using up his second substitute and making it Held, an attacker, for the full-back, Patzke.

Franz Beckenbauer, right arm in a sling – an injury which may have lost West Germany the semi-final against Italy.

It seemed, at first, another inspired alteration, for the blond Held, a star of the 1966 Final, produced just the running and finishing on the left that Germany needed. He had a tremendous drive kicked off the line, Seeler's fine header provoked a splendid save from Albertosi, and the match was in its third, breathless minute of injury time when Germany at last equalised. Grabowski crossed from the left, and the blond sweeper, Karl-Heinz Schnellinger, materialised in the goalmouth, to bang the ball home.

Now came extra time, and a period of mere basketball or sheer drama, according to the way one saw it. Italy now brought on Poletti for Rosato, but the most significant sight was that of Franz Beckenbauer with his arm strapped to his side. He had been brutally chopped down, not for the first time in the game, while in full, spectacular flight towards the Italian goal, accelerating with that sudden, irresistible power and grace which are so much his own. Technically, it was not a penalty, for the foul took place, by cunning intent, a few yards outside the box. Morally, it was a hundred times a penalty. As it was, Germany did nothing with the free kick, and crime emphatically paid, for the game was won and lost in that moment. Italian critics would later blame Schoen for his tactics and substitutions – *DANKE, SCHOEN!* one headline said; but the turning point was unquestionably the foul on Beckenbauer.

Extra time began well enough for Germany. Only five minutes had gone when Poletti clumsily and anxiously ran the ball away from Albertosi and almost over his own goal-line, for Muller to do, inevitably and typically, the rest.

Now the goals came thick and fast; as though it were indeed basketball. Tarcisio Burgnich, switched to centre-half, took a leaf out of Schnellinger's book by appearing in the goalmouth to score after Rivera's free kick on the left. Then Riva sharply pivoted to beat Schnellinger and drive home a low, left-footed cross shot from outside the box. So the first period ended with Italy again in the lead against a Germany now without a sweeper, and with Beckenbauer crippled.

Germany, and especially Seeler, were nevertheless far from done for. Once more, and at the same end, Seeler had a header saved by Albertosi. This time, however, when the corner came over, he met it on the far, left-hand post, nodded it across goal, and Muller flung himself to head the equaliser; his tenth goal of a tournament in which he would finish the leading scorer.

Six minutes of the second extra period had gone when Boninsegna got away on the left, went to the line, pulled the ball accurately back and little Rivera thumped it past Maier for the winner.

The Final Brazil v. Italy

So Brazil would play Italy in the Final; a meeting of two countries each of which had won the World Cup twice, even if the *azzurri*'s last victory lay thirty-two years in the past. Meanwhile there was the empty ceremony of the third-place match, in which West Germany were lucky to beat Uruguay 1–0. Wolfgang Overath, with his phenomenal left foot, was the star of an otherwise indifferent afternoon, and it was appropriate that he, and it, should score the only goal.

Dissatisfied with the talented but variable Maier, the Germans brought Wolter into goal, with somewhat comically unexpected results. Wolter had an abominable game, escaping time and again by sheer luck, till he made in the second half a glorious one-handed save from Ancheta's header, to save his team the match.

Brazil were so strongly favoured to win the Final that it was almost a burden for them. True – despite the indications of that strange semi-final – Italy had a strong, *catenaccio* defence. True, Burgnich and Facchetti, the Inter full-backs, were veterans of innumerable hard international matches for both club and country, even if the giant Facchetti was hardly the overlapping force he had been, and might find himself in trouble against Jairzinho. (Indeed he did; but not, as we shall see, quite as was expected.)

What was perfectly plain was that the Italians could hope to win only by playing as the Dr Jekyll of the quarter- and semi-finals, rather than as the destructive Mr Hyde of the eliminators. There was talent enough in midfield and up front. Riva had recovered his goal-scoring flair, Boninsegna was in splendidly incisive form, and how many teams in the world could afford the

Italy's team before the semi-final in Mexico City. Left to right, back row: Albertosi, Facchetti, Rosato, Domenghini, Boninsegna, Riva; front row: Bertini, Cera, Mazzola, DeSisti, Burgnich.

luxury of choosing between two such marvellous inside-forwards as Mazzola and Rivera?

The Brazilian defence was there to be attacked; even if Peru, the only team which had so far done so, had too porous a defence of their own to succeed. Felix's deficiencies were manifest. Carlos Alberto, the captain and right-back, was a great force when he was coming forward, but very much less impressive when he was against a winger who would take him on. Brito and Piazza could well be troubled by the thrust of Boninsegna and Riva, backed up by the sinuous dribbling of Mazzola or the winged passes of Rivera. As against that, Italy could scarcely expect to have again the advantage of such inept and permissive refereeing as one had seen from Señor Yamasaki, of Mexico and once of Peru, in the semi-final.

World Cup Final: Mazzola o Italy in a challenge with Brito and Gerson of Brazil

Indeed, the self-congratulation of the Referees' Committee seemed in precisely inverse ratio to the general level of refereeing in the competition. If the World Cup had been by no means quite as rough as many feared, nor had it been over-salubrious.

Speaking to the Italian players at their headquarters in the Hotel de la Ville, in Mexico City, however, suggested there was little or no chance of the leopard changing its spots. 'It's how we play in Italy,' said Facchetti, the captain, simply, 'so it's difficult to change it for one match. But shooting from thirty-five yards range is useful here. Usually it isn't, but here the speed is in-

Rivelino of Brazil admonished by the referee during the Final.

World Cup Final: no stopping Jairzinho, Brazil's right-winger.

creased by another fifty per cent. Tactics will be the same. Everybody marks his man. We'll attack a bit more, because the Brazilians aren't very strong in defence. England deserved to win against the Brazilians, but they missed those chances. . . . We've seen three or four of their games, but studying them does no good. I'll have my duel with Jairzinho; I'll go forward less than usual.' In retrospect, his last words have considerable irony.

Luciano Albertosi, the calm, tough, experienced goalkeeper, remarked, 'Brazil's defence isn't one of the strongest, but they have an attack that can score three or four goals, so the defence can permit itself the luxury of giving away two or three. As we have a rather strong defence, we hope to give away only one goal, and score two.'

No one, however, put the realities of the situation more succinctly than Francis Lee, who observed in Guadalajara: 'Against the Brazilians, you've got to push up and play. If you let them come at you, you're asking for trouble.'

Italy did let the Brazilians come at them, and trouble was inevitably what they got. For the game at large, however, the World Cup Final was a marvellous affirmation of what could still be done with attacking football, a splendid reassurance that cynicism, caution and negativity had not, after all, gained a stranglehold on football. The Brazilians won by playing beautifully, imaginatively and adventurously. They won despite the potential trauma of throwing away a silly, equalising goal, showing, as they did against Uruguay, that their morale was quite the equal of their phenomenal talent.

Pelé, who had sworn, after 1966, that he would never play in a future World Cup, and had changed his mind, would soon announce his retirement from all international football; but in this final he excelled himself. One might also call this match his apotheosis, such was his skill, audacity and sheer effectiveness. He scored a magnificent goal, he created two, evoking and fulfilling, in his second World Cup Final, all the immense promise of his first, twelve years before.

Italy's tactics were not only drearily negative but also strangely ineffectual; even in defence. They quickly switched Burgnich to centre-back, but never began to get to grips with Gerson, or with Carlos Alberto. Gerson, bewilderingly, was allowed infinite space and time in midfield, which he used with grateful and devastating mastery. Jairzinho, drawing Facchetti cunningly into the middle – Italy's man-to-man marking was inflexible – thus gave Carlos Alberto equal scope and leisure to advance down the empty right wing, for Italy were not playing with a left-winger.

After eighteen minutes Brazil took the lead. Rivelino crossed a long, high, unexceptional centre from the left; Pelé, being an exceptional player, got up above the Italian defence with a

Acrobatic celebrations by Brazil after the Final.

spectacular jump, and headed in as powerfully as he had done in Stockholm.

Though Mazzola was running and dribbling superbly, the very soul of Italy's resistance, and Boninsegna was responding vigorously to his clever passes, Italy's tactics made it seem most unlikely they could save the game. They needed a gift; and suddenly, seven minutes from half-time, they got it. Clodoaldo, intoxicated, perhaps, by his new-found freedom of expression, stupidly back-heeled the ball deep in his own half, at once putting Boninsegna clear through and the rest of his defence on the wrong foot. As Boninsegna swept in from the right of the goal, Felix dashed out, in futile desperation, was passed in his turn, and Boninsegna put the ball into the unguarded net.

That was the moment at which Italy might well, had they only had the character and courage, have turned the game. Pelé, visiting Rome a couple of years later, expressed his astonishment and relief that they had not pressed home their psychological advantage against a Brazilian team momentarily demoralised. But they did not. In the second half Brazil, despite Mazzola's continued excellence, steadily regained the advantage, until, after sixty-six minutes, Gerson, the artificer turned bombardier, pivoted to hit a tremendous low, left-footed cross shot from outside the penalty box, to make it 2–1.

That was the end of Italy. Five minutes later, Gerson took a free kick, Pelé touched it skilfully to Jairzinho, and he, pelting into the goalmouth, ran the ball in on the left-hand post. Italy

Carlos Alberto, Brazil's captain, displays the World Cup.

250

brought on Juliano for Bertini; then, six absurd minutes from the end, Rivera for . . . Boninsegna, surely the most mindless substitution of the tournament.

With so little time left, it was clearly all but impossible to save the game. Equally clearly, Valcareggi had been caught in a cleft stick over the Rivera-Mazzola duality. On this occasion it was quite unthinkable to take off Mazzola at the interval, so splendidly was he playing; at the same time, the non-appearance of Rivera would certainly inspire more sound and fury. Valcareggi's 'solution' was to put Rivera on in place of Boninsegna, the one Italian forward who, given the ineffectuality of Riva, seemed capable of scoring goals. So Brazil, three minutes from time, scored a fourth goal, in the way they had so often threatened. Jairzinho found Pelé, who laid the ball off immaculately to his right for Carlos Alberto to thunder on to it, and drive it past Albertosi.

The Brazilian jubilation afterwards was as spectacular and memorable as anything one had seen on the field: a joyful, dancing invasion of fans milling around their victorious players, pulling off their bright yellow shirts and hoisting them, bare to the waist, on to their shoulders. In this exuberance, this unconfined delight, one seemed to see a reflection of the way Brazil had played; and played was, indeed, the word. For all their dedication, all their passion, they and their country had somehow managed to remain aware that football was, after all, a game; something to be enjoyed.

So the Jules Rimet Trophy, won by them for the third time, went permanently to Brazil, who had shown that enterprise, fantasy, attacking play were still compatible with success; provided you had the talent. There could be no comparison with England's brave but ultimately sterile victory of 1966, a victory which had led only to myths of 'athletic football', 'work rate', the elevation of the labourer above the artist. It would take a couple of years for the new lesson to sink home in Europe, but sink it finally would, recalling Canning's boast that he 'brought into existence the New World to redress the balance of the Old'.

In Czechoslovakia and Belgium the immediate repercussions were less happy. The Czechs threw out and suspended Marko, their manager, and disqualified most of their World Cup players, initially till the end of 1971. In Belgium, Paul Van Himst and the left-winger, Wilfried Puis, insisted that they had been victimised and swore they would never play for their country again; though Van Himst would ultimately return.

These, however, were minor blemishes. Overall, despite the abominable conditions, the 1970 World Cup had been a marvellous triumph of the positive over the negative, the creative over the destructive. The Final itself took on the dimensions almost of an allegory.

Mexico 1970

Group I

Mexico 0, Russia 0 (HT 0/0)
Belgium 3, El Salvador 0 (HT 1/0)
Russia 4, Belgium 1 (HT 1/0)
Mexico 4, El Salvador 0 (HT 1/0)
Russia 2, El Salvador 0 (HT 0/0)
Mexico 1, Belgium 0 (HT 1/0)

	P	W	D	L	F	A	Pts
Russia	3	2	1	0	6	1	5
Mexico	3	2	1	0	5	0	5
Belgium	3	1	0	2	4	5	2
El Salvador	3	0	0	3	0	9	0

Group II

Uruguay 2, Israel 0 (HT 1/0)
Italy 1, Sweden 0 (HT 1/0)
Uruguay 0, Italy 0 (HT 0/0)
Sweden 1, Israel 1 (HT 0/0)
Sweden 1, Uruguay 0 (HT 0/0)
Italy 0, Israel 0 (HT 0/0)

	P	W	D	L	F	A	Pts
Italy	3	1	2	0	1	0	4
Uruguay	3	1	1	1	2	1	3
Sweden	3	1	1	1	2	2	3
Israel	3	0	2	1	1	3	2

Group III

England 1, Romania 0 (HT 0/0)
Brazil 4, Czechoslovakia 1 (HT 1/1)
Romania 2, Czechoslovakia 1 (HT 0/1)
Brazil 1, England 0 (HT 0/0)
Brazil 3, Romania 2 (HT 2/1)
England 1, Czechoslovakia 0 (HT 0/0)

	P	W	D	L	F	A	Pts
Brazil	3	3	0	0	8	3	6
England	3	2	0	1	2	1	4
Romania	3	1	0	2	4	5	2
Czechoslovakia	3	0	0	3	2	7	0

Group IV

Peru 3, Bulgaria 2 (HT 0/1)
West Germany 2, Morocco 1 (HT 0/1)
Peru 3, Morocco 0 (HT 0/0)
West Germany 5, Bulgaria 2 (HT 2/1)
West Germany 3, Peru 1 (HT 3/1)
Morocco 1, Bulgaria 1 (HT 1/0)

	P	W	D	L	F	A	Pts
West Germany	3	3	0	0	10	4	6
Peru	3	2	0	1	7	5	4
Bulgaria	3	0	1	2	5	9	1
Morocco	3	0	1	2	2	6	1

Quarter-finals

Leon

West Germany 3	**England 2**
(after extra time)	
Maier; Schnellinger,	Bonetti; Newton; Cooper;
Vogts, Hottges (Schulz);	Mullery, Labone, Moore;
Beckenbauer, Overath,	Lee, Ball, Hurst,
Seeler; Libuda	Charlton (Bell), Peters
(Grabowski), Muller,	(Hunter).
Loehr.	

SCORERS
Beckenbauer, Seeler, Muller for West Germany
Mullery, Peters for England
HT 0/1

Guadalajara

Brazil 4	**Peru 2**
Felix; Carlos Alberto,	Rubiños; Campos,
Brito, Piazza, Marco	Fernandez, Chumpitaz,
Antonio; Clodoaldo,	Fuentes; Mifflin, Challe;
Gerson (Paulo Cesar);	Baylon (Sotil), Perico Leon
Jairzinho (Roberto),	(Eladio Reyes), Cubillas,
Tostao, Pelé, Rivelino.	Gallardo.

SCORERS
Rivelino, Tostao (2), Jairzinho for Brazil
Gallardo, Cubillas for Peru
HT 2/1

Toluca

Italy 4	**Mexico 1**
Albertosi; Burgnich, Cera,	Calderon; Vantolra, Pena,
Rosato, Facchetti;	Guzman, Perez; Gonzalez
Bertini, Mazzola (Rivera),	(Borja), Pulido, Munguia
De Sisti; Domenghini	(Diaz): Valdivia, Fragoso,
(Gori), Boninsegna, Riva.	Padilla.

SCORERS
Domenghini, Riva (2), Rivera for Italy
Gonzalez for Mexico
HT 1/1

Mexico City

Uruguay 1	**Russia 0**
(after extra time)	
Mazurkiewicz; Ubinas,	Kavazashvili;
Ancheta, Matosas, Mujica;	Dzodzuashvili, Afonin,
Maneiro, Cortes,	Khurtsilava (Logofet),
Montero Castillo; Cubilla,	Chesternijev; Muntijan,
Fontes (Gomez), Morales	Asatiani (Kiselev),
(Esparrago).	Kaplichni; Evriuzhkinzin,
	Bychevetz, Khmelnitzki.

SCORER
Esparrago for Uruguay
HT 0/0

Semi-finals

Mexico City

Italy 4
(after extra time)
Albertosi; Cera,
Burgnich, Rosato
(Poletti), Facchetti;
Domenghini, Mazzola
(Rivera), De Sisti;
Boninsegna, Riva.

West Germany 3

Maier; Schnellinger;
Vogts, Schulz,
Beckenbauer, Patzke
(Held); Seeler, Overath;
Grabowski, Muller, Loehr
(Libuda).

SCORERS
Boninsegna, Burgnich, Riva, Rivera for Italy
Schnellinger, Muller (2) for West Germany
HT 1/0

Guadalajara

Brazil 3
Felix; Carlos Alberto,
Brito, Piazza, Everaldo;
Clodoaldo, Gerson;
Jairzinho, Tostao, Pelé,
Rivelino.

Uruguay 1
Mazurkiewicz; Ubinas,
Ancheta, Matosas, Mujica;
Montero Castillo, Cortes,
Fontes; Cubilla, Maneiro
(Esparrago), Morales.

SCORERS
Clodoaldo, Jairzinho, Rivelino for Brazil
Cubilla for Uruguay
HT 1/1

Third place match

Mexico City

West Germany 1
Wolter; Schnellinger
(Lorenz); Patzke, Fichtel,
Weber, Vogts; Seeler,
Overath; Libuda (Loehr),
Muller, Held.

Uruguay 0
Mazurkiewicz; Ubinas,
Ancheta, Matosas, Mujica;
Montero Castillo, Cortes,
Fontes (Sandoval);
Cubilla, Maneiro
(Esparrago), Morales.

SCORER
Overath for West Germany
HT 1/0

Final

Mexico City

Brazil 4
Felix; Carlos Alberto,
Brito, Piazza, Everaldo;
Clodoaldo, Gerson;
Jairzinho, Tostao, Pelé,
Rivelino.

Italy 1
Albertosi; Cera;
Burgnich, Bertini
(Juliano), Rosato,
Facchetti; Domenghini,
Mazzola, De Sisti;
Boninsegna (Rivera), Riva.

SCORERS
Pelé, Gerson, Jairzinho, Carlos Alberto for Brazil
Boninsegna for Italy
HT 1/1

Index

All matches are indexed to the name of the competing country appearing first in the alphabet.

Y

Z